D0456853

Israel
&
the Arabs:

The October 1973 War

Israel
&
the Arabs:

The October 1973 War

Edited by Lester A. Sobel
Contributing editor: Hal Kosut

DISCARDED
PASADENA CITY COLLEGE LIBRARY

FACTS ON FILE, INC.   NEW YORK, N.Y.

Israel
&
the Arabs:

The October 1973 War

© Copyright, 1974, by Facts on File, Inc.

All rights reserved. No part of this book may be
reproduced in any form without the permission
of the publisher except for reasonably brief
extracts used in reviews or scholarly works.

Published by Facts on File, Inc.,
119 West 57th Street, New York, N.Y. 10019.

Library of Congress Catalog Card No. 74-77485
ISBN 0-87196-173-3

9 8 7 6 5 4 3 2 1
PRINTED IN
THE UNITED STATES OF AMERICA

Contents

740181

Foreword

WAR BETWEEN ISRAEL AND ITS ARAB neighbors erupted Oct. 6, 1973 for the fourth time in the 25 years of modern Israel's existence. After eighteen days of fighting and international negotiations, the war was halted by an Oct. 22 cease-fire, with neither side winning a clear victory.

The causes of the 1973 war are generally recognized. They stem from the results of the first three Arab-Israeli wars—the war of 1948–49, from which Israel emerged as a state in a land that Arabs insist belonged wholly to Arabs; the Sinai-Suez campaign of 1956, in which the Israelis won control of virtually the entire Sinai Peninsula but which they returned to Egypt in at least partial reliance on international promises that, Israel claimed, were not kept; and the six-day war of 1967, in which the Israelis recaptured the Sinai Peninsula, took the Golan Heights from Syria and won the Jordanian-held Old City of Jerusalem and west bank of the Jordan River.

The Arab belligerents asserted that in 1973 they were fighting to regain Arab territories seized by Israel in 1967 and to restore "the rights of the Palestinians," the Arabs and descendants of Arabs who had lived in the land that became Israel. According to the Israelis, the dispute over the return of territories captured in 1967 should be settled by negotiation, not war, and the formula about the restoration of the rights of Palestinians was little more than a new code phrase for the goal Arabs had described previously as "pushing Israel into the sea."

As in the three previous Arab-Israeli conflicts, the ramifications of the war of 1973 extended far beyond the geographic area in which the fighting took place. In 1973, however, the conse-

1

quences of the hostilities produced international threats and disruptions considered more serious than had the previous Arab-Israeli encounters.

Statesmen and diplomatic observers had warned repeatedly that the chronic Arab-Israeli clashes could lead to a nuclear confrontation between the Soviet Union, which armed, advised and championed the Arab combatants, and the United States, whose admitted commitment to Israel's continued existence was the rationale for the sale of U.S. arms to the Jewish state. The U.S.-Soviet confrontation caused by the 1973 war went no further than verbal exchanges, a rivalry in the resupply of weapons and—most disquieting to some—a worldwide U.S. military alert generally recognized as a successful warning to the U.S.S.R. to cancel any plans for a unilateral dispatch of Soviet "peace-keeping" troops to the Middle East.

Another international consequence of the 1973 war had also been anticipated. Arab spokesmen had threatened to curtail the sale of Middle Eastern petroleum, on which much of the industrialized world was heavily dependent, unless the Western nations and Japan altered what the Arabs denounced as their pro-Israel policies. Arab oil-producers, fulfilling this threat, both reduced oil production and imposed an embargo on oil shipments to Israel's supporters, notably the U.S. Japan and several West European users of Arab oil indicated quickly that they were prepared to be more sympathetic to the Arab cause. It was asserted that the Arabs had been more successful in wielding their "oil weapon" than they had been in fighting with conventional weapons.

This book is a record of the war of October 1973, of the events that led to the war, of the negotiations that produced the cease-fire, of the aftermath of the war and of the various developments in Israel, in the Arab countries and in other parts of the world that are related to the conflict. The material of this book consists largely of the printed record compiled by FACTS ON FILE in its weekly reports on world events. Changes made in producing this book were made principally for the purpose of eliminating needless repetition, supplying necessary amplification or correcting error. As in all FACTS ON FILE works, great pain was taken to keep this volume free of bias and to make it an accurate and balanced reference book.

The War

Before

the War

Guerrilla Action & Retaliation

Violence Throughout 1972

Victory in the June 1967 war had meant territorial conquest but no peace for Israel. The Jewish state faced continued attacks from Arab guerrillas on all borders and from terrorists—not all of them necessarily Palestinian—in almost every part of the country. Israelis, their friends and innocent third parties were subject to aircraft hijackings, bombings, machine-gunnings and often indiscriminate homicidal attacks in virtually any part of the world.

The Israeli armed forces retaliated frequently by striking at commando bases.

During the nine months of 1973 before the October 1973 war and during the preceding year, repeated instances of virtually every type of terrorist attack and retaliatory operation took place.

These were among the violent events of 1972 that helped create the climate leading to the October 1973 war:

Israelis raid Lebanon again. An Israeli force Jan. 13, 1972 entered Lebanon the third time in a week to carry out a reprisal raid against Palestinian commando bases. The attackers struck at the town of Kafra, six miles north of the Israeli border, and blew up two houses reportedly used by guerrillas.

Lebanon claimed that four houses were blown up and that a Lebanese woman was seriously wounded. The latest Israeli thrust followed guerrilla shelling Jan. 12 of the northern Israeli town of Kiryat Shmona.

Lt. Gen. David Elazar, Israeli chief of staff, warned Lebanon Jan. 14 that the recent commando attacks from its territory were "liable to bring disaster upon the villages of south Lebanon." He called on the Beirut government and its army to "do their best to prevent such a grave development." Elazar attributed the recent upsurge of commando raids, following months of calm, to the massing of nearly 4,000 commandos at Lebanese bases near the Israeli border. He said intelligence reports told of Libyan instructors or advisers with the commandos. Elazar's statement was transmitted to Beirut in writing through the U.N. Mixed Armistice Commission.

The Palestinian commandos were reported Jan. 15 to have decided to refrain from firing on Israel while inside Lebanon. The guerrillas, whose leaders had conferred with Lebanese officials, agreed instead to operate from "mobile bases" and fire only when inside Israeli territory. The arrangement was worked out following a meeting Jan. 14 between commando leader Yasir Arafat and Lebanese military officials. The Lebanese reportedly feared an Israeli occupation

4

of the Arkub region aimed at neutralization of the commandos' main military bases.

Guerrilla attack in Gaza. One American was killed and another wounded in the ambush of their car by Palestinian guerrillas in the Gaza Strip Jan. 16. Mavis Pate, 46, a nurse at the Baptist hospital in Gaza was killed. The driver of the car, the Rev. Roy Edward Nicholas, 49, a minister at the hospital, was wounded.

Israeli jets attack Syria. Israeli planes bombed Palestinian commando concentrations in Syria Jan. 24. It was the first Israeli air strike on Syrian territory to be reported since clashes along the Golan Heights June 24–26, 1970.

The Israeli command announced that the planes attacked "concentrations of terrorists" north of Dera, in southwestern Syria, and scored direct hits. The assault, the command said, was in response to increased guerrilla attacks from Syria on civilian areas in Israel since September 1971. The command said that in the latest incident, the night of Jan. 23, three infiltrators crossed the cease-fire line but were killed by an Israeli patrol.

Syria confirmed the Israeli jet strike but claimed that its air defenses had driven off the attackers. Damascus said there were no casualties or property damage.

An Israeli military analyst estimated that about 2,000 guerrillas were stationed in Syria. The commandos were believed to have shifted their operations to the Golan Heights area after Beirut forced them to halt their activities along the Lebanese-Israeli border.

Arabs hijack, release jet airliner. A West German Lufthansa jumbo jet airliner enroute from New Delhi to Athens was hijacked by five Palestinians Feb. 21, 1972 and was diverted to Aden, Southern Yemen Feb. 22. All 172 passengers held hostage, including Joseph P. Kennedy 3rd, son of the late Sen. Robert F. Kennedy, were released later Feb. 22. The 16 crewmembers were freed Feb. 23 and the hijackers surrendered to Yemeni authorities.

The Palestinians described themselves as members of the Organization for Victims of Zionist Occupation, based in a refugee camp in the Israeli-occupied Gaza Strip.

Baghdad radio broadcast a political message which it claimed had been read by the hijackers to the passengers over the plane's public address system. The statement assailed "the flagging and defeatist attitude certain Arab regimes are adopting" on Israel and on West German aid to Israel. It pledged that "we will pursue the enemy everywhere and strike him and uproot him throughout the world."

The West German government disclosed Feb. 25 that it had paid $5 million in ransom for the release of the Lufthansa jet airliner and its crew.

Transport Minister Georg Leber said the Palestinian commandos had demanded the money in a letter addressed to Lufthansa and mailed at Cologne Feb. 22. It had stipulated that the ransom be carried by messenger to a secret meeting place outside Beirut, Lebanon. The West German government, which was a majority shareholder in the airline, complied with the request.

Leber identified the hijackers as members of the Popular Front for the Liberation of Palestine.

The Middle East News Agency reported that the five hijackers were released by Yemeni authorities Feb. 27.

Israelis battle commandos in Lebanon. Israeli air and ground forces carried out heavy reprisal operations against Palestinian commandos in southeastern Lebanon Feb. 25–28, 1972. Israel said that about 60 guerrillas were killed and more than 100 wounded. Israel placed its losses at 11 slightly wounded. The guerrillas admitted 20 of their men were slain and 36 were wounded.

The attackers pulled out after the U.N. Security Council had adopted a resolution earlier Feb. 28 demanding Israeli withdrawal from Lebanon.

Jerusalem said the operation was in retaliation for the recent infiltration of commandos into northern Israel from

Lebanon. Three Israeli soldiers and a civilian couple were killed and several others were wounded in guerrilla ambushes Feb. 22–23.

The Israeli thrust was centered on a number of guerrilla strongholds in the Arkoub Valley, an area between the Hasbani River and the western flank of Mount Hermon. An estimated 2,000–5,000 commandos were believed deployed there.

An Israeli report Feb. 28 said the four-day offensive had left the guerrilla forces in disarray and that much of their equipment had been captured. Buildings, installations, base camps and headquarters were destroyed from the air or dynamited on the ground.

Some of the Israeli ground patrols had come under fire by guerrillas from nearby Syria Feb. 27.

Lebanese troops Feb. 28 quickly moved into the commando areas evacuated by the Israelis. "This time we intend to occupy the guerrilla positions and keep them," a high-ranking Lebanese officer was quoted as saying.

A guerrilla spokesman Feb. 29 acknowledged the Lebanese army's right to control the area, saying "under no circumstances will we infringe on this sovereignty." Lebanese Premier Saeb Salam told a news conference Feb. 29 that despite the developments of the past four days his government's relations with the commandos remained strong.

The drive into Lebanon had been preceded by a Feb. 24 Israeli warning to the Beirut government of possible reprisal actions. Lt. Gen. David Elazar, chief of staff, charged that Lebanon was "responsible" for the latest guerrilla attacks on Israel. Elazar said the recent lull in commando raids that had followed the Israeli retaliatory strikes into Lebanon Jan. 13–14 had been agreed to by Premier Salam and guerrilla leaders.

U.N. emergency meeting—At Lebanon's request, the U.N. Security Council convened in emergency session Feb. 26 to consider the Israeli attack. All permanent Council members, with the exception of the U.S., criticized the Israeli action. Soviet delegate Yakov A. Malik called for sanctions against Is-

rael and Council consideration for expelling Israel from the U.N. as "an aggressor and incorrigible violator of the U.N. Charter."

Israeli delegate Jacob Doron said his country had been forced to act in self-defense against the "encampments of terrorists, from which they set out their forays against targets on Israeli soil."

After adjourning, the Council reconvened Feb. 28 and adopted by a 15–0 vote a resolution calling on Israel to stop its attacks and withdraw from Lebanon.

Golan Heights clash. Israeli forces followed up their four-day attack on Palestinian commandos in Lebanon with air and artillery strikes March 1 on suspected guerrilla bases in the southern and central part of the Israeli-occupied Golan Heights. Syrian planes retaliated later in the day with raids on Israeli settlements about two miles inside the heights.

An army spokesman in Jerusalem said the bombing of the suspected commando strongholds was in response to mortar attacks on Israeli settlements during the night. A Damascus broadcast said the Syrian air assaults were in retaliation for Israeli shelling of three Syrian villages in the heights and an air raid on a guerrilla camp near Dera in Syria, close to the border with Jordan. Three commandos and one Syrian civilian were killed in the attacks, the broadcast said.

Damascus radio warned that Syrian forces would "retaliate against any Israeli aggression . . . aimed at Syrian targets" or at Palestinian commandos in Syria.

Syria claimed March 2 that its planes and antiaircraft guns that day had driven off Israeli jets that flew over the Latakia area in the northwestern part of the country, not far from the Turkish border.

Lebanon urged to curb commandos. Defense Minister Moshe Dayan warned March 3 that Israel "reserves the option" of maintaining an indefinite presence in Lebanon if Beirut failed to curb attacks by Palestinian commandos on Israel from Lebanese soil.

Speaking in a television interview, Dayan described as a "fundamental change" in Lebanon's policy to have its army take control of former commando areas on the slopes of Mount Hermon from which the guerrillas had been operating against Israel since 1968. The defense minister expressed confidence that the Lebanese "will try at least to restrict, perhaps to control immediately the area, and not allow the Fatah to act either from Lebanon or to cross the border."

Lebanese Premier Saeb Salam said March 7 that his government had received another warning from Israel the previous week through the U.N. Mixed Armistice Commission. Salam declined to disclose the contents of the Israeli statement, but it presumably concerned commando attacks from Lebanese soil. Jerusalem had said an Israeli village had come under rocket assault only 24 hours after Israeli forces had ended their four-day operation against guerrilla bases in southeastern Lebanon.

The executive committee of the Palestine Liberation Organization was reported to have decided at meetings in Beirut March 1-2 to order their guerrilla forces out of populated centers in southern Lebanon and to abandon their fixed bases. The action was aimed at avoiding confrontations with the Lebanese army, which had moved into the former commando-held areas.

Israelis raid Lebanon. Israel's armed forces renewed attacks on Palestinian commando bases in southwestern Lebanon March 9. An Israeli spokesman said the raids were in retaliation for Lebanon-based guerrilla attacks on Israel March 8. An undisclosed number of shells fell in empty fields near the Israeli villages of Sasa and Baram.

Jerusalem authorities said Israeli artillery first responded with bombardments in the central sector of the front, between the Lebanese villages of Yarun and Ramasiah. This was followed by Israeli air strikes on guerrilla encampments in the village of Kfar Azait, seven miles inside Lebanon, a military spokesman added.

A Lebanese military spokesman reported that two civilians were injured and nine buildings were destroyed in an Israeli air attack in the Hasbaya region, west of Mt. Hermon. A commando spokesman said guerrilla antiaircraft had driven off 18 Israeli jets attempting to raid the Hasbaya area and that Israeli artillery earlier had shelled the village of Majdal Slim in the Tyre district in the southwest.

Agence France-Presse quoted Israeli officials as saying March 8 that the 1949 Israel-Lebanon armistice agreement no longer existed. A Lebanese Foreign Ministry communique March insisted the armistice was still in effect.

Israel thwarts Arab hijackers. Israeli paratroopers broke into a hijacked Belgian airliner at Lod Airport in Tel Aviv May 9, killing two of four Palestinian commandos and rescuing all 90 passengers and 10 crewmen.

The plane, operated by Sabena Airlines, had been seized May 8 by the four Arabs, including two women, after taking off from Vienna en route to Tel Aviv. The hijackers, armed with guns and grenades, were identified as members of the Black September Organization, a splinter commando group.

On landing at Lod, the Arabs, with International Red Cross representatives acting as intermediaries, began negotiating with Israeli authorities in the field's control tower. They demanded the release of 317 Palestinian guerrillas in Israeli prisons in exchange for the safety of the plane and its passengers and crew. The Arabs threatened to blow up the aircraft with all its hostages unless their demands were met. The negotiations and subsequent rescue operation were directed by Defense Minister Moshe Dayan, who was in the control tower with Lt. Gen. David Elazar, chief of staff, and other Israeli officials.

After the rescue had been carried out, Elazar disclosed that the negotiations with the commandos had been a ploy to gain time for preparing the plan to take over the plane, that Israel had no intention of meeting the hijackers' demands.

According to witnesses, Israelis crawled under the aircraft in the darkness and damaged it, making it unable to take off. They offered to repair the airliner so it could fly on to Cairo with the hostages, as the hijackers later demanded. Eighteen Israeli paratroopers, disguised in the overalls of aircraft repairmen, were driven to the plane in an airlines service vehicle. The soldiers climbed ladders onto the wings, opened two emergency doors and burst into the jet. A 10-second exchange of gunfire with the Arabs ensued. Two of the hijackers were shot to death, one of the women commandos was wounded, and the second woman hijacker surrendered.

Terrorists attack Israeli airport. Three Japanese gunmen hired by a Palestinian commando group attacked the Lod International Airport near Tel Aviv the night of May 30, 1972, killing 24 persons and wounding 76. The death toll was 28 by June 24. One attacker was slain by his own grenade, another was shot to death, apparently by bullets fired by his own companions, and the third was captured by an El Al airliner mechanic.

The captured attacker told Israeli authorities he was a member of "the Army of the Red Star," (also referred to as the United Red Army) a left-wing Japanese group recruited by the Arab guerrilla movement. In Beirut, the Marxist Popular Front for the Liberation of Palestine claimed credit for the assault.

The three Japanese had debarked with 116 other passengers from an Air France plane flight from Paris and Rome. They had boarded at Rome. Entering the passenger lounge, the three men picked up two valises from a conveyor belt, unzipped them and whipped out machineguns and grenades. Then they began firing and lobbing grenades indiscriminately at a crowd of about 300 in the waiting room. One of the terrorists fired at aircraft on the runway from an opening of the baggage conveyor, and the other, who eventually was captured, raced out to the tarmac shooting everyone in sight and at jets parked near the terminal. Witnesses said the attack lasted 3–4 minutes.

The Japanese embassy in Israel identified the captured man as Daisuke Namba, 22, and the others as Ken Torio, 23, and Jiro Sugizaki, 23.

Tokyo police June 1 reported that Daisuke Namba's name actually was Kozo Okamoto, brother of another Red Army member who had taken part in the hijacking of a Japanese airliner to North Korea in March 1970. The two slain Japanese were correctly identified later as Rakeshi Okudeira and Yoshuyiki Yasuda.

Among the dead were 16 Puerto Ricans who arrived on a pilgrimage to the Christian holy places. Eight Israelis were slain, including Dr. Aharon Katzir-Katchalski, 58, one of the country's leading scientists who had headed a research department at the Weizmann Institute.

Arab commandos claim credit—In a statement issued from its Beirut headquarters May 31, the Popular Front for the Liberation of Palestine said it was responsible for the Tel Aviv airport attack.

The PFLP "announces its complete responsibility for the brave operation launched by one of its special groups tonight in our occupied land," the statement said.

PFLP spokesman Bassam Zayid said in Beirut May 31 that the front had instructed the three Japanese gunmen not to fire on the Air France plane passengers, but on those debarking from an El Al flight due to arrive 10 minutes later and those waiting for them. "We were sure that 90%–95% of the people in the airport at the time the operation was due to take place would be Israelis or people of direct loyalty to Israel," Zayid said. "Our purpose was to kill as many people as possible at the airport, Israelis, of course, but anyone else who was there."

An Egyptian broadcast from Cairo May 31 boasted that "the heroes proved they can penetrate the conquered territories to avenge the blood of others. Now Israel has no alternative but to close down Lydda [Lod] Airport and to prevent tourist visits if she wishes to protect her borders."

Lebanese connection? In a letter to the U.N. Security Council June 1, Israel charged that Kozo Okamoto, the captured Japanese gunman, had been trained for his mission in Lebanon at a camp about 12 miles from Beirut.

A more detailed Israeli account of the background of the three Japanese assailants, provided June 5, further underlined the allegation that Lebanon was harboring persons responsible for attacks on international aviation. Mordechai Tabor, chief of Israel's national police, gave the following account based on interrogation of Okamoto:

Okamoto and his two companions were contacted in Japan earlier in 1972 by a representative of the Popular Front for the Liberation of Palestine. Okamoto left Japan Feb. 29 and arrived in Beirut by way of Montreal, New York and Paris. His two companions had preceded him to the Lebanese capital. After training exercises in the use of light arms, the three men received their final instruction May 16 for the trip to Tel Aviv to carry out their mission. They had agreed they would commit suicide afterwards.

Lebanon again denied June 5 that its territory had been used as a haven for the three Japanese terrorists.

Guerrillas kill Israeli soldier. The Israeli military command announced June 5 that an Israeli soldier had been killed the same day in an ambush by Arab guerrillas near Quneitra, on Syria's occupied Golan Heights. The attack was the first reported on the Syrian front since February.

Israel, Egypt claim jets shot down. Israel and Egypt June 13 gave conflicting reports of an air battle over the Mediterranean in which each nation claimed to have shot down two of the other's aircraft. It was the first such clash since the Suez Canal ceasefire of August 1970.

An Israeli military spokesman said two Egyptian MiG-21's were shot down over international waters about 25 miles northeast of Port Said when the MiGs intercepted a patrol of Israeli F-4 Phantoms. Two Egyptian pilots were seen parachuting into the sea, but all Israeli aircraft returned safely from the area, the spokesman said.

An Egyptian statement released after the Israeli report claimed eight Egyptian interceptors shot down two Israeli Mirage jet fighters when 16 Israeli planes invaded Egyptian airspace about 35 miles west of the Suez Canal, near the seaside resort of Ras el Bar. The state-

ment acknowledged that two Egyptian planes were hit but did not indicate whether they had crashed.

Israelis raid Lebanon. An Israeli armored force struck into southern Lebanon June 21 and captured five Syrian officers, a Lebanese officer and three military policemen. The strike coincided with an Israeli air and artillery attack against a suspected Palestinian commando base at Hasbaya in southeastern Lebanon. The Israeli military action followed by a day resumption of guerrilla attacks across the border after a four-month lull. Two civilians were killed in the ambush of a tourist bus.

According to Beirut's account of the incident: Four Lebanese policemen were killed and two civilians were wounded during the capture of the Syrians and Lebanese at the village of Ramieh about 100 yards from the Israeli border. The Syrians and their Lebanese escorts were ambushed by five Israeli tanks and three other armored vehicles. One Lebanese vehicle was destroyed and two Syrian limousines were captured. (The Associated Press reported that one of two wounded Lebanese who escaped later died.) Another Israeli armored force simultaneously entered the nearby village of Batishya but withdrew after a two-hour search.

Reporting on the Hasbaya attack, the Lebanese said the Israeli planes and artillery killed 14 civilians and wounded 25 others. Commando sources reported that 30 of their men had been killed and 30 wounded in the raid.

A Syrian communique broadcast by Damascus radio said the captured Syrian officers were in Lebanon "as part of the visits exchanged" by the Syrian and Lebanese armies.

An Israeli military spokesman said the Israeli operations against Lebanon were "connected with information we had in recent weeks of preparation" for more guerrilla attacks against Israel from Lebanese territory. The capture of the Syrians came as a surprise and was "evidence of joint Syrian-Lebanese planning against Israel," the spokesman said.

In a previous encounter, Israel reported that its forces June 15 had killed four Arab infiltrators in the occupied Golan Heights. The men were said to have worn uniforms largely identical with Syrian army uniforms.

Israelis raid Lebanon again. Israeli planes and artillery June 23 struck at suspected Palestinian commando bases in Lebanon for the second time in three days, inflicting heavy casualties. That raid and a previous attack on guerrilla concentrations in Lebanon June 21 were condemned by the U.N. Security Council June 26 following three days of acrimonious debate.

The latest Israeli attack followed the commando shelling earlier June 23 of Kiryat Shmona, an Israeli town seven miles from the Lebanese border.

A Lebanese communique said 18 Lebanese civilians were killed and 12 wounded in the Israeli assaults. The Palestinian Resistance Movement in Beirut reported "scores of guerrillas" killed or wounded in the attacks. Seventeen of the Lebanese fatalities occurred during Israeli jet strikes on Deir el Ashayer on the Syrian border, according to Lebanese authorities. The communique said the other Lebanese was killed by an Israeli rocket attack near Marjoun, directly opposite Kiryat Shmona.

Justifying the Israeli action, Premier Golda Meir said June 23 "if the danger [to Israeli lives] is from over the border and the Lebanese government is unable to handle it, we don't have any choice but to do it ourselves."

U.N. condemns Israel—The U.N. Security Council, called into emergency session June 23 at Lebanon's request, approved a resolution June 26 condemning "the repeated attacks of Israeli forces on Lebanese territory and population." The vote was 13–0, with the U.S. and Panama abstaining.

The resolution, sponsored by Belgium, Britain and France, called on Israel to refrain from future attacks on Lebanon and urged it to release the five Syrian officers and one Lebanese officer captured during a raid into southern Lebanon June 21.

The U.S. and Panama explained that their abstentions were based on the resolution's failure to also condemn the Arabs for their attacks on Israel.

Prior to voting for the resolution, Chinese delegate Huang Hua had criticized it because it contained modifying phrases included to avoid an outright U.S. veto. (One phrase deplored "the tragic loss of life from all acts of violence and retaliation." Another "profoundly deplored all acts of violence.")

Soviet delegate Yakov Malik also assailed the resolution's modifying phrases and attacked Israeli government leaders.

Israeli delegate Yosef Tekoah deplored the Council's action, charging that the resolution "ignores the murderous attacks on innocent civilians, the assaults on villages and towns, the crimes of air piracy perpetrated by Arab terrorist organizations." Tekoah took the Council to task for disregarding the May 30 Lod airport massacre "as if it never happened."

At the Council's June 24 meeting, Tekoah had rejected the demand for the return of the captured Syrian officers, claiming that they were prisoners of war. The Syrians, Tekoah said, had been on the Lebanese-Israeli border "to collect military data and work on guidelines for future operations," according to military papers found in possession of one of the men.

The Security Council July 21 approved a resolution again calling on Israel to release the Lebanese and Syrian officers. The vote was 14–0 with the U.S. abstaining.

The resolution, sponsored by Guinea, Somalia, Sudan, Yugoslavia and India, instructed Secretary General Kurt Waldheim and Council President Carlos Ortiz de Rozas to continue their efforts to get the six prisoners released.

Israel continued to boycott the debate, having refused to take its seat at the Council's July 18 meeting after its request for discussion of a full exchange of war prisoners held in the Middle East was rejected. In a statement made outside the chamber, Israeli representative Yosef Tekoah charged "We have witnessed the most sorry spectacle of the Security Council at work. A number of member states, by a parliamentary maneuver, has caused the Council to disregard the rights of a member state in an unabashed ravage of freedom of speech."

Israel had complained to the Council July 6 that Egypt and Syria continued to rebuff its requests for the exchange of prisoners. A letter sent to the Council by representative Yosef Tekoah asserted that "the policy of Egypt and Syria of persistent refusal not only to release Israeli prisoners but also to see their own nationals home again is not acceptable to civilized opinion."

Tekoah said Egypt held 10 Israeli prisoners of war and Syria three. He said Israel was holding 61 Egyptians, 45 Syrians and five Lebanese.

Syria and Lebanon July 4 had requested a meeting of the Council to press for the release of the Lebanese and Syrian officers. Tekoah later responded to the Lebanese-Syrian move by stating that "the only way there will be repatriation is through the release of all prisoners of war by all parties in accordance with the Geneva convention."

Israeli Foreign Minister Abba Eban had denounced the Council's June 23 resolution at a meeting July 3 with the ambassadors of Belgium, Japan and Argentina and the charge d'affaires of Britain. Their nations were members of the Council. Eban told the envoys there could be no unilateral release of prisoners. He assailed the Council's persistent failure to take note of Israelis killed by commandos while condemning Israel when it retaliated.

Israeli-Arab naval clashes—Israeli gunboats operating off the coast of Lebanon June 23 fired on a commando vessel and set it ablaze.

Beirut reported that in another naval clash Israeli warships June 24 sank a Lebanese fishing boat off the coast and fired machine guns at a Lebanese army post. The Lebanese returned the fire and forced the Israeli ships to withdraw.

A commando communique said an Israeli ship was sunk by a guerrilla vessel June 24 after the Israelis attempted to attack a Palestinian refugee camp at Rashiya.

Commando-Lebanese accord—Beirut sources reported June 26 that Palestinian commandos in Lebanon had agreed to a government request to temporarily suspend attacks on Israel to spare Lebanon from reprisal attacks by Israel. The decision was confirmed by Premier Saeb Salam, who said "we are in an understanding with the commandos and we shall remain so."

Salam had said June 24 that his government had no intentions of cracking down on the commandos. He declared: "Let Israel hear this: There will not be a clash between Lebanon and the Palestinians in any way."

Salam made his statement after conferring three times in the previous 24 hours with commando leader Yasir Arafat.

A formal agreement barring Palestinian commando raids on Israel from Lebanon was reached June 27 by Salam and Arafat.

A guerrilla splinter group declared June 28 that it would not abide by the Beirut accord for freezing operations against Israel. A statement signed in Damascus by the Popular Front for the Liberation of Palestine, General Command, which had broken away from the PFLP in 1968, said its forces would continue attacks on Israeli-held areas, but would carry out the raids "in the depth of enemy territory" and not near the cease-fire lines.

A British decision to permit the Palestine Liberation Organization to open an office in London was assailed by Israel July 4.

Commando leader assassinated. A leader of the Popular Front for the Liberation of Palestine, Ghassan Kanafani, 36, was killed in an explosion in a car in Beirut July 8, 1972. The blast killed his 17-year old niece when Kanafani started the vehicle.

Kanafani had been a spokesman for the front, but recently had said he no longer held that position. He had said he was only editor of its weekly journal, Al Hadaf.

The PFLP July 11 claimed credit for a grenade explosion that day at the central bus terminal in Tel Aviv. The blast wounded nine persons. The front said the explosion was in reprisal for Kanafani's death.

Israeli jets attacked. Israel reported that two of its jets flying over the Sinai Peninsula July 24 were the targets of four Egyptian surface-to-air missiles fired from the western bank of the Suez Canal. The planes were not hit or damaged and returned safely to base, the Israelis said.

Egypt claimed that one of four Israeli jets that crossed over the canal in the Qantara-Ismailia area was shot down by its air defenses on the waterway.

Israeli plane bombers arrested. Police in Rome Aug. 19 arrested two Arabs as suspects in a bomb explosion aboard an Israeli passenger plane Aug. 16. The bomb, contained in a record player stored in the baggage compartment of an El Al airliner, exploded 10 minutes after the plane's take-off from Rome for Tel Aviv. The damaged airliner returned safely to Rome after the explosion, with four passengers slightly injured.

The two men seized by police were identified from their passports as Ahmad Zaid, 32, of Baghdad, Iraq, and Adnan Mohammed Ali Hashan, 29, of Amman, Jordan. They had been traced as a result of information given to Italian police by two British women passengers who said they had been given a package containing the record player as a farewell gift from the two men at whose apartment they had stayed in Rome. Zaid and Hashan were identified from photographs taken by the two women—Audrey Wilton and Ruth Watkin, both 18. They said they were unaware that the record player contained an explosive charge. Judicial authorities in Rome Aug. 18 declared the two women innocent.

Arabs kill 11 Israelis at Olympics. Seventeen persons, among them 11 memvers of the Israeli Olympic team, were shot to death Sept. 5, 1972 in a 23-hour drama that began when Arab commandos broke into the Israeli dormitory at the Olympic village in Munich, West Germany. Nine of the Israelis, seized by the Arabs as hostages, were killed along with five of their captors in an airport gun battle between the Arabs and West German police.

The other two Israelis were killed in the initial Arab attack on their living quarters. The 17th victim was a West German policeman.

In Cairo, an Arab guerrilla organization called Black September claimed responsibility for the attack.

The Arabs and their hostages had been taken by helicopter to the airport 15 miles west of Munich where a jet was being made ready to fly them all to Cairo.

The tragic event began at 4:30 a.m. Sept. 5, when the commandos scaled an eight-foot wire fence that surrounded the Olympic village compound. The raiders made their way to Building 31, which housed the Hong Kong, Uruguayan and Israeli teams.

At about 5:30 a.m. the commandos burst into the quarters where the Israeli athletes were staying. As they rushed in, they were intercepted by Moshe Weinberg, the Israeli wrestling coach, who held a door against the commandos while shouting for the Israeli athletes to flee. Seconds later the Arabs broke in, killing Weinberg, 33, and Joseph Romano, 33, a weight lifter.

Six of the fifteen Israelis managed to escape the building. The nine, who were trapped inside their quarters, were reported to have fought the attackers for a time with knives. The Arabs, however, overpowered the Israelis, seizing them as hostages.

Once in control of the Israeli quarters in Building 31, the Arabs made known their demand: they wanted the release of 200 Arab commandos imprisoned in Israel.

Throughout the late morning and afternoon, West German officials negotiated with the Arabs on the patio of the Israeli dormitory, in full view of onlookers. One of those who met with the Arabs was Hans-Dietrich Genscher, West Germany's interior minister.

Throughout the negotiations Munich police were positioned outside the apartments where the Israelis were held. Some of the policemen, dressed in athletic attire, were stationed on top of Building 31.

At ground level, armored police vehicles were brought in to surround the building.

The stalemate was broken at about 9 p.m. when the West Germans succeeded in persuading the terrorists to move out of Building 31 with the hostages. As part of the bargain, the West Germans agreed to have three helicopters transport the Arabs and the nine Israelis to the military airport at Furstenfeldbruck.

When the convoy arrived at the airport, two of the terrorists walked from the helicopters to inspect a Boeing 707 jet that was to take them to Cairo. As they walked back to the helicopters, German riflemen reportedly opened fire. The Arabs, armed with automatic weapons, returned the fire.

Israel raids southern Lebanon. An Israeli armored patrol, supported by helicopters, struck more than a mile inside southern Lebanon Sept. 7, 1972 in search of Arab commandos.

Israeli military sources said the attack followed clashes on Israeli territory late Sept. 6 and early Sept. 7 in which two Arabs and an Israeli were killed. Sources denied the raid near the village of Yarun, which lasted eight hours, was related to the Munich shootings.

Military sources in Lebanon also said three formations of Israeli military planes flew sorties as far north as Tyre and Marjioun in Lebanon.

Raids reprisal for Munich killings. An estimated 50–80 Israeli planes carried out a damaging attack Sept. 8 against 10 Arab guerrilla bases and naval installations deep in Syria and Lebanon in retaliation for the Munich slayings. The raids, lasting 17 minutes, were the heaviest by Israel since the 1967 war. They were followed by a clash between Syrian and Israeli planes over the Golan Heights the following day.

The U.N. Security Council met in emergency session Sept. 10 on the Israeli air strikes, but separate vetoes cast by the U.S., and the Soviet Union and China blocked passage of any peace resolution.

An Israeli military officer, reporting on the air assaults against Syria and Lebanon, said initial accounts indicated that "scores" of Arab guerrillas had been caught in their camps and were killed or wounded. The Palestinian commando news agency in Damascus said Sept. 9 that the air strikes had killed 66 persons and wounded more than 40, mostly civilian women and children.

The planes dropped bombs and fired rockets on what Israeli military authorities described as troop concentrations, training centers, supply depots and headquarter units of Al Fatah, the principal guerrilla organization. Although the Munich attack was carried out by the Black September organization, the Israelis regarded that guerrilla organization as an integral part of Al Fatah.

Among the targets struck in Syria were El Hameh, regarded as the principal Al Fatah base in that country, located on the edge of a refugee camp four miles west of Damascus. Three Al Fatah naval installations on the Syrian coast were hit, including Burj Islam, the chief naval base a few miles north of Latakia.

Among the targets pounded in Lebanon were Nahar el Bard, a naval training base of Al Fatah north of Tripoli, Rashya el Wadi, a regional Al Fatah headquarters, and Rafid, an Al Fatah maintenance base, both in southern Lebanon. Civilians were reported to have suffered heavy casualties in Rafid.

Israeli authorities reported that in another action Sept. 8 one of their navy missile boats sank a small commando attack vessel off the southern Lebanon coast. The communiqué said the Israelis destroyed the Palestinian craft after the guerrillas opened fire with bazookas and machine guns.

In the air clashes over the Golan Heights Sept. 9, the first since June 26, 1970, the Israelis claimed three Syrian jets were shot down and another damaged, while reporting all of its planes returning safely to base. Syria conceded the loss of three planes, but claimed three Israeli jets also were downed by Syrian air and ground fire. The Damascus report said Israeli positions in the Golan Heights suffered heavy damage and casualties as a result of Syrian air and artillery strikes. Israel said the loss of the three Syrian planes raised to 29 the number of Syrian aircraft its pilots had downed since the end of the 1967 war. It placed its own losses by Syria during that period at one plane.

A spokesman in Amman, Jordan said 18 persons were killed and 13 houses were destroyed or damaged when four rockets fell on a Jordanian village near the Syrian border during the Israeli-Syrian dogfight. Israel said the rockets had been jettisoned by Syrian planes attempting to escape the pursuing Israeli aircraft.

In an assessment of the Israeli air strikes, Lt. Gen. David Elazar, Israel's chief of staff, said Sept. 10 that the raids on Syria and Lebanon were not only in retaliation for the Munich killings, but also for the increasing attacks on Israel's borders from those two countries. "These actions were part of a continuous war" that should not be regarded "as begun today and finished tomorrow," Elazar said. Replying to Arab charges that many civilians had been killed in the raids, the general said "We make every effort to avoid hurting civilians but many terrorist bases are situated in the vicinity of civilian settlements."

Big 3 veto U.N. resolutions. The U.N. Security Council meeting in emergency session Sept. 10 on the Israeli air attacks on Syria and Lebanon failed to take any action as the U.S., China and the. Soviet Union vetoed resolutions dealing with the crisis. The session had been called by Syria and Lebanon.

One resolution, sponsored by Guinea, Somalia and Yugoslavia, called on "the parties concerned to cease immediately all military operations and exercise the greatest restraint in the interests of international peace and security." It was approved by 13 members with only Panama abstaining.

U.S. representative George Bush vetoed the resolution on the ground that it failed to mention the Arab terrorist attack at Munich that had led to the Israeli reprisal air strike.

Bush called the resolution one-sided and asserted that similar ones adopted by the Council did not promote peace but encouraged "perpetrators and supporters of acts of terrorism to believe they can escape the world's censure." Bush then offered a compromise resolution that never came to a vote. It condemned "the senseless and unprovoked terrorist attack in Munich" and urged all parties concerned "to take all measures for the immediate cessation and prevention of all military operations and terrorist activities ..."

In a previous round of voting, a compromise resolution drafted by Belgium, Britain, France and Italy that deplored all acts of violence in the Middle East was vetoed by China and the Soviet Union.

Israel was not represented at the meeting because of a Jewish holiday.

Deep Israeli thrust into Lebanon. Israeli forces carried out a major ground and air attack against Palestinian commando bases in southern Lebanon Sept. 16–17, 1972. About 3,000 troops, spear- headed by about 50 tanks and other armored vehicles and with air support provided by about 25 jets, thrust 15 miles across the border in the deepest penetration of southern Lebanon.

Israeli authorities reported that during the 33-hour operation "at least 60" guerrillas were killed, 16 Arab villages were searched for terrorists and more than 150 houses believed to have quartered the commandos were destroyed. Israel placed its losses at three killed and six wounded. The Lebanese army as well as the guerrillas put up strong resistance. Many of the guerrillas fled north after the Israeli attack began.

Lt. Gen. David Elazar, Israeli chief of staff, Sept. 17 described the operation as "a major battle" in "our continuing war against the terrorists." It followed the killing of two Israeli soldiers Sept. 15 by Arab raiders in the Golan Heights.

Arab sources said the Israelis killed at least 35 guerrillas, 18 Lebanese soldiers and 23 Lebanese civilians. A Beirut communique said Israeli jets had destroyed two major bridges over the Litani River, which cut across Lebanon about 15 miles north of the Israeli frontier. Planes of Lebanon's small air force attempted to intercept the superior

Israeli jets, some of which had flown over Beirut.

Describing the ground action, the Lebanese said the Israeli troops and armored units struck in the southeast up to Adiesse and Taiybe in the direction of Marjioun and drove past Bin Jbail up to Tibnine and Ghandouniye. In a second thrust to the west, the Israeli force pushed as far as Kana, 15 miles south of the port of Tyre, according to the report.

Two American newsmen who accompanied the Israeli force reported Sept. 17 that heavy Lebanese and guerrilla resistance had delayed the return of some units to Israeli territory for at least 12 hours. Thomas Cheatham of UPI and Andrew Meisels of the American Broadcasting Co. said one attacking element scheduled to return to its base Sept. 16 had to "fight its way out" of the Arab village of Jouya, which was defended by both Lebanese soldiers and commandos. The unit finally made its way back to Israel early Sept. 17. Lebanon claimed that 17 Israelis were killed in the two-day operation and that seven tanks were knocked out of action.

Beirut curbs commandos. In the aftermath of the Israeli foray, Lebanon Sept. 17 ordered the commandos to evacuate all villages in southern Lebanon. The Palestine Liberation Organization (PLO) was reported Sept. 20 to have acceded to the Beirut government's demands. The agreement followed mediation moves by Mahmoud Riad, secretary general of the Arab League, who had arrived in the Lebanese capital on short notice Sept. 18.

According to the text of a Lebanese directive released Sept. 17 by the Al Fatah office in Cairo, the guerrillas were to remain confined to their camps in sectors where they had previously been restricted. They were to carry arms and wear their battle dress only after coordination between their command and the Lebanese army.

Al Fatah leader Yasir Arafat was reported at first to have challenged the commando curbs in a meeting with Premier Saeb Salam.

Shortly after the Israeli forces withdrew from southern Lebanon, government troops moved back into the area to block guerrilla reoccupation of their former bases.

Commando acceptance of the Lebanese military restrictions was confirmed by commando sources in Beirut Sept. 20. It was said that Arafat and other PLO officials had acquiesced in meetings with Mahmoud Riad. Kamal Nasser, chief PLO spokesman in Beirut, told newsmen: "The Palestinian resistance movement has full confidence in [Lebanese] President Suleiman Franjieh and his understanding of its role and his true belief in the justice of the Palestinian cause."

Bomb kills Israeli aide in London. An envelope bomb apparently mailed by Arab guerrillas exploded and killed a diplomat in the Israeli embassy in London Sept. 19. The incident was followed by the discovery of similar booby-trapped envelopes destined for Israeli officials in at least eight other cities. All bore Amsterdam postmarks. None of these detonated.

The Israeli official, Dr. Ami Shachori, 44, counselor for agricultural affairs, was killed by the explosive device in an envelope he was opening. He was hit in the chest and abdomen by the charge. Another official in the office was slightly injured. He was Theodor Kaddar, who had arrived recently to replace Shachori. Three more explosive devices in envelopes addressed to senior Israeli embassy members were discovered by Israeli security men. Israelis told police that one of them contained a leaflet from the Black September terrorist group.

Four more explosive letters addressed to members of the Israeli embassy staff were found in a London post office later September 19.

A security check of mail at the Israeli embassy in Paris Sept. 19 turned up two large envelopes containing explosives. They were defused.

Additional bomb letters were intercepted Sept. 20 in New York, Montreal, Ottowa, Brussels and Jerusalem. This brought to 32 the number of such devices mailed to Israeli officials. Three found by U.S. Customs employes at a New York post office were addressed to officials of Israel's U.N. mission. Two of four envelopes discovered in Jerusalem bore the names of Communications Minister Shimon Peres and Moshe Katz, head of the Welfare Ministry.

Israel opposes anti-terror groups. Following the death Sept. 19 of an Israeli diplomat in London by an Arab letter bomb, the Israel branch of the Jewish Defense League (JDL) announced the formation of an anti-terrorist organization to combat Arab guerrilla groups and institutions in Europe and the U.S. The Israeli government immediately cracked down on the JDL and individuals attempting to take action on their own.

Israeli authorities Sept. 21 disclosed the arrest of Amihai Paglin, a former leader in the underground struggle against British rule in Palestine, in connection with a secret shipment of arms that had been intercepted at the Tel Aviv airport. The weapons, including machine guns and grenades, were meant for use against Arabs abroad. The JDL claimed responsibility for the arms shipment, but its leader, Rabbi Meir Kahane, was later said to have told Justice Minister Yacov Shapiro that it was wrong to involve Israel. Israeli authorities also arrested JDL member Abraham Hershkowitz on charges of attempting to ship the arms out by air.

Police Sept. 22 raided JDL's Jerusalem headquarters, seized documents connected with the alleged arms smuggling operation and arrested the league's secretary, Joseph Schneider.

Israeli police acknowledged Sept. 26 that some arms shipments meant for the anti-terrorist campaign against Arabs had slipped out of the country and reached their destinations.

The Israeli government issued an injunction Sept. 22 against Kahane and 19 other JDL members ordering them to keep out of the West Bank and the Gaza Strip. The order was said to be aimed at preventing the JDL from conducting "any activities liable to disrupt order or endanger security in those areas."

U.S.-Israeli talks on terrorism. The U.S. Sept. 22 backed Israel's contention that priority must be given to combatting international terrorism, although "options must be kept open" for a Middle East peace settlement. The announced American position followed a report Sept. 21 that Israel had informed friendly governments that it would refuse to participate in further peace negotiations until all Arab terrorism was crushed.

The U.S.-Israeli agreement on terrorism was reached in talks in Washington between Secretary of State William P. Rogers and Foreign Minister Abba Eban. After the meeting a State Department spokesman said Rogers had agreed with Eban that "individual governments must act effectively to combat this challenge to world social order." Eban, the spokesman said, had outlined the measures Israel was taking to fight terrorism.

After meeting with Rogers, Eban emphasized to newsmen that his country was determined to combat terror tactics because "it has always been our policy to hit where we can those who make war against us."

"It is not our policy or duty," he said, "to wait for the saboteurs to kill us or our children." Eban charged that Egypt, Syria and Lebanon had engaged "in a new form of warfare" against Israel by supporting the Arab commandos.

The Sept. 21 report that Israel would refuse to negotiate pending the elimination of the Arab terrorist threat also said that Israel was preparing new blows against the Palestinian commandos. According to the Israeli source, in the coming months Israel would launch a "major military effort" in the Middle East to destroy the terrorist groups. It would also take preventive action anywhere in the world if necessary, particularly in Europe, where the Arab guerrillas were becoming more active.

Gromyko assails Arab terrorists. In the strongest Soviet criticism of Arab terrorism, Foreign Minister Andrei Gromyko told the U.N. General Assembly Sept. 26 that some Palestinian terrorists had turned to "criminal actions."

Gromyko called for an end to Israeli occupation of Arab territory, reiterating the Soviet Union's support of "the just struggle of the Arab people of Palestine for the restoration of their inalienable rights recognized by the United Nations." But he added, "it is certainly impossible to condone the acts of terrorism by certain elements from among the participants in the Palestinian movement which have led, notably, to the recent tragic events in Munich."

"These criminal actions," Gromyko said, "deal a blow also to the national interests and aspirations of the Palestinians; these acts are used by the Israeli criminals in order to cover up their bandit-like policy against the Arab peoples."

Jerusalem supermarket blast. Three persons were slightly wounded when a bomb exploded in a Jerusalem supermarket Sept. 29. Police rounded up 134 persons, mostly Arab workers from a nearby construction site, for questioning. It was the first serious Arab terrorist incident in the Israeli capital in two years.

Arabs send more letter bombs. More Arab guerrilla letter bombs addressed to Israeli diplomats were found in several cities of the world Sept. 21. All were defused.

Ten of the booby-trapped letters, postmarked from Amsterdam, were intercepted in a Jerusalem post office. Others were received at the Israeli embassies in Kinshasa, Zaire; Brussels and Buenos Aires.

Amsterdam police theorized Sept. 21 that the Arabs had slipped into the Netherlands the previous week and fled the country after carrying out their mission.

Amsterdam police said Sept. 22 that the British police would coordinate international efforts to investigate the letter-bomb activities. Authorities in the Netherlands and other countries agreed to forward pertinent information to Scotland Yard in London.

A Jordanian government spokesman said Sept. 23 that the Amman post office that day had intercepted and defused four letter bombs addressed to four Jordanian officials. The spokesman said the letters bore Amsterdam postmarks.

Arab letter bomb explodes. A postal clerk was injured Oct. 14, 1972 when a letter bomb similar to the ones sent by Arab terrorists exploded in a New York post office. The man's hands were maimed by the blast.

The letter, bearing a Malaysian postmark, was addressed to an unidentified former national officer of Hadassah, the women's Zionist organization.

Two other New York women also active in American Zionist circles had received letter bombs Oct. 10. The recipients opened the envelopes but the bombs did not explode. Both letters bore Malaysian postmarks. Similar letters were mailed Oct. 10 to Jewish families in Bulawayo, Rhodesia.

A letter bomb delivered Oct. 4 to the Rome office of United Hias Service, a Jewish immigration office, was defused by Italian explosive experts. The letter, mailed from Malaysia, bore inscriptions which said "Black September," the Arab guerrilla group.

Israeli jets bomb Lebanon, Syria. Israeli planes Oct. 15 bombed Palestinian Al Fatah commando bases in Syria and Lebanon. It was the first time that Israeli forces had attacked targets in Arab countries without immediate provocation. In explaining the new policy, an Israeli spokesman said "we are no longer waiting for them to hit first. This is the operative phase of our pledge to hit the terrorists wherever they are, and they are in Lebanon and Syria."

The new Israeli strategy was further stated in a broadcast by Chaim Herzog, former chief of staff. He said: "We are not engaged in reprisal, but a war against terror. The very presence of terrorists in the area between the border and the Litani River is a provocation" and Israel, therefore, considered itself "free to act against them."

Premier Golda Meir said the attacks on Syria and Lebanon were carried out because it was in those countries that the guerrillas had planned the Munich killings, the Tel Aviv airport massacre and the mailing of letter bombs to Jews.

Israeli military authorities said about 20 planes had bombed four guerrilla installations in Lebanon and one in

Syria. The targets in Lebanon were a naval base at the coastal town of Ras Naba Muhiliv; a command post north of Bakifa; Deir Ashayer, a base on the principal road leading from southern Lebanon to Syria; and a central motor pool for vehicle repairs near Saida on the coast. The target struck in Syria was an Al Fatah training camp one mile east of Masyaf.

A Lebanese communique said the Israeli raid had killed two civilians and wounded 16.

Letter bombs aimed at Nixon, Arabs. Letter bombs were addressed Oct. 24–27 to U.S. officials, including President Nixon, and to Palestinian Liberation Organization leaders and other Palestinians in four Arab countries. Several of the latter bombs were opened and exploded, injuring a number of Arabs.

Israeli postal authorities in the northern town of Kiryat Shmona Oct. 24 intercepted three letter bombs intended for President Nixon, Secretary of State William P. Rogers and Defense Secretary Melvin R. Laird.

Letter bombs bearing Belgrade, Yugoslavia postmarks were received Oct. 25 in Lebanon, Libya, Algeria and Egypt. A letter opened in Beirut exploded and injured the secretary of a trading company known to have arranged arms deals with Arab countries. The envelope was addressed to a Palestinian partner in the firm who was traveling outside Lebanon. A Beirut postman was blinded after one of the letters he was sorting exploded in his face. Palestine Liberation Organization official Abu Khalil was injured in Algiers when he opened a booby-trapped parcel. Another PLO official, Mustafa Awad Abu Zeid, the organization's secretary in Libya, was blinded by a parcel bomb opened in Tripoli. Two other persons received less serious injuries. Egyptian authorities intercepted a parcel bomb at the Cairo airport. The package was addressed to a PLO official.

Three other letter bombs exploded at the Cairo airport Oct. 26, seriously injuring an Egyptian security officer, who was examing the envelopes after intercepting them. The letters were intended for three officials of the PLO office in Cairo.

Dutch authorities Oct. 25 detained and then released a Jordanian with an Algerian diplomatic passport who was found to be carrying unaddressed letter bombs, hand grenades and explosives in his luggage. The Jordanian, intercepted at the Amsterdam airport, told a magistrate that he was unaware of the contents of the suitcases. He said he thought his luggage contained documents for an Algerian embassy in South America.

The Beirut office of the newspaper of the Popular Front for the Liberation of Palestine was the intended target of a letter bomb Oct. 27. The device was intercepted at the city's post office and rendered harmless.

Arabs force release of Munich slayers. Two Arab guerrillas of the Black September group hijacked a West German airliner over Turkey Oct. 29, forcing the Bonn government to release the three Arab commandos held in the Sept. 5 murder of 11 Israeli athletes at the Olympic Games in Munich. The freed killers were later flown to Tripoli, Libya.

The released Arabs who faced trial for the killings were Mahmud el-Safadi, 21, Samer Mohammad Abdullah, 22, and Ibrahim Badran, 20.

The aircraft, a Lufthansa Boeing 727 with 13 passengers and seven crewmen, was commandeered by the two guerrillas after it left Beirut, Lebanon for Ankara, Turkey. Threatening to blow up the plane and its occupants unless their demands were met, the commandos forced the pilot to fly to Munich with fuel stopovers at Nicosia, Cyprus and Zagreb, Yugoslavia. As the plane circled the heavily-guarded Munich airport, however, the hijackers ordered it flown back to Zagreb. It circled the airfield there for an hour and did not land until a smaller jet carrying the three guerrillas released by the West Germans arrived at the Yugoslav airport. The three freed prisoners then boarded the hijacked airliner which flew on to Tripoli. The Lufthansa plane was released and flew back to West Germany with the passengers and crew Oct. 30.

The Israeli government reacted sharply to the release of the Munich commandos. A Foreign Ministry spokesman said Oct. 29 that "every capitulation encourages the terrorists to continue their criminal acts." After a Cabinet meeting on the incident, Minister Without Portfolio Israel Galili assailed Bonn's decision as "unforgivable from the Jewish and Israeli point of view."

Israeli Foreign Minister Abba Eban protested to Bonn Oct. 30. The message, conveyed through West German Ambassador to Israel Jesco von Puttkamer, charged "capitulation to terrorists," and said Israel questioned whether "there has been a change in German policy regarding terrorists and their actions."

In reply to Eban's charge of "capitulation," a West German government spokesman said Oct. 30 that the foreign minister had "missed the point" that 20 lives were at stake.

Israeli jets raid Syria. Israeli jets Oct. 30 bombed four Arab guerrilla bases near Damascus and returned later to attack a Syrian army camp at Tel Kalakh, 100 miles north. At the same time, Syrian forces shelled Israeli positions in the Golan Heights.

Israel denied the air strikes were in retaliation for the Arab hijacking of a West German airliner Oct. 29. An Israeli military spokesman said one Israeli was wounded in the Syrian shelling of the heights. Lt. Gen. David Elazar, chief of staff, said Israeli artillery had not returned fire because "we wanted to make the point that Israel will choose her own time and place to fight."

Syrian authorities reported that more than 60 civilians had been killed and 70 wounded in the first Israeli air strike, which they claimed included the bombing of Palestinian refugee camps. Palestinian commandos placed their losses at 15 dead.

Israeli jets raided Syrian targets again Nov. 9 after clashes in the Golan Heights.

Israel claimed its pilots shot down two Syrian MiG-21 fighters before returning safely to base. Damascus admitted the loss of the two aircraft, but claimed the downing of four Israeli planes, two apparently by antiaircraft fire.

The latest fighting followed two incidents involving Arab guerrillas in the Golan Heights. An Israeli civilian was wounded in the northern section

Nov. 8 when his tractor hit a commando-planted mine. In the second incident, an Israeli patrol Nov. 9 clashed with a group of 18 commandos attempting to set up an ambush position in the southern part of the heights. Israeli jets then retaliated by striking at two Syrian army positions near the Golan truce line where the 18 infiltrators had passed through. The Syrian army responded with a three-hour artillery barrage against two Israeli settlements in the heights, killing one soldier and causing considerable property damage. Israeli planes then attacked Syria for the second time, striking at four army forward positions, two artillery concentrations and a surface-to-air missile battery on the northern part of the truce line.

Damascus reported that the pilots of its two downed planes had bailed out over Syria. The communique said pilots of two of the four downed Israeli planes had been picked up by an Israeli helicopter after bailing out. Israel claimed the downing of the two MiGs brought to 33 the number of Syrian planes destroyed since the 1967 war. Israel listed its air losses in that period at three fighter-bombers.

Defying Israeli threats of further retaliation, the Syrian government declared Nov. 10 that its "aid to the guerrillas will continue regardless of Israeli reprisals."

Letter bombs intercepted. Numerous letter bombs, apparently sent by Arab guerrillas, were intercepted Oct. 31–Nov. 13 by authorities in various parts of the world. Most of the booby-trapped devices were addressed to Jewish firms, organizations and individuals in Britain.

The Malaysian Home Affairs Ministry confirmed Nov. 1 that 15 letter bombs meant for Jewish groups in London, Rome and the U.S. had been discovered in the Kuala Lumpur post office Oct. 31 and defused by army experts. Malaysian officials said Nov. 2 that a local Malay-Arab group was responsible for sending out 35 letter bombs, including the 15. The same group was said to have mailed out nine other explosive devices from Penang in October.

A letter bomb received by the Egyptian embassy in London Oct. 31 was rendered harmless. London police Nov. 2 defused a letter bomb destined for the British Technion Society, which was connected with the University of Haifa in Israel. It was postmarked Penang.

Another 19 letter bombs intended for Jews in London and Glasgow were received Nov. 10–13 bearing postmarks from New Delhi and Bombay, India. One of the devices which had not been intercepted was opened Nov. 10 at a London diamond trading company, exploding and wounding an official of the firm.

Swiss authorities intercepted five letter bombs at the airport postal center in Geneva Nov. 10. All bore New Delhi postmarks and were addressed either to the Israeli mission to U.N. agencies in Geneva or to Jews and Jewish organizations.

Addressing the House of Commons Nov. 13, British Home Secretary Robert Carr denounced the letter bombs and declared they "will not intimidate any section of the British public."

The Indian government was criticized by opposition leaders in parliament Nov. 13 for allegedly being lax in preventing dissemination of the letter bombs. Rightwing Jan Sangh party members charged that New Delhi's "pro-Arab policy" hindered government action in the matter. Communications Minister H. N. Bahgunua denied the allegations, saying that more than 50 letter bombs had been caught by Indian authorities.

Israel, Syria battle on truce line. Israeli and Syrian armed forces fought an eight-hour battle along the Golan Heights truce line Nov. 21, using planes, artillery and tanks. The clash, the second in less than two weeks, was the most serious between the two nations in more than two years. The fighting followed Israeli air strikes in retaliation for Arab commando attacks from Syria on Israeli settlements in the heights. Syria described the action as the start of a new "war of attrition."

According to the battle claims made by an Israeli military spokesman:

Israeli planes downed six Syrian MiG-21 fighters in a dogfight and knocked out 15 Syrian tanks. The jets also attacked guerrilla and Syrian army positions along a 40-mile front, knocking out a radar site and several artillery batteries and damaging two infantry division command posts. The Syrians had brought up "hundreds" of tanks to the frontier during the battle, and fired a "few thousand rounds" of artillery at Israeli positions. Two U.N. observation posts on the cease-fire line were hit and destroyed but there were no injuries. One Israeli civilian was killed and two civilians and one soldier were wounded during the Syrian shelling of settlements in the heights. No Israeli planes were lost during the day's operations.

According to Damascus' version of the battle as contained in a military communique:

Two Israeli planes and one Syrian jet were downed. The Syrian pilot bailed out over Syrian territory. Syrian forces destroyed 14 Israeli tanks and knocked out five artillery positions. A number of civilians were killed or wounded by Israeli air strikes in southern Syria.

Israeli sources said the fighting was precipitated by six commando incidents along the Golan Heights in the past several days. Two military vehicles had struck mines near the settlement of Nahal Al Nov. 17 and the nearby settlement of Nahal Golan was shelled Nov. 17 and 20. Two newly laid mines were found near Nahal Al earlier Nov. 21.

Fighting erupted Nov. 25 along the Israeli-Syrian truce line at the Golan Heights for the second time in four days. Damascus radio claimed that Syrian artillery shelled Israeli positions at Kafr Naffakh and El Quneitra after the Israelis had fired at Syrian positions earlier in the day.

In an unusual action, Israel Nov. 25 warned Egypt through the United Nation's truce supervisory staff in Jerusalem not to permit itself to "be drawn into the Syrian provocation." The statement, made by Maj. Eliahu Zeira, director of military intelligence, said the Syrian attack that day had been launched without Israeli provocation. "The Syrian shelling constitutes a clear violation of the cease-fire, being an intended provocation meant to intensify tension in Israeli-Syrian relations," Zeira said.

The Israeli declaration followed Egyptian threats to come to the aid of Syria in the event of further Israeli attacks. Foreign Minister Mohammed Hassan el-Zayyat had said Nov. 23 that Cairo's "well-known ties with Syria dictate what stand the Egyptian government should take toward this [Israeli] aggression."

Zayyat made the statement after summoning the British, French, Soviet and Chinese ambassadors and Joseph Greene, the chief U.S. diplomat in Cairo, to discuss the Nov. 21 clashes between Israel and Syria.

An Israeli commander in the Golan Heights had acknowledged that his troops, under higher orders, had deliberately shelled six Syrian villages during the day's fighting "to give the Syrians a signal that they should stop shelling our civilian settlements."

Arab diplomatic sources in Beirut reported Dec. 9 that Syria had ordered the Palestinians to stop using Syrian territory for raids against Israel. The order was a consequence of Israeli assaults on Syria Nov. 21 and 25 in retaliation for commando attacks.

Israelis raid Lebanon. An Israeli force, Nov. 24 pushed inside Lebanon and clashed with a Palestinian commando unit.

A guerrilla statement said four commandos were wounded in an exchange of fire with helicopter-borne Israeli troops near Khreibeh, less than a mile inside Lebanon near Mt. Hermon. A Lebanese army communique said the Israeli 'copters flew out of the area after government soldiers intervened and opened fire.

An Israeli command spokesman denied that helicopters were used in the operation.

Commando leader Yasir Arafat had said Nov. 18 that the guerrillas had suspended operations from southern Lebanon to spare the local Lebanese population from Israeli retaliation.

Lebanese, commandos clash. Palestinian commandos and Lebanese army troops clashed in the Arkoub section of southern Lebanon Dec. 8 and 9. Beirut said two soldiers were killed and five wounded in the first incident. Guerrillas placed their losses at four killed and five wounded. One commando was killed and five wounded in the second engagement.

The Lebanese Defense Ministry blamed the commandos for the outbreak of fighting Dec. 8, saying that one of their patrols came under guerrilla fire after the Palestinians had entered prohibited military zones. A commando statement said the Lebanese had first shelled their positions and they fired back.

The Defense Ministry recalled that the commandos' major force had withdrawn from the southern region after

Light shading indicates area seized by Israel in 1967 Middle East conflict—all of Sinai Peninsula and Gaza Strip, the Jordan bulge west of Jordan River and Syrian Golan Heights on Israel's northern border. Dark shading shows Israeli territory before the 1967 acquisition.

Israel's massive raid there Sept. 16–17 but that the guerrillas had returned Dec. 7. The fighting ensued after the commandos refused Beirut's order to leave the region by Dec. 8.

Israeli jets raid Syria. Israeli jets attacked Palestinian guerrilla bases and army positions in Syria Dec. 27.

One group of planes struck at a commando strongpoint near Dail, about 20 miles east of the Golan Heights cease-fire line, while another wave of fighter-bombers pounded two forward Syrian army positions and an artillery battery across the border from Nahal Golan. Damascus claimed three civilians were killed and two soldiers wounded.

An Israeli spokesman said the attacks, the first in five weeks, were in retaliation for five recent commando attacks in the Golan Heights. In the latest incident, an Israeli patrol Dec. 26 discovered a number of explosive devices near Nahal Golan that were primed to detonate when a vehicle approached.

Another round of attacks occurred Dec. 30 when Syrian forces shelled Israeli civilian settlements and army positions in the Golan Heights in reprisal for the Dec. 27 air strikes. The Syrian assault was quickly followed by an Israeli air raid on a Syrian army camp at Nebk, 120 miles inside the frontier. Damascus claimed one Israeli plane was damaged, but the Israelis said all their aircraft returned safely.

Arabs seize Israelis in Thailand. Four armed Palestinian commandos seized the Israeli embassy in Bangkok, Thailand Dec. 28, and held its six Israeli occupants hostage for 19 hours before releasing them. The Arab guerrillas, members of the extremist Black September group, freed the Israelis Dec. 29 after negotiations with Thai officials. The guerrillas were flown to Cairo in a Thai plane.

The seizure of the embassy began when two of the commandos climbed the wall of the compound and opened the gate for the two others. The guerrillas walked into the building and held the six Israelis at gunpoint, threatening to kill them and blow up the embassy unless 36 Palestinian prisoners held in Israel were freed by 8 a.m. Dec. 29.

Two Thai officials—Marshal Dawee Chullaspaya, the armed forces chief of staff, and Deputy Foreign Minister Chartichai Choonhavan—entered the embassy and conferred with the guerrillas while hundreds of Thai soldiers and police surrounded the building. They were assisted in the negotiations by Egyptian Ambassador Mourtafa el-Essaway. After the guerrillas were persuaded to give up the hostages and leave the country, the commandos, the negotiators and the six Israelis left by bus for the Bangkok airport, 18 miles away. The commandos, the two Thais and the Egyptian ambassador boarded the plane and arrived in Cairo later Dec. 29. The Israelis remained in the bus at the Bangkok airport. They included Nitzan Hadass, the embassy's first secretary, his wife, embassy staff members Dan Beeri and Pinhas Lavie, and Shimon Avimor, Israel's ambassador to Cambodia, who was visiting Bangkok at the time.

Thai officials said the guerrillas had been shamed into releasing their captives. A Thai officer said the Egyptian ambassador had told the commandos that Dec. 27 and 28 "were very important days for the Thai people," because ceremonies were being held for the investiture of the son of King Phumiphol Aduldet as crown prince, and "if anything happens it would make things very difficult."

'72 Israeli combat, terror toll. The Israeli command reported Jan. 11, 1973 that 19 Israeli servicemen and 34 civilians had been killed in combat and terrorist incidents in Israel and at the borders of or in occupied Arab territories in 1972. Fifty-nine soldiers and 124 civilians were wounded. (The civilian toll included the 28 killed and more than 70 wounded in the terrorist attack at the Tel Aviv airport in May.)

The command said there were 271 combat incidents in 1972, a majority of them along the frontier. A total of 122 were reported along the Syrian line, 18 inside Israel, six along the Suez Canal, 60 in the Gaza Strip and 22 on the West Bank of the Jordan River.

In 1971 there were 19 military deaths and 119 wounded. Ten civilians were listed as killed and 52 wounded.

Terrorism cuts Israeli tourist trade. A record 727,400 tourists visited Israel in 1972, the Israeli Tourism Ministry reported Jan. 3, 1973.

The flow of tourists had been running 32% ahead of the 1971 rate until the May 30 Tel Aviv airport massacre. Then it dropped sharply through December, the ministry said. The agency's statement said Israel "still managed an 11% increase overall for the year, but it would have been far greater had it not been for the terrorism and hijackings."

Violence Unabated in 1973

Israeli-Syrian jet clash. Israeli and Syrian jets fought a brief air battle over Lebanon Jan. 2, 1973. Israel claimed that one MiG-21 was shot down but all its planes returned safely. The Syrian aircraft was the 40th reported downed by Israel since the 1967 war.

The dogfight occurred as the Syrian jets sought to intercept the Israeli planes on a routine patrol flight. Damascus acknowledged one of its planes was hit but claimed one Israeli plane was shot down. The Lebanese Defense Ministry reported two planes crashed in the dogfight—one near Faraya, about 30 miles northeast of Lebanon, and the other into the sea off the northern port of Tripoli. The ministry announced that the first plane was Syrian but said it could not identify the second one.

Israeli-Syrian ground, air clashes. Israeli and Syrian forces fought extensive air and ground battles Jan. 8 along the Golan Heights cease-fire line and over Syrian territory.

Israel claimed six Syrian planes had been downed and six Syrian tanks and four radar stations had been knocked out. Syria acknowledged the loss of three MiGs but said its pilots shot down four Israeli planes and that its ground forces destroyed 15 Israeli tanks and 10 artillery positions. Israel said all its planes returned safely.

The fighting broke out after Israeli jets retaliated for Syrian-based Palestinian commando attacks on the Golan Heights Jan. 7.

The Israelis said the six Syrian planes had been downed during a dog fight involving more than a dozen aircraft from each side. It was described as the biggest air battle since the 1967 war. Among the other targets claimed by the Israelis to have been hit by the air strikes were two commando encampments, three Syrian army bases and 35 artillery positions. One raid was directed against a Syrian army brigade headquarters north of the port of Latakia, less than 30 miles from the Turkish border.

Israel reported two of its soldiers were wounded during the exchange of gunfire on the Golan Heights truce line and that two settlements on the heights were damaged by Syrian shelling.

Damascus said that in the day's action two Syrian soldiers were killed and eight were wounded and that two Syrian tanks and two radar stations were destroyed.

A military spokesman in Tel Aviv told newsmen that although Syria had lost 14 MiG-21s and mobile radar stations in the past seven weeks, the Soviet Union seemed to be replacing them "at least one for one."

During the day's fighting, Damascus radio repeatedly urged other Arab countries to "go into battle immediately with Israel and not let Syria stand alone and take the enemy blows." The fighting, the broadcast said, has now become "part of our daily life."

A further Damascus report Jan. 10 on the Israeli raid said more than 500 Syrian civilians had been killed. The report said one of the air strikes had killed the entire population of the village of Dail, near the Jordanian border.

The Israeli military command called the Syrian casualty claim a "lie."

Israeli Defense Minister Moshe Dayan warned Syria Jan. 12 that it risked major military blows unless it curbed Palestinian commando attacks from its territory. Dayan predicted that Syrian-Israeli border tensions were "liable to persist for quite some years" and blamed the situation on Syria's refusal to abandon claims to the Golan Heights.

U.N. inspects Syria raid damage—The U.N. Truce Supervisory Organization reported Jan. 12 that Syrian witnesses had testified that at least 125 civilians had been killed in the Israeli air strikes Jan. 8. An Israeli spokesman at the U.N. challenged the figures.

Maj. Gen. Ensio Siilasvuo of Finland, UNTSO head, said the observers had visited four villages Jan. 10 at the request of the Damascus government. In one village the truce inspectors had found more than 20 houses completely destroyed, and in another they were shown "mass graves" said to contain 69 civilians, Siilasvuo said.

The Lebanese newspaper Al Nahar reported Jan. 14 that Syria might threaten to withdraw from the three-nation Federation of Arab Republics if the other two members—Egypt and Libya—failed to come to its aid in event of another Israeli attack. Damascus radio condemned the passivity of other Arab states, stating that "only combined efforts of Arab countries can bring an end to Israeli arrogance."

Arab & Israeli slain in Cyprus. A representative of the Palestine Liberation Organization in Cyprus was killed by a bomb explosion in a Nicosia hotel room Jan. 25. Police said the victim, Hussain al Bathir, was apparently killed while handling a number of bombs. Police said Bathir had arrived in Nicosia Jan. 22 from Beirut and carried a Syrian passport and Lebanese identification documents.

An Israeli was shot to death March 12 in a Nicosia hotel by a man said to be a Jordanian, Cyprus police reported. The murdered Israeli, Simha Gilzer, 59, was described by police as a businessman.

The Iraqi news agency reported March 13 that Black September had claimed credit for Gilzer's slaying. According to the report, the Palestinian commando group said Gilzer was an Israeli intelligence officer responsible for al Bathir's death.

Israeli sources denied that Gilzer was an intelligence agent.

Israeli agent slain in Madrid. An agent of the Israeli security services was shot and killed by a Palestinian commando in Madrid Jan. 26. The Black September group claimed responsibility for the killing in a statement issued in Cairo Jan. 27. The statement said the Israeli had been shadowing Arab intelligence agents.

The Israeli government Jan. 30 acknowledged the death of the agent and identified him as Baruch Cohen, 37.

Gaza Arabs protest terrorism. Gaza Arabs Feb. 15 protested the recent outbreak of Palestinian commando terrorism in the Israel-occupied area.

Six members of the Shatti refugee council resigned to protest the murder of the council chairman Feb. 11. Other Gazans were circulating a petition calling on Arab world leaders to persuade the commandos to halt their attacks in the Gaza Strip. The petition followed an unsuccessful attempt Feb. 13 to assassinate former Gaza Mayor Rashid Shawa. Shawa was ambushed by gunmen but escaped with minor injuries.

Israeli authorities the previous week were reported to have seized 19 alleged members of the illegal Palestine Liberation Forces.

Suez air clash. Israeli and Egyptian jets clashed Feb. 15, 1973 over the Gulf of Suez for the first time in eight months. Israel said one Egyptian plane was shot down during an attempt to intercept Israeli aircraft over the gulf. Cairo said six Israeli planes had attempted to penetrate Egyptian air space but were turned back.

Israeli jets down Libyan airliner. Two Israeli jet fighters shot down a civilian Libyan airliner over the occupied Sinai Peninsula, about 12 miles east of the Suez Canal Feb. 21. The plane crash-landed and burned, killing 106 persons; seven survived. Three of the victims died in a Sinai field hospital, a fourth succumbed to his injuries on an Israeli helicopter flying him to a hospital in Beersheba and two others in the hospital. The death of two more of those injured raised the death toll to 108.

Most of the passengers were Egyptians and Libyans and five of the nine crewmen were French. The Libyan co-pilot and a French steward were among the survivors.

The plane, a 727 Boeing, was en route from the Libyan cities of Tripoli and Benghazi to Cairo when it apparently strayed off course. Israel claimed the plane was shot down after it ignored warnings to land. Egypt insisted that there had been no contact between the airliner and the Israeli pilots and that the Libyan aircraft was fired at without warning.

According to an initial Israeli communique Feb. 22, the Libyan airliner entered Israeli airspace in Sinai, flying over military installations along the canal and over a military airfield, 50 miles inside the territory. Attempts to contact the intruder by radio went unanswered. Israeli phantom jets then took off to meet the jetliner and "approached the plane and instructed it to land in accordance with the international regulations. When the plane took no notice of the instructions and the warning shots that were fired, it was intercepted by Israeli planes. The hit plane landed inside Sinai 20 kilometers and crashed."

In a statement, Premier Golda Meir expressed "deep sorrow at the loss of life resulting from the crash" and said she regretted that "the Libyan pilot did not respond to the repeated warnings."

Israel's air force chief, Maj. Gen. Mordechai Hod, told a news conference Feb. 22, "We did not mean to shoot it [the Libyan plane] down." Hod claimed the crew ignored several orders to land at a nearby Israeli air base "for inquiries" and "the more the pilot objected and the more he tried to get away, the more suspicious he became." It was feared the Libyan passenger plane might have been on a spy mission since it was flying over Israel's secret air base at Bir Gafgafa, Hod said. He said the surviving Libyan co-pilot had told interrogators that the crew was aware of what the Israeli interceptors wanted them to do but decided to go away when they saw the airfield below. Hod quoted the co-pilot as saying "Because of the relations between our two countries, we decided we'd better get away from here."

The two Israeli pilots involved in the interception of the Libyan plane appeared with Hod at his news conference. One said the airliner had flown over Bir Gafgafa and that he had "traded hand signs three times" with the plane's pilot, indicating that he wanted him to land at the base. The Israeli went on: The Libyan plane pilot gestured to show he was ignoring the request and was flying ahead. The two Israelis flew in front of the airliner, tipping their wings in another gesture and then fired three times in the direction of the aircraft to force a landing. These signals were also ignored. "When the canal was only one minute's flying time away, I shot at the wing to force him to land before he could reach the coast. Red flames and black smoke came from the wings."

One of the survivors at the Beersheba hospital, a French steward, told newsmen there had been no warning shots before the plane was struck.

Egyptian authorities told a news conference in Cairo Feb. 22 that the pilot of the Libyan plane who was among those killed, French Capt. Jacques Bourges, had informed the Cairo control tower that he had lost his way because of instrument failure. He thought he was over Egypt and was being followed by Egyptian MiGs. The pilot's version was contained on a tape described as a copy of a recorded exchange between the Libyan plane and the control tower. According to the message playback, Bourges told the control tower of his navigational problem. Then he said "We have now four MiG fighter planes behind us. Can you give us a radar fix?" A few moments later the pilot shouted "We are shot at by the fighters." Then radio contact was lost.

Aeronautics director Capt. Hassan Selim told the news conference that the Cairo airport had no record of any contact between the pilot and the Israelis, refuting Israel's contention that it had been in contact with the plane for 15 minutes. Selim indicated that heavy clouds at the time could have affected the plane's navigational instruments. The area in which the plane was shot down was about 60 miles from the Cairo airport.

Selim's report appeared to differ somewhat from the account of the incident first reported by Cairo radio Feb. 21: the pilot had acknowledged that he was being pursued by Israeli planes, and not by Egyptian MiGs as reported in Bourges' taped message. According to the broadcast, the jetliner was coming in for a normal landing at Cairo and was in radio contact 20 minutes before arrival time. Five minutes later the plane turned east instead of flying to the northeast and lost radio contact with the tower, Cairo radio said. "When contact was resumed," according to the broadcast, "the captain said he was lost and surrounded by Israeli fighters over Sinai. Contact was cut off again, which means the Israeli planes shot down the Libyan aircraft."

Israel Feb. 24 accepted partial responsibility for the airliner's destruction. Israeli officials had previously insisted that the airline's pilot was totally at fault.

At a Tel Aviv news conference, Defense Minister Moshe Dayan acknowledged that "in this case we erred—under the most difficult of circumstances—but that does not put us on the guilty side." He conceded that the Israeli air force had misconstrued the nature of the intrusion of the Libyan aircraft and its intentions. But Dayan said the pilot of the plane, French Capt. Jacques Bourges, who was killed, was guilty of "serious irresponsibility." Dayan noted that Bourges had strayed more than 100 miles off course, became completely lost, failed to distinguish between Israeli and Egyptian plane insignia and disregarded Israeli orders to land. The defense minister also blamed the Cairo control tower for misinforming Bourges that "he was over Egypt when they told him they would give an order to the Egyptian MiGs to stop firing."

Despite Israel's responsibility for the loss of the Libyan jet, Israel should not compensate the families of the victims because that would imply guilt, the defense minister said. He proposed a hot line between Tel Aviv and neighboring Arab countries to prevent a recurrence of a similar disaster.

Lt. Gen. David Elazar, Israeli chief of staff, told the same news conference he had given orders to shoot down the Libyan plane because in the short time available Israeli authorities "could not discount the possibility that a civilian aircraft could come into our territory on a hostile mission." "Had we known it was a civilian aircraft, carrying live passengers, we would not have used force to make it land," Elazar said.

The airliner's automatic flight recorder was retrieved from the wreckage of the plane Feb. 23. Its contents confirmed Cairo's initial contention that Bourges had believed he was inside Egyptian air-

space and that the planes intercepting him were Egyptian. The Israelis Feb. 24 released the tape recorded message of the last minutes of the plane's movements and the conversation inside the cockpit. At one point, three burst of cannon fire and the sound of passing jet fighters could be heard on the tape. The pilot told the Cairo control tower that his plane was "shot by your fighters twice." A second later, the Libyan co-pilot, Ayad el Mahadi, realized what was happening and shouted "It's Israeli fighter, an Israeli fighter."

The Israeli Cabinet Feb. 25 disregarded Dayan's suggestion and announced it had decided to compensate the families of the victims. A spokesman said the payments would be made voluntarily "in deference to humanitarian considerations." A government official said later that this meant Israel was making restitution without any implications of guilt.

The Israeli government then announced March 6 that it would pay $30,000 in compensation to the families of each victim of the disaster and $10,000–$30,000 to each of the injured, depending on the extent of the injuries.

The Libyan airliner's co-pilot said April 15 that the aircraft's captain had heard the warning shots fired by Israeli interceptors and had planned to land, "but at the last minute changed his mind" and attempted to head back to Egypt. The statement was made by Ayad el Mahadi, who had recovered from his injuries and was about to return to Libya.

Mahadi said the plane had lost its way when it intruded into Israeli airspace and he conceded it was a "mistake" not to obey the Israeli signals to land. Mahadi's remarks supported Israeli claims that their jets had fired at the airliner only after it refused orders to land.

While visiting Washington, Israeli Premier Golda Meir said in a speech at the National Press Club March 1 that Israel would not have shot down the plane if it had known that civilian passengers were aboard.

Mrs. Meir viewed "this tragedy against the background of Arab terrorist activity." Meir said Israel had received in January "warnings from various important intelligence agencies in the world that Black September [the extreme commando group] was planning a dramatic act in Israel." She said the plan called for an explosive-filled plane to crash into an important military installation or a major city.

U.N. body condemns Israel—Israel's action in shooting down the Libyan airliner was condemned Feb. 28 by the General Assembly of the U.N.'s International Civil Aviation Organization by a 105-1 vote. Israel cast the lone dissenting vote. Only two nations—Colombia and Malawi—abstained.

The U.N. Commission on Human Rights had denounced Israel's downing of the Libyan plane in a message issued in Geneva Feb. 27.

Israeli force raids Lebanon. Two Palestinian commando bases near Tripoli, Lebanon were attacked Feb. 21 by Israeli amphibious and airborne troops. The raiders struck the bases near refugee camps at Nahar el Bard and El Badawi, 112-125 miles north of the Israeli-Lebanese border and just south of the Lebanese-Syrian frontier.

The Palestine news agency Wafa said 31 Arabs were killed, including 13 civilians. The Israelis claimed about 40 guerrillas were killed in several hours of fighting at both camps, and that a Turkish guerrilla had been captured. Israel said eight of its men had been wounded. A building housing a commando headquarters at El Badawi was destroyed by a demolition charge.

The Israeli troops landed from helicopters believed to have taken off from frigates in the Mediterranean off Nahar el Bard. Other troops came ashore from small rubber boats.

Lebanon Feb. 21 lodged a complaint with the United Nations Security Council, accusing Israel of having committed "barbaric acts" against refugee camps. Israeli Ambassador Yosef Tekoah rejected the complaint, and accused Lebanon instead of harboring "some 5,000 terrorists, belonging to various terror organizations."

An Israeli general staff spokesman said Feb. 21 that the raids were aimed at thwarting Palestinian commando plans to attack Israelis overseas. The spokesman said Israel had "detailed information" that some of these attacks were to have been carried out soon. "We have good reason to believe that at least some of them will be forestalled by the raids conducted last night," the spokesman said.

Another Israeli military official was critical of the U.N. Relief and Works Agency for Palestinian refugees, which administered the Nahar el Bard camp. He said the "raids made it a proven fact that UNRWA is acting as host to a gang of terrorists."

An Al Fatah guerrilla captured during the raids was sentenced to seven years in prison by an Israeli military court Aug. 8. Faik Buluk, a Turk, became the first suspected commando captured outside Israel to be convicted under an Israeli law extending the jurisdiction of Israeli courts to crimes committed abroad.

U.S. ambassador & 2 other diplomats slain in Sudan. Three diplomats—two U.S. and one Belgian—were murdered March 2, 1973 in Sudan by terrorists of the Black September group who had seized the Saudi Arabian embassy the previous day during a reception for one of the men later slain.

The Arab terrorists took over the Saudi Arabian embassy in Khartoum March 1 and held six diplomats hostage, demanding the release of Arab prisoners in various countries. When the terrorist demands were refused during negotiations which followed, they murdered three of the hostages—U.S. Ambassador Cleo A. Noel, Jr.; George C. Moore, the departing U.S. chargé d'affaires; and Guy Eid, the Egyptian-born charge at the Belgian embassy.

The terrorists ended their three-day occupation of the embassy at dawn March 4, surrendering to Sudanese authorities, who promised only that they would not be killed immediately.

The attack began about 7 p.m. March 1 when a Land Rover with diplomatic plates, later identified as belonging to Al Fatah, drove up to the gates of the embassy, where a party celebrating Moore's departure was in progress. The eight invaders, led by Abu Salem, second-ranking official at the Fatah office in

Khartoum, crashed the gate and entered the building firing machine-guns and revolvers.

Many of the guests escaped by jumping over the embassy wall. Others hid and then fled, while some identified themselves and were released. Noel suffered an ankle-wound from a ricocheting bullet, and Eid was shot in the leg. According to Shigeru Nomoto, the Japanese charge d'affaires who described the attack in a March 3 statement, the commandos "tightly bound Ambassador Noel and Mr. Moore with ropes they had brought with them and punched and kicked them unmercifully." Also held in the attack were Sheik Abdullah el-Malhouk, Saudi ambassador and host to the party; his wife and four children and Adli el-Nazir, the Jordanian chargé d'affaires. The guerrillas were apparently persuaded to release the Saudi ambassador's children and his wife, who later returned to be with her husband.

Several hours later the guerillas issued an ultimatum that they would kill the six hostages within 24 hours unless certain demands were met. They insisted on the release of Abu Daoud and other members of Fatah imprisoned in Jordan as well as of Maj. Rafeh Hindawi, a Jordanian officer under life sentence for plotting against the Amman government. They also demanded the release of Sirhan Sirhan, convicted assassin of U.S. Sen. Robert F. Kennedy; all Arab women detained in Israel; and members of the Baader-Meinhof urban guerrilla group in West Germany "because they supported the Palestinian cause."

Telephone contact with the commandos was maintained by Sudanese Interior Minister Mohammed el Baghir who informed them early March 2 that the Jordanian government had refused demands for the release of Daoud, Hindawi and the others.

Shortly after the Jordanian refusal, the commandos read a statement in which they gave up their demand for the release of prisoners in Israel, "since Sudan cannot contact the Zionist enemy," and for the "German comrades," because the West German ambassador, who left the party early, "was not present as we had hoped." The dispatch concluded: "We insist and reconfirm that we will not leave the embassy or release the hostages or even guarantee their lives except if the Palestinian prisoners held in the prisons of the reactionary regime of Jordan are freed."

At a Washington news conference March 2, President Nixon said that while the U.S. would "do everything we can" to have the hostages released, it would "not pay blackmail." He announced that William B. Macomber Jr., deputy under-secretary of state for management, was being sent to Sudan.

Meanwhile, Sudanese troops kept the building surrounded, and the terrorists wired explosives to the embassy floor, warning that the building would be blown up if the soldiers attempted to enter.

The three Western diplomats were killed March 2 at about 9:30 p.m., the Sudanese government announced the following day. A Sudanese officer, who entered the embassy with permission from the terrorists, confirmed that the men had been taken to the basement and shot repeatedly.

The commandos remained in the embassy throughout March 3, occasionally speaking through a bullhorn to Sudanese soldiers outside and refusing to hand over the bodies of the slain diplomats unless the government guaranteed the commandos safe conduct to an unspecified Arab capital. Baghir told the terrorists later in the day that an emergency Cabinet session had rejected their request for an airplane and that they would be given until dawn the following morning to surrender. The commandos surrendered on that schedule.

(According to the Washington Post March 6, Sudanese Information Minister Umar al-Hag Musa confirmed that a major role in the surrender of the commandos had been played by Yasir Arafat, leader of Al Fatah. The Post quoted Musa as having said: "He helped in the last part, when it became clear they had no way out.")

In Lebanon, Prime Minister Saeb Salam expressed March 3 "the regret" of his government but noted that the Palestinians "have an issue of fate which should be dealt with from its roots" and that the international community should "embark on finding positive solutions for this issue based on right, justice and the dignity of man."

The London Times March 5 reported a Black September statement it said had been mailed the previous day to the Beirut office of the Iraqi news agency. The Times quoted the statement as asserting that the three diplomats killed in Khartoum had taken part in "massacring our people and conspiring against our Arab nation." George Moore was accused of having been a CIA agent. The organization promised "every prisoner of our people that its war against Zionism, American imperialism and their hirelings will continue."

Ghassan Tueni, publisher of the Lebanese daily An Nahar, asked in an editorial March 5 whether "the recovery of Palestine" was "still the goal" or "has the revolution reached such a point of despair as to be without logic—namely to carry out commando action for its own sake?"

An Egyptian weekly, Rose el-Yussef, suggested March 4 that the existence of plans to build a joint Israeli-Belgian-U.S. aircraft and missile factory at Liege in Belgium had been a factor in the death of Guy Eid.

The Sudanese government announced June 15, however, that the trial of 10 Palestinian guerrillas charged with killing the diplomats had been postponed indefinitely.

Sudanese Interior Minister Mohammed el-Baghir had said March 10 that a confession by one of the terrorists revealed their attack against the Saudi embassy and the murder of the diplomats had been directed from the Beirut headquarters of Al Fatah, the main Palestinian guerrilla organization, with whom the terrorists were in radio contact.

Nimeiry accuses Fatah—In a radio and television address March 6, Sudanese President Mohammed Gaafar el-Nimeiry accused Al Fatah of being the principal force behind the operation which led to the killing of the diplomats.

Nimeiry revealed that Fawaz Yassin, Fatah's representative in Khartoum, had left Sudan on a Libyan airliner bound for Tripoli several hours before the Saudi embassy was invaded March 1. He asked that Yassin be extradited by "the Arab country where he may now find himself."

He described the killing of the diplomats as "a criminal, rash action devoid of revolutionary spirit and bravery." Nimeiry said Sudan had cooperated with Fatah because of a belief in "the legitimate right of the Palestinians to return to their homeland and determine their own future," but he insisted that the recent Black September operation "could in no way benefit the Palestinian people" and was designed solely to "humiliate" the Khartoum government.

Nimeiry expressed the belief that the Sudanese court trying the commandos would hand down "a just punishment."

(Foreign Minister Manzur Khaled had announced March 5 that the commandos would be tried in his country. Khaled said: "Murder is a capital crime. This was a clear case of murder....We want to finish this as soon as possible." U.S. Secretary of State William P. Rogers said in Washington the same day that he regarded the death penalty as "quite appropriate" for the terrorists and that he did not "know any other way to deal with this.")

Bombs in New York fail to explode. Police in New York March 7 discovered and defused three bombs in parked cars next to Israel's El Al Airlines terminal at Kennedy International Airport and near two Israeli-owned banks.

A U.S. federal warrant was issued March 15 for a suspected Black September terrorist believed to have escaped the country after planting the bombs. Federal Bureau of Investigation agents identified the suspect as Khalid Danham Al-Jawari, an Iraqi, and said he was the subject of an international search.

Gaza terror group wiped out. Israel reported March 9 that its security forces that day had wiped out a Palestinian guerrilla group responsible for the renewal of terror attacks in the Gaza Strip in February, the first outbreak in 18 months. A number of other commandos were arrested.

The three dead men, described as members of the Popular Front for the Liberation of Palestine, had been apprehended hiding in a bunker in the Gaza city home of Dr. Rashad Musmar. The men were found during a search that followed a guerrilla ambush March 8 of an Israeli patrol in which one soldier was killed. Large quantities of weapons were uncovered in the bunker and Musmar was detained. Musmar had previously been sentenced to five years in prison for harboring terrorists, but served only two years.

France deports guerrilla suspects. Two suspected members of the Palestinian Black September guerrilla movement who reportedly were part of a plan to blow up the Israeli and Jordanian embassies in Paris were arrested in France March 16. Dianne Campbell-Lefevre, a Briton, was deported to London March 22, and Jamil Abdelhakim, was flown to Damascus March 23.

Information on the two suspects and the reported bomb plot had been provided by two Arabs who had been arrested March 14 by French authorities near the Italian border with explosive equipment in their car. The two Arabs remained in custody.

PFLP man slain in Paris. A member of the Popular Front for the Liberation of Palestine (PFLP) was shot to death by two unknown assailants on a Paris street April 6. The victim was identified as Basil el-Kubaisi, an Iraqi.

A PFLP statement in Beirut said Kubaisi was on a mission for the organization and attributed his slaying to Israeli intelligence.

Arab attacks fail in Cyprus. A group of Arab guerrillas April 9 blew out the entrance to the Nicosia apartment building housing Israeli Ambassador Rahamim Timor and then attacked an Israeli El Al airliner in a futile attempt to hijack it before takeoff. Nine men participated in the raid.

No residents of the building were injured. The ambassador's family, but not Timor himself, and others were in their apartments at the time. The bomb exploded after it was placed at the entrance by an Arab who ran to a waiting car. Cypriot security guards opened fire as the automobile sped away and its three occupants were later arrested.

Shortly afterward, Arabs in two cars crashed through the gates of the Nicosia airport. One of the vehicles was stopped by police, but the other made its way to the Israeli plane about to leave with passengers for Tel Aviv. The Arabs began exchanging fire with Cypriot policemen and an Israeli security agent. The Israeli wounded three of the Arabs with automatic weapons fire; one of them later died. Two Cypriot policemen were wounded. One Arab assailant escaped and a total of seven were taken into custody. Dynamite and grenades were tossed at the plane but failed to explode. One of the plane's propellers was damaged by the Arabs' car.

Seven Arabs were sentenced in Nicosia July 27, 1973 to seven years in prison for the attack on the residence of the ambassador and on the airliner.

Lebanese capital raided. An Israeli force struck deep into Lebanon April 10, attacking Palestinian commando bases in the center of Beirut and in the coastal town of Saida to the south.

Lebanese Premier Saeb Salam submitted his resignation April 10 following the Israeli raid. He said he was doing so "in the public interest."

Operating under cover of darkness, the Israeli units drove into Beirut after landing on the coast in small boats and killed three prominent Al Fatah leaders in the capital. They were Abu Youssef (whose real name was Mohammed Yussef Najjar), one of two Fatah representatives on the executive committee of the Palestine Liberation Organization (PLO); Kamal Adwan, an organizer of Palestinian resistance in the occupied West Bank; and Kamal Nasser, an official spokesman of the PLO.

All three men and Youssef's wife were shot to death in separate apartments in two guarded houses that were entered by the attackers. The buildings were located in the Sabra refugee camp in the heart of Beirut, where most of the commando groups were headquartered. Other guerrilla targets struck in the city were the central offices of the Democratic Popular Front and workshops reportedly used to prepare explosives.

In the operation at Saida, the Israelis blew up a garage allegedly used to repair vehicles of guerrillas stationed in southern Lebanon.

After coming ashore near Beirut, the Israeli units were reportedly met by six Israeli agents, who were said to have entered Lebanon a week earlier as tourists with false British, Belgian and West German passports. They drove the raiders into Beirut in automobiles they had rented earlier in the week. A Lebanese communique said the vehicles were found later April 10 at the same coastal site where the Israelis apparently returned to their boats that took them back to Israel.

Lebanon said 12 persons were killed in the Israeli attack—four Palestinians, two Lebanese policemen, two Lebanese civilians, three Syrians and an Italian woman. In addition, 29 Lebanese, including nine policemen, were wounded, Beirut said.

A PLO statement in Beirut charged April 10 that the Israeli raiders had "relied on elements of American military intelligence" provided by the U.S. embassy in Beirut. The U.S. State Department denied the allegation in Washington.

The Israelis reported that two of their men were killed and two wounded in the operations.

Lt. Gen. David Elazar, Israeli chief of staff, told a news conference in Tel Aviv April 10 that the raid was carried out in retaliation for "the intensification of terrorist acts in Europe and other places in the last months." He said that although most of those commando raids had failed, "we had to act." He said the thrust into Lebanon could be considered in part a response to the Arab guerrilla attack in Cyprus the previous day, but he conceded the timing was "to some extent a coincidence."

Elazar would not comment on how the Israeli strike force had landed in Lebanon or how it made its way into Beirut. "We are not going to reveal the operational details because I am not sure that we will not be forced to continue this type of operation in the future." The Israeli military leader warned "there is no possibility of honoring the sovereignty of Lebanon and its capital as long as it is serving as a complete haven for terrorists."

■ The Lebanese army said April 17 that it had not been informed of the attack until it was over. The statement said that at first the police who rushed to the scene in Beirut "were confused," thinking the Palestinian commandos were fighting among themselves. It added that "the Palestinians thought they were being attacked by Lebanese security forces."

U.S. rejects complicity charge—The U.N. Security Council met in emergency session April 12 at Lebanon's request the previous day to consider the Israeli attack.

U.S. chief delegate John A. Scali denounced Arab guerrilla charges that the U.S. embassy in Beirut was harboring some of the Israeli forces that had taken part in the assault. Scali said "if this big lie succeeds, the responsibility will rest on those governments who heard the big lie and failed to speak up against it."

Israeli representative Yosef Tekoah criticized Lebanese representative Edouard Ghorra's demand that Israel be condemned. To do so would support "Lebanon's remaining base for murderous outrages in the Middle East and outside the region," Tekoah said.

The Arab charges of U.S. involvement in the Israeli attack were further assailed April 12 by Secretary of State William P. Rogers at a meeting in Washington with 13 Arab envoys. Rogers told the envoys of his displeasure with Arab government broadcasts of these "falsehoods" and urged them to transmit his "formal and authoritative denial" to their governments. The diplomats represented Algeria, Egypt, Iraq, Jordan, Kuwait, Lebanon, Libya, Mauritania, Morocco, Qatar, Saudi Arabia, Sudan and Tunisia.

Broadcasts of the U.S.' alleged involvement in the attack on Lebanon originated in Algiers, Tripoli, Cairo, Baghdad, Khartoum, Damascus and Amman. One broadcast from Algiers April 11 calling on Arabs to attack U.S. embassies everywhere and to "assassinate everyone who is American" drew a sharp protest from the U.S. government the same day.

■ Al Fatah leader Yasir Arafat April 13 again linked the U.S. embassy in Beirut with the Israeli attack, charging that an embassy station wagon with diplomatic license plates had been parked near a gasoline station in the vicinity of the buildings where three commando leaders were slain by the Israelis. The same vehicle, according to Arafat, was later seen transporting four people. Arafat said former U.S. Ambassador to Lebanon Armin Meyer headed an American intelligence team to "coordinate with Israeli intelligence against Palestinian guerrillas."

■ The Palestinian news agency Wafa said April 13 that a U.S. Air Force transport plane had arrived in Beirut the day of the Israeli attack, and left with 45 persons aboard, all Israeli raiders. The U.S. embassy denied the allegation, saying the plane had stopped off in Beirut to deliver supplies for the American mission.

■ Egyptian Foreign Minister Mohammed el Zayyat April 22 expressed doubt that the U.S. had assisted Israel in its attack on Beirut. Speaking on the CBS-TV program Face the Nation in Washington, Zayyat said "I'm not including myself" among the Arab officials who charged the U.S. with "complicity" in the raid.

Israel detains Arab suspects—Israeli security forces rounded up a number of suspected Arab guerrillas in Israel and in the occupied areas April 11-12 on the basis of documents reportedly captured by the Israelis in their raid on Beirut.

The documents were said to have been found in the apartment of Kamal Adwan, one of the three slain Fatah leaders. The papers reportedly told of plans for commando attacks in Israel to coincide with the celebration May 7 of Israel's 25th anniversary of independence. The documents also were believed to contain codes used by guerrilla broadcasts to communicate with agents in Israeli territory.

Arafat takes political powers—The Iraqi news agency reported April 21 that Al Fatah leader Yasir Arafat had taken over the leadership of the combined commando movement's political and governmental relations in the wake of the Israeli slaying of three Fatah leaders in Beirut April 10. Arafat replaced Abu Youssef, one of the slain men, as head of the political department of the Palestine Liberation Organization. The department was responsible for relations with Arab and foreign governments.

The Palestine National Council Jan. 12 had reelected Arafat as chairman of the executive committee of the PLO. The council announced its action at the conclusion of a six-day conference in Cairo.

The council was the parliamentary body of the PLO, which was the main political arm of the commandos. It also elected a new 10-member executive committee—two from Arafat's Al Fatah, four independents, one from the extremist Popular Front for the Liberation of Palestine and three from smaller groups.

A communique pledged "to continue armed struggle until the liberation of Palestine."

Israel warns Lebanon of new raids. In the aftermath of the Israeli attack on Lebanon April 10, Defense Minister Moshe Dayan warned the Beirut government April 13 that it would be held responsible for further Arab commando activity originating in Lebanon.

Dayan said in a state television interview that Israel would hold Lebanon accountable "as a state for actions of the terrorists running their operations from its territory, and we don't intend to act against terrorists only on a personal basis."

Security Council censures Israel. The U.N. Security Council April 21 approved an Anglo-French resolution condemning Israeli attacks on Lebanon and "all acts of violence which endanger or take innocent human lives." The latter phrase was understood to refer to Palestinian terrorist attacks in general.

The vote was 11-0, with the U.S., the Soviet Union, China and Ghana abstaining. The U.S. abstained because the resolution failed to provide "evenhanded condemnation" of Israel's April 10 attack on Beirut along with Palestinian commando assaults that had prompted the raid. The Soviet Union, China and Ghana did not vote for the resolution because they felt its condemnation of Israel was not strong enough.

In explaining his abstention, U.S. chief delegate John A. Scali said the resolution "concentrated too much on the meaningless exercise of apportioning blame." Referring to Council members' "one-sided references to the United States efforts to meet Israel's legitimate defense needs," Scali complained "there has been no reference to the fact . . . that major deliveries are being made by other powers to several countries in the area." "The United States does not propose to sit idly by as others pour arms into the area, thus encouraging some to think they can risk another round of fighting," he added.

Soviet delegate Yakov A. Malik replied that "assistance to the victims of aggression should not be put on the same footing as support for the aggressor any more than individual terrorism and state terrorism should be regarded as parallel."

Israeli delegate Yosef Tekoah had assailed the resolution before the vote, saying it showed that the Security Council still could not "deal equitably with questions pertaining to the Middle East situation."

A U.S. veto threat had prompted modification of the first version of the British-French resolution, which had condemned the Israeli raid on Lebanon and urged "all states to refrain from providing [Israel] any assistance that would facilitate such attacks." An Israeli spokesman had charged that this resolution "would subject Israel to sanctions." The U.S. had sought unsuccessfully to include mention of the Palestinian commando killing March 2 of three diplomats in Khartoum, Sudan.

U.S.-owned oil tanks bombed in Lebanon. An American-owned oil installation near Saida, on the Lebanese coast south of Beirut, was bombed and set ablaze April 14. Four oil tanks were blasted by explosive charges set by a group of 20 armed men who overpowered guards at the Zahrani oil terminal.

A previously unknown group calling itself the Lebanese Revolutionary Guard took credit for the attack, describing it as "a blow against American support for Israel." The statement accused the Lebanese army of "failing to protect the country against Israeli raids."

Palestinian guerrillas denied a Lebanese government statement intimating that they were responsible for the raid on the oil terminal. The Palestinians said Israelis had carried out the attack, but Israel denied the charge.

The blasted tanks were owned by the Trans-Arabian Pipeline Co. (Tapline) and the Mediterranean Refinery Co. Pumping of crude oil at the refinery resumed April 16.

Israel thwarts Arab 'suicide' mission. Israeli troops April 21 captured three Palestinian guerrillas from Lebanon who were said to have planned an attack on civilians at a bus station at Safad, Israel. Identified as members of Al Fatah, the three were seized two miles south of the Lebanese border and 14 miles northwest of their intended target.

One of the captured men, Shehada Ahmed Mustafa, told a news conference in Tel Aviv April 22 that he and his companions were on a "suicide mission to sabotage the bus station, a restaurant and other public places" and were under orders "to kill as many as we could and not permit ourselves to be captured."

Syria alerts forces. Syria placed its armed forces on full alert in anticipation of a possible Israeli attack in the Golan Heights, the Lebanese newspaper An Nahar reported April 28. The Syrian action followed the Israeli capture April 26 of five guerrillas attempting to infiltrate the Golan Heights. The Israelis also reported capturing that day 10 Al Fatah commandos in the West Bank.

Israel airline man slain in Rome. An Italian employe of the Israeli El Al airline office in Rome was shot to death by an Arab April 27. The victim was Vittorio Olivares. His accused assailant, who was arrested, was identified as Zaharia Abou Saleh, a Lebanese.

Saleh told Italian police he was a member of the Palestinian Black September and was sent to Rome by the organization on a mission to kill Olivares because he was an Israeli spy responsible for the slaying of an Al Fatah official in Rome in October 1972.

Lebanon foils U.S. embassy attack. Lebanese troops April 30 captured four Palestinian guerrillas approaching the

U.S. embassy in Beirut in a car loaded with arms and explosives for what authorities said they believed was an intended attack on the building. Five other armed Palestinians were later arrested in connection with the abortive raid.

Lebanese, commandos clash in Beirut. Lebanese army troops, using planes and tanks, engaged in heavy fighting with Palestinian commandos May 2–3. The clashes erupted in Beirut and quickly spread to other parts of Lebanon.

The fighting was halted briefly May 2 by a cease-fire agreed to by Al Fatah leader Yasir Arafat and Premier Amin Hafez. However, the truce broke down and the battle resumed May 3 following a guerrilla ambush of a Beirut police barracks in which three policemen were killed and seven wounded.

The fighting was the worst since the near-civil war in 1969 between Lebanese army regulars and the commandos.

The latest outbreak was precipitated by a breakdown in negotiations for the release of two Lebanese officers kidnapped by guerrillas May 1. The two officers were released after the first day's fighting. The men had been held as hostages for the release of seven Palestinian commandos arrested April 27 for carrying explosives at the Beirut International Airport.

The hostilities began May 1 near Beirut's Shatila camp, which housed 5,000 Palestinian refugees, and spread to the nearby Burj-al-Barajineh camp, which housed 7,700 refugees.

A Defense Ministry communique May 3 said air strikes had been ordered against guerrilla bases after "army positions and barracks came under sudden shelling by armed men."

The clashes expanded to southern Lebanon May 3 and were particularly fierce in the Arkub region, a commando stronghold which had been used for operations against Israel. Capt. Riad Awad, guerrilla commander in the Arkub region, and three other commandos were reported to have been killed when their jeep attempted to run through an army roadblock at Hasbeya. Other clashes in the south raged in the Yanta and Rasheiya areas between government forces and the Syrian-backed As Saiqa guerrilla group.

Two large groups of Palestinian forces crossed from Syria into Lebanon to join the combat. The first group, numbering several thousand men, entered Lebanon May 3 and skirmished with government soldiers but withdrew to Syria after a truce was worked out May 4.

The breakdown of the May 4 truce precipitated the resignation May 8 of Premier Amin Hafez and his Cabinet.

The cease-fires had been worked out through the mediation efforts of Egypt, Iraq, Algeria and Kuwait. Arab League Secretary General Mahmoud Riad, Kuwait Foreign Minister Sheik Sabah al-Ahmad al-Jaber and Hassan Sabry al-Kholy, Egyptian President Anwar Sadat's special envoy, traveled between Beirut and Damascus, meeting with all sides in the dispute.

Lebanese President Suleiman Franjieh told Arab mediators in Beirut May 5 that his government would not permit the guerrillas in his country to terrorize and kidnap people "as if they were above the official authority." Franjieh informed the representatives of the presidents of Syria, Egypt and Iraq that the Palestinian refugee camps in Lebanon harbored illegal arms and served as the headquarters of subversive guerrilla organizations. He said Beirut was opposed to giving the commandos special privileges to organize attacks against Israel from Lebanon.

The truce broke down completely with the resumption of full-scale fighting in Beirut May 7. The clashes were centered around the Shatila and Burj al-Barajineh refugee centers. The camps came under heavy government cannon, rocket and automatic weapon fire for more than an hour, and jet planes struck at commando positions around the camps. Casualties in the Burj al-Barajineh camps were high. The Palestine news agency Wafa said 17 persons were killed in one of the camps.

The renewed violence prompted Premier Hafez to declare a state of emergency May 7, placing the country under martial law.

The hostilities in Beirut were largely curtailed by a new cease-fire negotiated May 8, but incidents continued in southern Lebanon.

Syria closed its border with Lebanon May 8, accusing Beirut of complicity in an anti-Palestinian plot of "foreign design." A government statement broadcast by Damascus radio threatened intervention, saying that Syria would "carry out its full commitment in confronting and foiling this conspiracy."

Libya May 8 pledged to give the commandos its "entire potential" in their struggle with Lebanon. The offer was contained in a cable sent by Col. Muammar el-Qaddafi to Al Fatah leader Yasir Arafat.

A guerrilla force from Syria moved into Lebanon May 9 for the second time in eight days. The commandos, said to number several thousand, took up positions in the southeastern Rasheiya area and set up gun emplacements between Rasheiya and Massna, about 15 miles to the north. The guerrillas came under rocket and strafing attacks later in the day by Lebanese planes. Meanwhile, joint government-commando patrols were enforcing the truce in Beirut, which was largely quiet except for a number of explosions.

Government jets May 10 bombed commando positions in northern Lebanon and in the Rasheiya sector in the south. An army communique said the raids followed commando assaults on three army positions on the eastern bank of the Hasbani River in the south and on a government checkpoint at Arida and on an airbase at Klaitat, near the Syrian frontier in the north.

Israel warns Syria not to intervene— Israel warned that it might be obliged to take counteraction if Syria or any other Arab state intervened in the fighting in Lebanon or if the guerrillas took over the Lebanese government.

Premier Golda Meir declared May 6 that if Syrian forces joined the guerrillas, as they did briefly in the fighting in Jordan in 1970, then "We will also have to see that we are protected."

Similar warnings were issued May 9 by Foreign Minister Abba Eban and Defense Minister Moshe Dayan. Eban, in Washington for consultations with U.S. officials, noted that there was "now an effort by the Lebanese government to assert its sovereignty over its own capital." Dayan said "if the Syrians move into Lebanon and face us on a new border, we shall consider ourselves free to act." Dayan stressed, however, that Israel "will

not and should not act as the policeman of the Arabs. We shall not defend the sovereignty of Lebanon."

Lebanese-commando tensions ease— Lebanon began to return to normal as the May 8 truce took effect, with the ex-

The cease-fire was marred May 12 when a government custom post at Chadra on the Syrian border in the north was shelled. One guard was reported killed. In Beirut three persons were killed when a taxi carrying four persons was blown up by a land mine near the Shatila refugee camp.

The Palestinian guerrilla force that had entered Lebanon from Syria during the height of hostilities May 9 was reported May 12 to have withdrawn from the Rasheiya area in the southeast.

Lebanese security forces arrested 35 persons in Beirut May 12 on charges of stirring up trouble between the Lebanese army and the guerrillas. Among those seized as "agents provocateurs" were a number of West Europeans and citizens of other Arab states. During the fighting in Beirut both sides had claimed that a "third force" was firing at govenment and Palestinian forces to provoke more clashes.

The government and the Palestinian commandos announced May 17 an agreement that ended two weeks of fighting in which at least 250 persons were reported killed. In another development that reflected a return to normal conditions, Amin Hafez agreed May 19 to withdraw his resignation as premier and again head the Cabinet.

The peace agreement was worked out in two days of talks between a team of three Lebanese army officers and representatives of three major guerrilla organizations—Al Fatah, the Popular Front for the Liberation of Palestine and the Popular Democratic Front. The accord contained these points:

■ The Palestine Liberation Army's 5,-000-man Yarmuk Brigade and other guerrillas who had entered Lebanon from Syria at the height of the fighting were to leave the country. (Their withdrawal was completed May 18.)

■ The 15 camps housing 90,000 Palestinian refugees were brought under Lebanese sovereignty and their status as "isolated zones" on Lebanese territory was ended.

■ Guerrillas were barred from carrying arms or wearing uniforms outside the refugee camps.

■ The commandos were banned from establishing roadblocks, making arrests or conducting interrogations.

■ Joint Lebanese army and guerrilla inspection teams were to see to it that no heavy weapons were stored in the refugee camps.

Three guerrilla leaders denounced the accord May 20 and warned they would not abide by the key demands that the commandos withdraw from populated areas and that heavy weapons be prohibited in the camps. The opponents of the agreement were identified by the semi-official Palestine News Agency as Salah Khalef, Abu Maher and Yasir Abeid Rahboh.

The Lebanese army announced May 19 that 53 soldiers and policemen were killed in the two weeks of fighting and that 169 were wounded.

The state of emergency was lifted by the Cabinet May 23.

Israeli, Arab prisoner exchange. Three captured Israeli pilots were exchanged June 3 for 56 Syrian and Lebanese prisoners. Forty-six Syrians were returned at a border crossing in the Golan Heights, while 10 Lebanese were turned over at Rosh Haniora, a frontier crossing on the Mediterranean coast. The exchange, the biggest since the 1967 war, followed six months of secret negotiations by the International Committee of the Red Cross in Geneva, Beirut, Damascus and Jerusalem.

The Israelis also freed Golan Heights Druse leader Kemal Assad Kanj, who was pardoned after serving two years of a 23-year jail term for espionage. Assad Kanj, a former member of the Syrian Parliament, chose to remain in the Israeli-occupied Golan Heights rather than return to Syria.

The three freed Israeli pilots had been captured by the Syrians in 1970 following air battles over the Golan Heights.

Among the released Syrians were five ranking intelligence officers captured in

an Israeli raid into Lebanon June 21, 1972.

Most of the other Syrians had been taken during an Israeli armored thrust into Syria June 1970. The 10 Lebanese had been captured in the same raid and in another border clash Sept. 16, 1970.

The three Israeli pilots said they had been tortured and interrogated by their Syrian captors. The Syrian Defense Ministry charged in a statement June 4 that the Israelis had subjected the 46 Syrian POWs to physical and psychological torture. The Lebanese said they had been well-treated.

An Israeli denial of the Syrian torture charges was issued June 5 by Lt. Gen. David Elazar, chief of staff. Elazar said he had talked with the five senior Syrian officers just before they were released and they had told him they were well-treated.

As a result of the latest prisoner trade, there no longer were any Israeli captives in Syria or Syrians or Lebanese held by the Israelis.

Israeli aide slain in U.S. The air and naval attache of the Israeli embassy in Washington, Col. Yosef Alon, 43, was murdered July 1 by a group of unknown assailants who escaped in a car. Alon was shot five times as he was parking his auto outside his suburban home in Chevy Chase, Md. after returning from an embassy party. Mrs. Alon, who was accompanying her husband, was unharmed.

A broadcast later July 1 by the Voice of Palestine Radio in Cairo said Alon had been "executed" in reprisal for the "assassination" June 28 of an alleged Palestinian Black September representative in Paris. Identified by French police as an Algerian, Mohammed Boudia, 41, was killed when his automobile exploded as he started the engine. The Cairo broadcast said Boudia was murdered "at the hands of the Zionist intelligence element." Boudia had been sought by Italian police in connection with the sabotage of petroleum installations in Trieste in 1972.

Defense Minister Moshe Dayan July 2 accused Arab terrorists of killing Alon. Speaking at the Tel Aviv airport where the colonel's body had arrived aboard a U.S. military plane, Dayan said Israel would "attempt to liquidate these terrorist activities by striking at the terrorists and not at the diplomatic corps of governments which harbor or support them in Arab countries."

Terrorism committee opens talks. The Special Committee on International Terrorism opened a four-week meeting at United Nations headquarters in New York July 16, with representatives of all 35 member nations attending.

A Syrian statement asserted "the international community is under legal and moral obligation to promote the struggle for liberation and to resist any attempt to depict this struggle as synonymous with terrorism and illegitimate violence."

On the other hand, Japan stressed the "immediate peril endangering innocent lives and fundamental human rights " and urged the U.N. to "make every effort to avoid a situation where the adoption of preventive measures is hampered by delay in studying the underlying causes" of terrorism.

The Japanese view was echoed July 24 by the U.S. representative, W. Tapley Bennett Jr., who urged the committee to focus its attention on "the most serious criminal threat" and avoid "extended conceptual controversy" and the "consideration of abstract definitions."

The British representative, John R. Freeland, joined Bennett in his call for action, stressing that the study of terrorism's underlying causes was "inevitably a long-term matter" and should not "become a brake on progress with measures to protect the innocent."

Arab delegates, who did not participate in the early debate, maintained no action should be taken against terrorism without a study of its causes, according to the New York Times July 25.

Arab blocked in Athens raid. An armed Arab terrorist who failed in an attempt to attack an El Al Israeli airlines office in Athens July 19 was later flown out of Greece in exchange for the release of 17 hostages he had held in a nearby hotel for more than five hours.

The gunman was prevented from entering the El Al office by a guard inside who pressed the security lock that closed the inner glass doors. The Arab then fled to the hotel with two policemen giving chase. Armed with a submachine gun and grenades, the Arab threatened to kill the hostages in the lobby unless Greek Deputy Premier Styliànos Patakos escorted him to the Athens airport for safe conduct out of the country. Patakos refused the demand.

The release of the hostages was negotiated by the ambassadors in Athens of Egypt, Libya and Iraq, who spoke with the gunman in the lobby for two and a half hours. The gunman was taken to the airport and flown to Kuwait.

Japanese jet hijacked, destroyed. A Japan Air Lines 747 passenger jet en route to Tokyo was hijacked July 20 by pro-Palestinian guerrillas shortly after take-off from Amsterdam and was diverted to the Persian Gulf sheikdom of Dubai, a state in the Union of Arab Emirates. The plane remained on a desert airstrip for three days, and was then flown July 24 to Benghazi, Libya, where it was blown up by the hijackers minutes after they and the 137 passengers and crew evacuated the aircraft.

The hijackers, identified as three Palestinians and one member of the terrorist Japanese Red Army, were arrested by Libyan authorities.

During the flight to Dubai, the hijackers variously described themselves as members of the Organization of Sons of Occupied Territories, the Mount Carmel Martyrs, "the Japanese Red Army acting for the People of Palestine," and "Palestine commandos and members of the Japanese Red Army."

The major Palestinian commando groups in Beirut disclaimed any knowledge of these groups and disassociated themselves from the hijacking. A statement issued July 24 by the Palestine Liberation Organization condemned the plane's seizure as "harmful to the Palestinian revolution."

Although the hijackers publicly made no specific demands, they were reported to have said during the flight to Dubai that they sought the release of Japanese Red Army terrorist Kozo Okamoto, serving a life sentence in Israel for the 1972 massacre at Tel Aviv's Lod International Airport.

A statement signed and distributed clandestinely by the Organization of Sons of Occupied Territories in Beirut July 26 said the Japanese plane was hijacked and destroyed in retaliation for the $6 million the Japanese government had paid Israel in compensation for the victims of the Lod incident. The statement said the seizure of the plane was meant to demonstrate the "unity of the world revolutionaries" in the struggle against imperialism, "which is an ally of international Zionism."

Israeli Transport Minister Shimon Peres declared July 21 that his government would not turn Okamoto over to the hijackers. "The position of Israel that we don't give in to blackmail still holds," he said.

Israeli officials said July 24 that unspecified precautions had been taken to prevent the Japanese plane from entering Israeli air space in preparation for a possibility that the hijackers might carry out previous commando threats to crash such a plane into an Israeli city on a suicide mission.

The hijackers had boarded the plane earlier July 20 in Paris. They commandeered the aircraft 30 minutes out of Amsterdam. Shortly afterward a woman hijacker was killed and the plane's Japanese purser was wounded when the hand grenade she was holding exploded accidentally.

The terrorists first tried to have the plane land in Beirut, but Lebanese officials refused permission. Then they flew on to Basra, Iraq, where the runway was regarded as too short for a jumbo jet. The plane headed for Bahrain in the Persian Gulf, but authorities there also denied the hijackers the right to land. The plane finally touched down at the Dubai airport.

Sheik Mohammed bin Rashid, defense minister of the Union of Arab Emirates, boarded the plane July 21 to negotiate for the release of the hostages. The terrorists rejected this request and subsequent appeals over the control tower loudspeaker.

The Dubai control tower July 23 relayed to the hijackers a message reported by authorities to have been sent by a clandestine terrorist group in West Germany. The message said: "If you intend to kill the passengers on board ... tend to kill the passengers on board ...

do it at once, otherwise be human enough to release them... Please give up your intentions. There are other means of unbloody possibilities to reach your political aims."

Shortly after receiving the message, the hijackers demanded and Dubai authorities agreed to refuel the plane. The plane took off July 24. The hijackers' request to land at Baghdad was rejected by Iraqi officials. Syrian officials granted the plane permission to land at Damascus, where it refueled and took off a few hours later for Benghazi.

The plane landed at the Libyan field later July 24, all on board slid down the emergency escape chute. Two minutes later, the aircraft was rocked by an explosion, starting a fire that quickly destroyed the jet. The hijackers were captured by Libyan troops.

The captain of the plane, Kenzi Konuma, said the hijackers had received a relayed message from other guerrillas in Amsterdam to blow up the plane on landing in Benghazi. The message had been sent via the air control towers in Bahrain and Kuwait, the captain said.

Arab slain in Norway. A Moroccan suspected of being a member of the Palestinian Black September organization was shot to death by two assailants July 21 in the Norwegian town of Lillehammer, 115 miles north of Oslo.

Oslo police said six persons of various nationalities, including two Israelis, were arrested in connection with the slaying of Ahmed Bouchiki, 30, who had lived in Norway several years.

An Oslo newspaper (Aftenposten) reported Aug. 1 that Bouchiki had been killed after being mistaken for a Black September leader by an extremist Israeli counterterrorist group called the Wrath of God, an offshoot of the militant Jewish Defense League. The newspaper said that two Israeli undercover agents had infiltrated the group and had been in telephone contact with diplomat Yigal Eyal and other Israeli officials in Oslo. The two Israelis were arrested in Eyal's Oslo apartment July 25.

The Israeli counterterrorist group was believed to have carried out the killing of Bouchiki as part of an Israeli plan to thwart a Black September effort to assemble a group in Norway and then hijack an El Al Israeli airlines jet in Denmark.

An Israeli Foreign Ministry official denied July 26 that his government had any connection with the men arrested for Bouchiki's death.

Arabs raid Athens airport terminal. Two Arab terrorists attacked the crowded Athens airport terminal with machine guns and hand grenades Aug. 5, killing three persons and wounding 55. One of the wounded died Aug. 15. The Arabs, identifying themselves as Black September guerrillas, surrendered to Greek police after releasing 35 hostages they had seized following the killings.

The two Arabs were charged in an Athens court Aug. 7 with "premediated murder" and faced a mandatory death sentence if convicted. They were identified as Shafik el Arid, 22, and Tallal Khantouran, 21, both from Jordan. They told the court prosecutor they were "carrying out orders to hit at emigrants to Israel because they kill our wives and children." Court officials said Arid and Khantouran had flown to Athens from Benghazi, Libya Aug. 3 to survey the transit lounge. Then they took off for Beirut and returned Aug. 5 to carry out the attack.

Police said the two Arabs drew guns and started shooting as they were about to undergo a routine search by a Greek security inspector. The terrorists fired at a line of passengers about to board a Trans World Airlines plane bound for New York and others waiting in the terminal. Arid and Khantouran admitted to police Aug. 6 that they had meant to fire at the passengers of another TWA flight for Tel Aviv.

The Greek government filed a complaint with Arab states Aug. 7, charging that such "criminal terrorist acts" as the Athens incident could have "unfavorable repercussions" on their relations.

Israeli-Egyptian air, naval clashes. Egypt claimed that its jet fighters hit one of six Israeli planes that penetrated Egyptian air space over the Suez Canal Aug. 9. The Israeli command said its planes were patrolling the Gulf of Suez at the time mentioned in the Cairo communique, but said "all our aircraft returned to base safely."·

Israeli and Egyptian naval vessels exchanged gunfire in the Gulf of Suez Aug. 13 for the first time in almost six years. The Israeli command claimed that one of its two patrol boats was attacked first by two Egyptian vessels northwest of Ras Sudar in the eastern part of the gulf on the Israeli side of the truce line. The command said the Israelis returned the fire and disabled one of the gunboats.

According to Cairo's version, Egyptian patrol boats intercepted Israeli naval units attempting incursions near Ismailia in the Suez Canal and just south of Adibiya in the Gulf of Suez, forcing them to flee.

Israelis force down Iraqi jet. An Iraqi Airways passenger jetliner enroute from Beirut to Baghdad Aug. 10 was intercepted by two Israeli jet fighters 25 miles north of the Lebanese capital and forced to land at a military airfield in northern Israel near Haifa. The plane was permitted to continue its scheduled flight to Baghdad after a two-hour security search by Israeli authorities.

Israeli Defense Minister Moshe Dayan said Aug. 11 that the purpose in forcing down the Iraqi plane was to capture several commando leaders, including George Habash, head of the Popular Front for the Liberation of Palestine (PFLP), believed to be aboard. Dayan called Habash a "master of murder" and said the PFLP was responsible for the July 20 hijacking of a Japan Air Lines plane to Libya and the Aug. 5 attack on the Athens airport terminal.

An Israeli military spokesman had conceded earlier Aug. 11 that the wrong plane had been intercepted. He said Israel had planned to divert another Beirut-to-Baghdad plane about the same time as the intercepted flight. That aircraft had been delayed a few minutes in taking off and reportedly carried several leaders of the commando movement.

A spokesman for the Palestine Liberation Organization, the umbrella commando group, said Aug. 11 that George Habash and his deputy, Salah Salah, were to have been on the plane, but canceled their reservations shortly before its departure as a routine security precaution. Other reports said Habash, who suffered from heart trouble, had left the plane because he felt ill.

The airliner, carrying 74 passengers and seven crewmen, was leased from Lebanon's Middle East Airlines. A Beirut communique said Lebanese antiaircraft guns opened fire as the two Israeli jets intercepted the airliner. The statement said at the same time other Israeli jets were "violating Lebanese airspace over Merj Uyun, Tyre and over the sea."

The chairman of the Israeli pilots union, Capt. Yitzhak Shaked, Aug. 11 criticized the forcing down of the airliner. He said his group was opposed to such actions because the union "fights against hijackings and interference with civil aviation."

Israel's chief of staff, Lt. Gen. David Elazar, warned Aug. 15 that Israel would carry out further plane interceptions. He said Israel had the "right of self-defense" to "get those that advocate the liquidation of Israel."

U.N. Council condemns Israel—The United Nations Security Council Aug. 15 approved by a 15–0 vote a resolution condemning Israel for "violating Lebanon's sovereignty and territorial integrity" and for "the forcible seizure" of the Iraqi airliner in Lebanon's airspace. The Council said the act constituted "a serious interference with international civil aviation and a violation of the Charter of the United Nations."

The resolution warned Israel that "if such acts are repeated, the Council will consider taking adequate steps or measures to enforce its resolutions."

Explaining his endorsement of the resolution, U.S. delegate John A. Scali said it "in no way represents a change in my government's view on the problems and possibilities for a solution in the Middle East. Nor should it be interpreted as endorsing the principle of sanctions as a means of dealing with this problem."

Israeli delegate Yosef Tekoah said despite the Council's condemnation of his country, Israel would continue "its struggle against Arab terrorism," giving "no quarter to the ruthless killers of the innocent."

Scali and Lebanese delegate Edouard Ghorra had worked closely in drawing up a resolution that would be satisfactory to both nations. The U.S. had threatened to veto any resolution that called for sanctions against Israel, as demanded by several Council members, including Egypt, China, India, the Soviet Union and Yugoslavia.

Arabs raid Saudi embassy in Paris. A group of five armed Palestinian commandos broke into the Saudi Arabian embassy in Paris Sept. 5 and seized 13 diplomats and employes as hostages. After 28 hours of protracted negotiations, the guerrillas agreed to release all but four Saudi hostages, and left Paris Sept. 6 with their captives aboard a plane provided by Syria. The aircraft landed in Kuwait Sept. 7 after a refueling stop in Cairo.

The commandos described themselves as belonging to a hitherto unknown group called Al Icab. After storming the embassy, they threatened to blow up the building or kill the hostages unless their demands were met. They called for the release of Abu Daoud, an Al Fatah leader serving a life term in Jordan for terrorism. The gunmen later dropped this demand and insisted only that they be given safe passage by plane to an Arab country.

The impasse was finally broken Sept. 6 when Syrian President Hafez al-Assad agreed to put a Syrian Arab Airlines plane at the disposal of the commandos.

The terrorists with the four hostages transferred later Sept. 7 to a Kuwaiti Boeing 707 plane and circled over Riyadh, Saudi Arabia, threatening to throw their captives out of the aircraft unless the Saudis took action to help secure Abu Daoud's release. Saudi officials refused. Jordan announced Sept. 7 that it would not free Daoud.

Returning to Kuwait, the gunmen asked for another Syrian plane to fly them to Damascus. Ali Yassin, PLO representative in Kuwait, who was serving as mediator between the commandos and the Kuwaitis, was seized as a hostage by the commandos. In further negotiations Sept. 8 Kuwait offered to give the commandos safe passage to Iraq in a car if the commandos freed all the hostages. The guerrillas insisted on taking Yassin or a Kuwaiti security official with them. This demand was refused. Yassin was freed two hours later. The commandos surrendered later Sept. 8, released the four Saudis and were taken into custody.

Israel condemns commando missiles. The U.S. at Israel's insistence protested to the Soviet Union over Palestinian commando possession of Soviet-made surface-to-air missiles, an Israeli government source reported Sept. 9. The weapons, along with five Arab guerrillas who planned to use them to attack Israeli passenger planes, were seized by Italian police Sept. 5. The police said the Arabs had planned to shoot down an Israeli El Al airliner at Rome's international airport at Fiumicino.

One of the Arabs was seized in an apartment at Ostia, four miles from the airport, along with two light-weight launchers for ground-to-air missiles, according to the police. The four others were arrested later in Rome.

An Israeli government communique Sept. 9 said Israel had called the U.S.' attention "to the significance of the supply of sophisticated Soviet weapons for the purpose of international terrorism." Foreign Minister Abba Eban said Israel's diplomatic missions abroad had been instructed to demand that foreign governments condemn the commando plan to shoot down Israeli planes.

Defense Minister Moshe Dayan had said Sept. 8 that the possession of the missiles by the guerrillas posed a new threat to international civil aviation. He deplored the "alliance of the terrorists with the countries from which they had received these weapons."

Israeli, Syrian jets clash. Israel claimed that 13 Syrian jets were shot down and admitted the loss of one of its own Sept. 13 in the biggest air battle between the two countries since the 1967 war. Syria said its pilots had shot down five Israeli jets and acknowledged that eight of its planes were "hit."

According to Israel's version of the dogfights, as given to newsmen by Maj. Gen. Binyamin Peled, air force commander:

Israeli Phantom and Mirage fighters were on a routine patrol over international waters of the Mediterranean 150 miles north of Haifa when they were intercepted and fired on by Syrian MiG-21s. The Syrians lost nine planes and the Israelis one Mirage in this first encounter. Israeli planes providing cover for a helicopter rescue of the downed Israeli pilot were later intercepted by four Syrian jets. All of the Syrian aircraft were destroyed by additional Israeli planes that joined the battle, Peled said. The Israeli pilot as well as a downed Syrian pilot nearby were rescued by the helicopter. A total of 12-16 MiGs and 12 Israeli jets were involved in the air clashes. Peled described the Israeli patrol as routine "to find out what's going on in the Mediterranean waters."

A Damascus military communique said 64 Israeli planes had "violated Syrian airspace over the coastline" between the ports of Latakia and Tartus. "Our fighter planes intercepted them and air battles developed, . . . Five enemy planes were shot down and eight of ours were hit." The communique said the clashes lasted three hours.

As a result of the latest air battle, Israel claimed that Syria had lost 60 planes since the 1967 war. It placed its own losses on the Syrian front during that period at four.

Hostages used to curb Austrian transit of Soviet Jews. Yielding to terrorists, the Austrian government announced Sept. 29 it would no longer allow group transit of Soviet Jewish emigrants through Austria, and would close Israeli-run facilities that housed emigrants awaiting transfer to Israel. The decision was made in return for the release of one Austrian and three Soviet Jewish hostages, whom Arab guerrillas had held under threat of murder at the Vienna airport. Austrian chancellor Bruno Kreisky refused to modify his decision during an Oct. 2 meeting with Israeli Premier Golda Meir.

The three Jewish hostages were seized Sept. 28, along with a woman who later escaped with her infant son, on a Moscow-Vienna train carrying 40 Jewish emigrants in Czechoslovak territory at the Austrian border. The two heavily armed guerrillas, who said they were members of a group called the Eagles of the

Palestinian Revolution, left the train at the Austrian customs station, where they seized a customs official, commandeered a car and drove to Vienna's Schwechat airport.

Israeli Acting Premier Yigal Allon said in Jerusalem Oct. 1 that "certain elements" in Czechoslovakia might have co-operated with the guerrillas, since they had entered the train with arms and ammunition in a country "subject to tight control and surveillance."

During several hours of negotiations, the Austrian Cabinet offered to fly the guerrillas to the Middle East but refused their demands to take the hostages with them. The hostages were released early Sept. 29, after Austrian Chancellor Bruno Kreisky agreed to close the Schoenau Castle transit facility outside Vienna, run by the Jewish Agency of Israel, and to bar "group transports" of Jews through Austria, according to Interior Minister Otto Roesch in a radio broadcast Sept. 29.

The guerrillas were given a twin-engine plane with two Austrian pilots and were allowed to land in Libya only after they had been refused by Tunisia and Algeria and had threatened to blow up the plane. The plane had made refueling stops in Yugoslavia and Italy. In a statement issued at Schwechat, the guerrillas said they had acted "because we feel that the immigration of Soviet Union Jews constitutes a great danger to our cause."

Austria's government-run television said Sept. 29 that the offer to close Schoenau had been a compromise suggested by Arab governments, "especially Iraq." Kreisky, in several interviews that day, said he had refused demands to bar all future Jewish emigrants from entering Austria and said "all people with proper papers" would be allowed to pass through. Nearly all the 70,000 Jewish emigrants who had left the European Communist countries since 1971 had passed through Austria in groups, without Austrian visas.

Kreisky, Jewish-born, said he had acted solely to prevent loss of life but said Austria "would sooner or later have had to order a modification" of the emigration procedures because of the threat of violence and the presence of "armed men from both sides."

Austria had been criticized by Arab and Communist governments for permitting the transit facilities. Three Arabs had been arrested as suspected terrorists early in 1973, only to be released after the Austrian embassy in Beirut received a terrorist bomb threat. Austrian security officials were reported to have opposed the Schoenau operation, in existence for 11 years. Four armed Israeli security agents were detained and then released by Austrian police Sept. 29 at the Czechoslovak border, where they were guarding a group of emigrants.

Israeli officials condemned Austria's decision on the transit issue. Israeli Ambassador Yitzhak Patish, recalled to Tel Aviv Sept. 29, said the incident was the first success by Arab terrorists in forcing a government to change its policy.

Israeli Premier Golda Meir asked the Austrian government to reconsider its decision in an Oct. 1 address to a meeting of the Assembly of the Council of Europe in Strasbourg, France. She called the Austrian decision "the greatest encouragement to terrorism throughout the world," although she said Israel was "strongly grateful" for Austria's past role as a transit point for refugees.

But Meir failed to convince Kreisky to reverse his decision when she met with him in Vienna Oct. 2.

After their meeting, Kreisky told newsmen that resisting the terrorists would have not discouraged future terrorism, since "by now, even if they are indicted and convicted, terrorists know the events that follow—that they will be liberated anyway," referring to the release of terrorists by several European countries, including West Germany and Switzerland, after pressure from other guerrillas.

United Nations Secretary General Kurt Waldheim informed Austria Oct. 2 that the Office of High Commissioner for Refugees could not assume responsibility for the Schoenau facility under existing U.N. rules, as Kreisky had suggested in his meeting with Meir. Waldheim said approval for a takeover would have to come from the General Assembly, since the Jews, who had legal Soviet exit visas and assurances of asylum in Israel, did not come under existing U.N. definitions of refugees.

Peace Efforts
& Diplomatic Moves

Little Progress During 1972

Little tangible progress was reported during 1972 toward the goal of bringing lasting peace to the Middle East. Instead, terrorism and military clashes continued, and both sides made efforts to build up their military strength.

Israel approves talks with Egypt. Israel Feb. 2, 1972 agreed to a new American proposal for indirect talks with Egypt on reopening the Suez Canal. The actual start of the negotiations, however, remained uncertain since the U.S. had not yet sought Egyptian approval of the plan.

The proposed discussions, described as "proximity talks," would possibly be held in the same or nearby hotel in New York with U.S. Assistant Secretary of State Joseph J. Sisco acting as a go-between, shuttling between Israeli and Egyptian representatives. This formula had been proposed by Secretary of State William P. Rogers in his Oct. 4, 1971 appeal to both sides to work out an interim agreement on the reopening of the canal.

Israeli approval of the American proposal followed weeks of discussion in Washington between Sisco and Israeli Ambassador Yitzhak Rabin. These meetings had overcome Premier Golda Meir's two principal objections to the American proposal.

Mrs. Meir had held that Washington's refusal to sell Israel additional Phantom jets would put her government at a military and psychological disadvantage in future negotiations with Egypt. She also had taken issue with specific ideas outlined by Rogers in his Oct. 4 statement, which she claimed differed from some of Israel's positions. These objections were cleared up in the Israeli-U.S. exchanges in which Washington agreed to supply Israel with more planes and military equipment and assured Jerusalem that Rogers had not intended to "impose" his views on future Israeli-Arab talks.

The U.S. State Department Feb. 2 welcomed Israeli agreement to enter into talks with Egypt and reaffirmed the U.S.' availability "to help this process if that is the desire of the parties concerned."

Egypt asserted Feb. 2 that Israel's approval of the U.S. proposal and Washington's welcome of its agreement were a maneuver aimed at misleading world opinion.

Premier Meir had insisted Jan. 28 that there was "no linkage" between Israeli willingness to enter into negotiations with Egypt and its request for

American Phantom jets. "When we demand or ask for Phantoms . . ., we are negotiating for something which we believe is essential to our security," Mrs. Meir said in a New York Times interview. The Israeli leader expressed willingness to participate in the renewal of negotiations under the supervision of U.N. mediator Gunnar V. Jarring, but she complained that the talks had stopped because the Egyptians "were not negotiating with Israel at all, even indirectly. They were negotiating with Dr. Jarring . . ."

Asserting that Israel would not return to the borders before the 1967 war, Mrs. Meir said her country would keep all of Jerusalem, the Golan Heights and Sharm el Sheik. She opposed any form of Islamic "territorial" control of the Moslem holy places in Jerusalem but did not rule out Moslem "administration."

Egypt, U.S.S.R. urge U.N. peace move. Egyptian President Anwar Sadat conferred with Soviet officials in Moscow Feb. 3–4. A joint communiqué issued at the conclusion of the talks appealed for resumption of U.N. efforts to settle the Middle East crisis but made no specific promise of additional Soviet military equipment for Egypt. The announced objective of Sadat's visit was to obtain more Soviet arms.

On the matter of military aid, the joint statement said only that both sides had "considered measures" in the area for "further strengthening" Egyptian military capabilities against Israel "and outlined a number of concrete steps in this direction." In his talks with Soviet leaders in Moscow in October 1971, Sadat had received a specific pledge of Soviet arms shipments.

The communiqué, blaming Israel for the Middle East impasse, said that U.N. mediator Gunnar V. Jarring "should immediately" resume his separate discussions with Israeli and Arab representatives to promote a political settlement involving total Israeli withdrawal from occupied Arab territory. The statement did not mention the U.S.-proposed "proximity talks" approved by Israel Feb. 2 but regarded with disfavor by Egypt and the Soviet Union.

(The weekly Moscow News expressed displeasure with U.S. mediation Feb. 3, saying "The plans of the 'honest broker' were utterly exposed by the U.S. decision to supply dozens of Phantoms and Skyhawks to Israel . . .")

Both countries "reaffirmed their intention to continue to strengthen Soviet-Egyptian friendship and cooperation in every way," the communique said. It also assailed "the aggressive expansionist policy pursued by Israel with the support of the United States."

Sadat, who had arrived in Moscow Feb. 2, conferred with Premier Alexei Kosygin, Communist party General Secretary Leonid Brezhnev and other Soviet leaders during his three-day stay.

Before returning to Cairo, Sadat stopped in Yugoslavia, Syria and Libya, where he briefed leaders on his Moscow talks. He conferred with Yugoslav President Tito Feb. 4–5 and with Syrian President Hafez al-Assad and Libyan leader Muammar el-Qaddafi Feb. 6.

Israel-Jordan contacts hinted. Israeli government spokesmen reported Feb. 10 that Premier Golda Meir had conferred in January with Anwar Nusseibeh, a former Jordanian defense minister and confidant of King Hussein. Mrs. Meir's office said the meeting was a "courtesy call" and took place at Nusseibeh's request.

Confirming his meeting with Mrs. Meir, Nusseibeh said Feb. 10 that its only purpose was "simply to get acquainted and exchange ideas."

The announcement on the Meir-Nusseibeh discussion followed Israeli press reports that Israeli officials were maintaining contacts with Hussein through Nusseibeh to work out a possible peace agreement between the two countries.

Israel-Jordan air pact. An Israeli-Jordanian agreement on air traffic cooperation was disclosed by Israeli civilian aviation authorities Feb. 20. Under the pact, radio communication was to be established between the Israeli airfield at the southern port of Elath and a new Jordanian field opening near Aqaba, six miles away. The control towers of both airfields were to advise each other on traffic to prevent air collisions.

Egypt rejects Israeli contact. Premier Golda Meir's office disclosed Feb. 15 that Egypt had recently turned down an Israeli offer to hold high-level talks. The discussions were to have been arranged by an unidentified mediator through Nahum Goldmann, a former president of the World Jewish Congress. Mrs. Meir's office said she had asked Goldmann to establish the contact but that Cairo spurned the proposal.

Goldmann denied in Paris Feb. 15 that he had been designated as the go-between. He said another person, whom he refused to identify, had been involved in the projected meeting but that the Egyptians said the time was not yet ripe for such talks after Mrs. Meir had given approval.

Goldmann had figured in a previous unsuccessful attempt to establish Israeli-Egyptian contacts in March 1970.

Jarring visits Mideast capitals. U.N. Middle East envoy Gunnar V. Jarring intensified his efforts to resolve the Arab-Israeli conflict with visits to Cairo Feb. 18–19, Amman Feb. 23 and Jerusalem Feb. 25. He conferred with Secretary General Kurt Waldheim in Geneva Feb. 27 before returning to U.N. headquarters in New York the following day to report on his latest mission.

Jarring met with Egyptian Foreign Minister Murad Ghaleb in Cairo Feb. 18 and described the talks as successful. He conferred in Amman Feb. 23 with Jordanian King Hussein, Premier Ahmed al-Lawzi and Foreign Minister Abdullah Salah. Amman radio said the discussions centered on the implementation of the 1967 Security Council resolution calling for Israeli withdrawal from occupied Arab territory in exchange for a peace treaty.

Following his meeting with Israeli officials in Jerusalem Feb. 25, Foreign Minister Abba Eban said Jarring "did not ask for new commitments" and "his mission will certainly continue."

Israel favors wider Jarring mission. Foreign Minister Abba Eban said March 7, 1972 that Israel was seeking to reactivate Jarring's mission but preferred the U.S. initiative for an interim Egyptian-Israeli agreement on the reopening of the Suez Canal.

In a major review of foreign affairs during parliamentary debate on the annual budget, Eban indicated that Jarring had not shifted from his original position, first expressed Feb. 8, 1971, which called for an Israeli commitment to quit Egyptian territory before negotiations were started on a peace treaty. "We have neither accepted nor shall we accept this condition," Eban said.

Eban disclosed that Israel had informed the U.S. in a hitherto secret memo sent April 19, 1971 that Israel would not accept as final a new cease-fire line in the Sinai Peninsula that would be established in a proposed accord to reopen the canal but would withdraw later to permanent and agreed borders to be set in a peace treaty. This position was in contrast to Egypt's demand for an Israeli pullback from the canal as the first phase of a total withdrawal from all occupied areas.

Mrs. Meir visits Rumania. Israeli Premier Golda Meir conferred with Rumanian officials in Bucharest May 4–6. On her return to Tel Aviv May 7, Mrs. Meir confirmed that President Nicolae Ceausescu, who had visited Egypt in April, had clarified President Anwar Sadat's Middle East position to her in one of their meetings. The Israeli leader said Rumania could help bring the disputing parties together, but she emphasized that Bucharest had no intentions of acting as a "go-between."

A joint statement by Mrs. Meir and Premier Ion Gheorghe Maurer, made public May 7 in Jerusalem and Bucharest, stated that "the two heads of government stood for the continuation of the efforts toward the peaceful settlement of the conflict."

Mrs. Meir, who became the first Israeli premier to visit a Communist country, revealed that Maurer had agreed to return the visit and that an invitation also had been extended to Ceausescu.

Foreign Minister Abba Eban had disclosed in Washington April 21 that Rumania had advised Israel that it planned to use its "position of mutual confidence" in Cairo and Jerusalem to clarify the positions of the two governments to each other. Israel lauded the Rumanian effort as a "contribution to peace" and would cooperate with it, Eban said.

OAU summit held. The annual Organization of African Unity (OAU) summit conference ended June 15 in Rabat, Morocco. Attended by representatives from 40 African countries, including 23 heads of state, the meeting opposed Israel's position.

Delegates unanimously passed a resolution June 14 denouncing Israel's "negative and obstructive attitude," which was said to be preventing resumption of the Gunnar Jarring peace mission in the Middle East. OAU members were asked to "give Egypt every assistance" and U.N. members were asked "to refrain from giving Israel any arms or military equipment or moral support."

Israel proposes Sinai truce line. Israeli Defense Minister Moshe Dayan Aug. 17 offered an interim peace agreement with Egypt based on a truce line dividing the Sinai Peninsula.

Dayan noted that his suggestion represented a pullback from Israel's previous insistence that it would exchange the current truce lines only for "secure, recognized and agreed borders, determined under a peace treaty." Now, he said, Israel was prepared for interim settlements "by stages" in the absence of an over-all agreement. Dayan, however, was not specific as to where the proposed truce line would be drawn and whether Israel and Egypt would be allowed to station troops along the buffer strip.

Although his proposal meant some relinquishment of territory captured by Israel in the 1967 war, Dayan said Israel had no intention of giving up all the former Arab territories. "Such is not the reward of aggression," he said in accusing Egypt, Jordan and Syria of having instigated the war.

Dayan warned that if the Egyptians "refuse to meet us part way, we will have to go on acting in the way we have adopted for the five years" since the war.

Israel, Jordan peace bids. Israeli Premier Meir Sept. 8, 1972 offered King Hussein of Jordan what she described as a "generous" offer to end the impasse between their two countries. Mrs. Meir said that "under a peace settlement," Israel was prepared to give Amman "port facilities in Gaza or Haifa, open skies to its planes and free passage."

"But since we shall never return to the pre-1967 war boundaries, then Hussein must give up territories," Mrs. Meir said.

Jordan appeared to ease its demands for sovereignty over East Jerusalem as a precondition for peace with Israel, according to remarks made Sept. 7 by Foreign Minister Salah Abu Zaid. In an interview published Sept. 9, Zaid, in reply to a question about Jordan's long-standing demand for a return of at least nominal control over East Jerusalem, said: "Let us not be imprisoned by words. I think the acknowledgment of the rights of Jordan in Jerusalem is by itself an achievement. We talk about our right in Jerusalem, not about controlling it the way some people think."

Zaid also was conciliatory about Israel's demands for demilitarization of the Jordan River and the West Bank area around Jerusalem as its condition for peace. He said this proposal would be "one of those details that must not stand in the way of peace."

Israel backs talks with Jordan. Israeli Foreign Minister Abba Eban said Dec. 2 that Jordan would benefit from negotiations with Israel. Such talks, Eban stressed, could provide the Amman government with "peace, population, territory, and a special status for the Moslem places of Jerusalem."

Israel was not prepared to yield on the sovereignty or unity of Jerusalem, but this did not mean that it claimed "exclusive jurisdiction or unilateral responsibility over the holy places of Islam" in the Israeli capital, Eban said. The foreign minister said that although it would be logical for Israel to conclude a peace pact with Egypt first, his government would not rule out an initial accord with Jordan if such an agreement were attainable. But Eban expressed doubt that the Amman government had "the strength and stability of policy necessary" to reach a compromise settlement.

Eban's friendly overture to Jordan followed a statement by King Hussein in a Le Monde interview published Nov. 3 in which he had said he was ready to conclude a "total peace" with Israel. His remarks, however, were qualified by his previous demands that although "minor adjustments on the basis of reciprocity" could be made, he would oppose any Israeli annexation of Jordanian territory, including the former Jordanian section of Jerusalem. Hussein said if Israel recognized Jordan's "inalienable rights of sovereignty" over Jerusalem, "we could discuss a formula which would make Jerusalem a city of peace and cooperation among the three monotheistic religions."

Premier Golda Meir said Nov. 11 that she believed Hussein "sincerely wants peace" with Israel. She stated that by becoming the first Arab leader to call for peace with Israel, Hussein "has taken an almost revolutionary step." But she said there can only be a settlement if the king conceded some of his territory lost to Israel in the 1967 war.

1973's Mediation Efforts Fail

International attempts to settle the Arab-Israeli dispute proved futile during 1973, and war erupted in October. Among peace efforts and other diplomatic activities that took place during 1973 before the renewal of hostilities:

Hussein presses U.S. on peace. King Hussein of Jordan urged the U.S. Jan. 7 to take initiatives to promote peace in the Middle East.

In an interview published by U.S. News & World Report, Hussein said: "I don't know just what the United States is prepared to do specifically, but I am rather hopeful that within the near future the United States will show a greater interest. I am really quite optimistic about the trend. I feel we may be on the threshhold of important developments."

Pompidou, Brezhnev meet in U.S.S.R. French President Georges Pompidou and Soviet Communist party General Secretary Leonid Brezhnev held two days of talks at a country estate in the village of Zaslavl, near Minsk, Jan. 11–12, 1973. A joint communique issued at the end of the talks proposed, among other measures, a resumption of the Middle East mediation mission of Dr. Gunnar V. Jarring, the United Nations special envoy.

Israeli premier meets Pope. Israeli Premier Golda Meir held an unprecedented meeting with Pope Paul VI in the Vatican Jan. 15. They discussed peace efforts in the Middle East, the status of Jerusalem, Palestinian refugees, Arab terrorism and the condition of Jews in the Soviet Union.

A Vatican communique issued after the meeting said the Pope had recalled "the history and the sufferings of the Jewish people" before stating his positions on the principal topics discussed with Mrs. Meir. A simultaneous "verbal declaration" made by Federico Alessandrini, the Vatican press spokesman, minimized the importance of the occasion, saying that Mrs. Meir's audience with the Pope had not been a "preferential or exclusive gesture," and that it did not imply any change in "the attitude of the Holy See concerning the Holy Land." (The Vatican favored a special international status for Jerusalem and holy places in Israel.) Alessandrini noted that the pontiff had met with Arab leaders, including King Hussein of Jordan, and that the meeting with Mrs. Meir, therefore, did not mean the Pope was taking sides in the Middle East dispute. Alessandrini said Mrs. Meir had requested the audience and the Pope accepted because he felt it was his duty to act for peace and human rights in the

Middle East. Israeli newspapers and officials had reported Jan. 14 that Paul had extended the invitation to Mrs. Meir.

Giving her version of the meeting, Mrs. Meir told a news conference at the Israeli embassy in Rome that the Pope had called their meeting an "historic occasion" and had "expressed his appreciation the way Israel is taking care of the holy places." The premier said her meeting with Paul had been arranged through "constant contacts" between the Vatican and Israel's ambassador to Italy, Amiel E. Najar. Asked by newsmen whether she considered Alessandrini's statement "a diplomatic slap in the face," Mrs. Meir replied: "I didn't break into the Vatican, I came because the meeting had been arranged. I have no excuse to offer for my coming."

The chief rabbi of Rome, Elio Toaff, asserted Jan. 16 that the Vatican had committed a "grave discourtesy" with its attempt to play down the importance of the meeting between Mrs. Meir and the Pope. Toaff said the Allessandrini statement was made in response to Arab pressure, that there were reports that "five or six" diplomats of Arab countries had called on the Vatican immediately after the announcement Jan. 14 that Mrs. Meir was going to confer with the Pope.

Mrs. Meir said her meeting with the Pope was marked by tension, according to an interview published in the Israeli newspaper Maariv Jan. 19. She was quoted as saying: "I didn't like the opening at all. The Pope said to me at the outset that he found it hard to understand how the Jewish people, which should be merciful, behaves so fiercely in its own country."

Saying that "I can't stand it when we are talked to like that," Mrs. Meir disclosed she had told the pontiff: "Do you know what my earlier memory is? A pogrom in Kiev. When we were merciful and when we had no homeland and when we were weak, we were led to the gas chambers."

Mrs. Meir said she was "satisfied with the fact" that the Pope thanked her for "the guarding of Christian holy places" in Jerusalem.

Meeting with African leader—Following her meeting with the Pope, Mrs. Meir

flew to Geneva, where she conferred Jan. 16–17 with Ivory Coast President Felix Houphouet-Boigny. The discussions were said to have dealt with Israel's concern at deteriorating relations with African states. Since April 1972, the Congo Republic, Chad, Niger and Mali had severed diplomatic relations with Israel.

Mrs. Meir ended her six-day European trip and returned to Israel Jan. 17.

Meir at Socialist International—On her first visit to France as Israeli premier, Mrs. Meir had arrived in Paris Jan. 12 to attend an unofficial Socialist International congress Jan. 13–14. Her presence sparked a series of clashes between several hundred anti-Israeli demonstrators and Paris police Jan. 13–14 after the anti-Zionists defied an official ban on all demonstrations during the meeting.

The demonstrators—mainly students— hurled rocks and bottles at the police, who dispersed them with clubs and tear gas grenades.

Massive security precautions were ordered for Mrs. Meir following an increase of tension in Paris between pro- and anti-Israel groups. Arab supporters had called for street protests following the death Jan. 9 of Mahmoud Hamchari, the Paris representative of the Palestine Liberation Organization. Hamchari had been wounded by a bomb blast in his apartment Dec. 8, 1972, for which Arabs blamed "Zionist terrorist groups." (The Black September Movement, an extremist Arab guerrilla group, claimed responsibility for a bomb attack Jan. 9 which severely damaged the Paris offices of the Jewish Agency, an organization responsible for aid and immigration to Israel. No one was injured in the blast.)

Nixon meets King Hussein. King Hussein of Jordan conferred with President Nixon in Washington Feb. 6 and received assurances of continued U.S. economic and military assistance. The two leaders also reviewed efforts to achieve a Middle East peace settlement in their 70-minute meeting.

Hussein said Feb. 7 that the U.S. had "agreed in principle" to supply Jordan with 30 F-5E jet fighter planes. Fifteen of the aircraft had been promised in 1972 but had not yet been delivered. The king said Jordan needed the additional arms as "a point of stability" and as "a deterrent in its own self-defense." Hussein said Jordan was prepared to enter into separate negotiations with Israel if agreement could be reached in advance on "general principles," particularly the future status of Jerusalem.

Before departing for the U.S., Hussein had declared in a televised address in Amman Feb. 3 that he would seek American assistance to obtain "a peace based on justice which generations after us can accept and live under." He ruled out any "partial solution" or separate peace between Jordan and Israel that ignored the problem of Egyptian and Syrian territory occupied by Israel since the 1967 war. That kind of a settlement, he said, would be "a deadly stab at the Arab cause and national interest."

Nixon meets Ismail, Meir. U.S. efforts to help achieve peace in the Middle East were spurred by separate talks President Nixon held in Washington Feb. 23 with Hafez Ismail, Egyptian President Anwar Sadat's national security adviser, and March 1 with Israeli Premier Golda Meir.

A White House spokesman said after Nixon's 1½ hour discussion with Meir that the President had assured her of "continuing United States support." The Israeli premier was seeking $515 million in new credits and American assistance.

White House Press Secretary Ronald L. Ziegler summed up Nixon's talks with Meir, Ismail and King Hussein of Jordan Feb. 6 by stating that "it would be inadvisable to expect any immediate results from these conversations."

Meir said after the meeting, also attended by Henry A. Kissinger, Nixon's national security adviser, that Israel "had a great friend at the White House and nothing has happened to change my mind."

U.S. claims 'rapport' with Egypt. U.S. officials said President Nixon, Secretary of State William P. Rogers and other Administration leaders had established a "good rapport" with Egypt after several hours of high-level talks with Hafez Ismail Feb. 23. The State Department said both

sides "recognized that dramatic results were not to be expected as the result of today's discussions. We look forward to a continuation of our discussions through diplomatic channels."

In welcoming Ismail, President Nixon said the U.S. goal was to end the impasse in the Middle East, which he described as "this very troubled and explosive area of the world." Ismail brought a message to Nixon from President Anwar Sadat, but its contents were not disclosed.

Ismail told newsmen after his separate talks with Rogers that progress had been made and, as a result, U.S.-Egyptian relations were "more relaxed."

U.S. officials said in Paris Feb. 25 that despite improved relations between the U.S. and Egypt, the talks with Ismail had brought no substantive progress in breaking the Middle East deadlock. The officials said Rogers, in Paris for the international conference on Vietnam, reported that Egypt continued to oppose American suggestions for proximity talks with Israel through a third party to obtain an interim agreement for reopening the Suez Canal. Cairo reiterated that it would not enter such talks unless Israel committed itself in advance to withdrawal from all Arab territories.

Following Ismail's talks in Washington, Sadat assured other Arab countries Feb. 24 that he would not make a separate peace with Israel at the expense of its Arab neighbors. Sadat's views were conveyed through Mahmoud Riad, secretary general of the Arab League.

U.S. to press peace moves. The U.S. State Department said March 29 that Washington was still interested in promoting an interim solution of the Middle East conflict.

Assistant State Secretary Joseph J. Sisco made the announcement in the Administration's first policy statement since President Nixon's meeting earlier in the year with Jordanian, Egyptian and Israeli officials. Sisco said Israeli and Egyptian stands were too far apart to be reconciled by an overall settlement, and so the best approach would be to work for a limited solution—the reopening of the Suez Canal with an Israeli withdrawal from the waterway to a certain distance. He said Egyptian President Anwar Sadat had not rejected diplomatic action to end the deadlock.

A report from Cairo April 2 quoted a government source as saying that Egypt's "dialogue with the United States has not stopped, and we have no intention to stop it."

Bonn minister visits Arab states. West German Foreign Minister Walter Scheel made a plea for a Middle East peace settlement in visits to Egypt, Jordan and Lebanon May 20–25, 1973.

Scheel conferred in Cairo May 20–22 with President Anwar Sadat and other Egyptian officials, with King Hussein in Amman May 23–24 and with Lebanese leaders in Beirut May 24–25. Scheel reportedly assured the Egyptians that the U.S. and Soviet Union were pressing for a quick solution of the Middle East deadlock.

He told a news conference in Beirut May 25 that his assessment of the Middle East situation was based on his participation in West German-Soviet leadership talks in Bonn May 18–22 and on meetings Chancellor Willy Brandt held with President Nixon in Washington May 1–2. Scheel said his tour of the three Arab states convinced him the Arabs had a deep desire for peace.

During Scheel's visits agreements were signed providing Egypt, Jordan and Lebanon with West German financial and technical aid.

U.S. favors Arab-Israeli talks. The U.S. warned May 29 against any change of the United Nations Security Council's 1967 resolution on the Middle East that might discourage direct or indirect Arab-Israeli negotiations to achieve a peace settlement. John A. Scali, U.S. ambassador to the U.N., made the statement preparatory to an extensive Security Council debate on the Middle East.

Noting that both sides had accepted but given different interpretations of the 1967 resolution, Scali said the U.S. nevertheless believed it constituted "a fundamental framework whose continued existence is essential." The Council, therefore, "must avoid any action which would have the effect of altering its substance and delicate balance," Scali said. He recalled that whenever the U.N. sought to interpret the resolution, "or have suggested procedures not acceptable to both sides, they have impeded rather than promoted negotiations between the parties."

A State Department official later said that one purpose of Scali's statement was to warn Egypt and its supporters that the U.S. would block approval of a new resolution that could be interpreted as putting additional pressure on Israel.

U.N. issues peace-effort report. Secretary General Kurt Waldheim issued a report May 21 reviewing the U.N.'s peace efforts in the Middle East. The 41-page summary was aimed at preparing the groundwork for the Security Council's full-scale debate on all aspects of the Arab-Israeli dispute.

The report was prepared for Waldheim by Gunnar V. Jarring, his special envoy to the Middle East. Its principal focus was on the Security Council's Nov. 22, 1967 resolution, which called for Israeli withdrawal from Arab territories and an end to a state of belligerency.

Waldheim said Israeli and Arab interpretations of the resolution remained fundamentally unreconciled. Israel, he noted, regarded the resolution as meaning that "a settlement of the Middle East question could be reached only through direct negotiations between the parties culminating in a peace treaty and that there could be no question of withdrawal of their forces prior to a settlement."

Egypt and Jordan, on the other hand, continued to insist that "there could be no question of discussions between the parties until Israeli forces had been withdrawn to the positions occupied by them" before the 1967 war.

Waldheim proposed a "new appraisal of the possibilities and procedures" of the Security Council and "an exploration of all the means by which the framework of the United Nations might be used" to reach a settlement. The Council, he said, was "the only forum where all the parties to the conflict have been able to meet together in the same room."

The report said the Council had met 72 times to consider 17 Middle East truce violations.

Israeli Ambassador Yosef Tekoah took issue with the part of the report that lauded the Council as a vehicle for achieving peace. Tekoah said the report's "salient fact is that throughout the years, the United Nations have not succeeded in bringing Israel and the Arab states into a meaningful dialogue."

U.N. Council opens Mideast debate.

The United Nations Security Council began a general debate June 6 on the Middle East. The debate continued until June 15, then recessed and resumed July 20. Among developments June 6:

Egyptian Foreign Minister Mohammed H. el-Zayyat reiterated his government's demand for "an immediate Israeli withdrawal from occupied Arab territories." He said the "aspirations of the Palestinian nation will have to be satisfied and their rights guaranteed," including their right "to live in peace within recognized and secure boundaries."

The minister appeared to soften Cairo's policy of refusing direct talks with Israel when he said: "Israeli leaders keep insisting on direct negotiations with the Arab states 'with no prior conditions.' I accept, Egypt accepts to have talks without prior conditions." Then Zayyat added: "Do not let us be fooled. Everything, they claim, would be negotiable. In the same breath, the Israeli government ... poses a very heavy precondition" by refusing to withdraw or to commit itself to withdraw from Arab territories.

In reply, Israeli Ambassador Yosef Tekoah noted "that Egypt accepts direct negotiations without prior conditions. Much that Minister Zayyat said after that destroyed the significance of this declaration and turned it into another seemingly polemical argument. However, this is an opportunity that the Security Council must not and cannot miss." Tekoah repeated Israel's call for direct negotiations with the Arabs. "The alternative," he said, "is the continuation of the impasse."

Zayyat said June 7 that there could be no peace in the Middle East until the Palestinian refugees were given their own homeland, whose borders were drawn up by themselves. Zayyat said the 1947 U.N. resolution that established "the Jewish state" also gave the Palestinians the right to self-determination.

Israeli Ambassador Yosef Tekoah replied that Zayyat's proposal "would necessitate the dismemberment of Jordan" since Jordan had taken over the areas allotted to the Palestinians in the war that followed the U.N.'s 1947 partition plan.

Tekoah also said the Egyptian proposal would interfere with the U.N.'s 1967 Middle East resolution, which made no specific mention of recreating a Palestinian state but merely referred to settling the refugee problem. "Changing the substance or the interpretation" of that resolution "will create a complete void in the United Nations framework as far as the Middle East is concerned," Tekoah said.

In another reply to the Egyptian proposal for establishment of a Palestinian state, Tekoah said June 13 that historically "only the Jewish people saw the land of Israel as a distinct political entity." To support his argument that the Palestinians already had a state, Tekoah quoted King Hussein as declaring in 1963 that "Jordan is Palestine and Palestine is Jordan." The allegations that the Palestinians had no state were not true since "the Arabs of Palestine exercise these rights in the Palestinian state of Jordan," Tekoah said.

The state minister of the Union of Arab Emirates, Adnan Pachachi, replied that the Arabs who had lived in Palestine for the past 1,300 years were "entitled to self-determination there—not the people [the Jews] who resided there 2,000 years ago."

The U.S.' chief delegate, John A. Scali, June 14 rejected Arab demands that Israel withdraw from the occupied territories as a precondition for negotiations between the Arabs and Israelis. Scali noted that the 1967 resolution called for agreement between the two sides and that this could not be achieved "without an ongoing serious negotiating process, either direct or indirect, which engages the parties themselves."

Scali as well as Tekoah accused Soviet delegate Yakov A. Malik of expressing his government's views while claiming to speak for the entire Security Council. As Council president for June, Malik said he was speaking for the entire body when he cited provisions of the U.N. charter and resolutions of the Security Council and General Assembly that tended to support the Arabs on the inadmissibility of acquiring territories by force and the right of peoples to self-determination.

Tekoah accused Malik of misusing his office as Council president.

Chinese delegate Huang Hua demanded that Israel withdraw "from the Arab territories." Huang charged that "the 1967 war of aggression by the Israeli Zionists was launched with the support, connivance and acquiescence of one or two superpowers," which, he said, "could do what they please to manipulate and dominate the situation."

U.S. vetoes U.N. resolution. The U.S. July 26 vetoed a United Nations Security Council resolution that deplored Israel's continued occupation of the Arab territories taken in the 1967 war. The resolution also expressed "serious concern at Israel's lack of cooperation" with Gunnar V. Jarring, the U.N. secretary general's special representative in the Middle East.

The resolution was approved by 13 members: Australia, Austria, Britain, France, Guinea, India, Indonesia, Kenya, Panama, Peru, Soviet Union, Sudan and Yugoslavia. China did not vote because, it said, the resolution was not sufficiently strong or explicit.

U.S. representative John A. Scali said he vetoed the resolution because it "would have done irrevocable harm and permanent damage" to "the only agreed basis for a peaceful solution" in the Middle East. Scali was referring to the Council's Nov. 22, 1967 resolution that called for Israeli withdrawal from occupied territories and the right of all states in the area to "live in peace within secure and recognized boundaries."

Israeli delegate Yosef Tekoah said the U.S. veto had "averted a grave development in the Middle East situation." He repeated Israel's call for direct negotiations between the parties to the conflict.

Egyptian President Anwar Sadat July 26 condemned the U.S. veto, asserting it was meant to force the Arabs to negotiate with Israel.

Tunisian, Israeli contacts reported. Efforts were under way to arrange a possible secret meeting between Tunisian President Habib Bourguiba and Israeli Premier Golda Meir to discuss the Middle East crisis, the Los Angeles Times reported June 14. A Tunisian government official confirmed that it was "possible" such contacts were in progress.

An Israeli government statement June 14 said "since Israel announced her readiness a few weeks ago that Mrs. Meir meet with President Bourguiba, no response has been received."

The statement referred to Foreign Minister Abba Eban's declaration May 30 that "It goes without saying that the Israeli government is ready to meet with President Bourguiba, and we will be pleased to have President Bourguiba's thought with respect to the timing."

Eban noted that Bourguiba "does not want to be a mediator and, furthermore, would not be acceptable to Israel as such because of Tunisia's one-sided engagement in the Middle East conflict so far." Eban's remarks were in reference to Bourguiba's latest policy statement on the Middle East expressed in late May in an interview with the Italian newspaper Corriere Della Sera.

Bourguiba called on the Israelis and Arabs June 19 to enter into negotiations for "a just and lasting peace" that would recognize the right of Palestinians and the right of Israel "not to be exterminated and cast into the sea." Speaking to the annual assembly of the International Labor Organization in Geneva, Bourguiba said the Arabs had the right "not to be occupied and humiliated" and the Palestinians had the right "not to be deprived of a homeland." He described the Palestinians as "patriots who are fighting to regain the rights of which they have been despoiled."

Saudi Arabian King Faisal was said to have approved Bourguiba's position in a meeting with the Tunisian leader in Tunis June 13. Libya had expressed opposition to the peace move.

Eban again called for Israeli-Tunisian contacts in commenting on Bourguiba's Geneva speech June 20. Eban said "if the Tunisian leader is ready for a dialogue, it will be fruitful if any Tunisian representative would make contact with any Israeli representative in any capital or international agency."

Premier Meir disclosed June 20 that Israel had asked a third country to contact Tunisia to explore the possibility of arranging a meeting with Bourguiba. The go-between was reported to be Italy.

Israeli and Tunisian envoys were making secret political contacts in Geneva in a new attempt at peace in the Middle East, Time magazine reported in its July 16 issue. The private meetings were said to have been disclosed by Tunisian Foreign Minister Mohammed Masmoudi.

According to the Times article, President Habib Bourguiba had proposed a four-stage plan for peace negotiations: public probes already concluded; the current secret contacts between Israeli and Tunisian officials to seek a basis for peace talks; a public summit meeting between Bourguiba and Israeli Premier Golda Meir; and the entry of the Palestinians and Egyptians into the discussions with the Israelis, followed by the Tunisians' withdrawal from the talks.

Israeli Foreign Minister Abba Eban had complained June 30 that Tunisia had made no effort to contact Israeli representatives despite Bourguiba's proposals for such meetings. "Although Israel has expressed its willingness" to participate in such talks, "nothing tangible has materialized," Eban said.

Bourguiba had been quoted in a June 29 newspaper interview as saying that his proposal for Israeli-Tunisian contacts had broken down because of Israeli rejection of his suggestion that the talks be based on the U.N.'s 1947 partition plan.

The Israeli government said July 8 that it would no longer reply to public declarations on Middle East peace contacts by Bourguiba.

U.S. presses Israel, Egypt on peace. The U.S. was reported Aug. 6 to be urging Israel to propose some new ideas to break the Middle East stalemate. Egypt also was asked to adopt a new approach.

U.S. prodding of Israel was said to have stemmed in part from the U.S.' July 26 veto of an anti-Israel resolution in the U.N. Security Council. Many Arab states and some European nations criticized the American veto. The U.S. also was concerned about its relations with Saudi Arabia and other oil-rich Arab states, who had been pressuring Washington to drop its support of Israel.

American pressure against Israel had been recently applied by Assistant Secretary of State Joseph J. Sisco in talks with Simcha Dinitz, Israel's ambassador to the U.S., and in interviews with the Israeli press and television. In one TV interview, Sisco said that although the U.S. supported Israel, Washington also had "important political, economic and strategic interests in the entire area" of the Middle East, including the oil-producing Persian Gulf and Arabian Peninsula. Sisco said U.S. concern "over the energy question" was "a factor in the situation."

Israel opposes U.S. prodding on peace. Israeli Foreign Minister Abba Eban took issue Aug. 18 with the U.S. suggestion that his country propose new peace initiatives to break the Middle East impasse, asserting that Israel's current policy of offering Egypt unconditional talks had been a success.

Eban made the statement during a stopover in New York on his return to Israel from a Latin American trip. The foreign minister said Israel's "objective is to induce a change in the attitude of Arab states by loosing off options that are sterile and unacceptable." He said his government was "maintaining a balance of strength and developing international support for the cease-fire" as means of preventing an Arab "war of revenge."

Eban denied there was an "energy problem arising from the Arab-Israeli conflict." The Arab sale of oil was "the essential condition of their economic survival" and was not "an act of disinterested altruism," he said.

Waldheim mission to five nations. United Nations Secretary General Kurt Waldheim visited Syria, Lebanon, Israel, Egypt and Jordan Aug. 27–Sept. 4 to determine the prospects for peace in the Middle East.

Waldheim had said during a stopover in Geneva Aug. 26 that he did not expect to return from his five-nation tour "with a solution to this very complex . . . problem," nor was it his "intention to present specific proposals." He visited the Swiss city to confer with his special Middle East representative, Gunnar V. Jarring.

The secretary general conferred in Damascus Aug. 27 with Syrian officials, including President Hafez al-Assad. He met in Beirut Aug. 28–29 with Lebanese President Suleiman Franjieh and then went to Israel where he met Aug. 30–31 with Premier Golda Meir and members of the Israeli Cabinet. Waldheim traveled to Cairo Aug. 31 and talked with Egyptian President Anwar Sadat Sept. 1. On leaving Cairo Sept. 2, the U.N. leader flew to Amman, the last leg of his journey. He met Sept. 3–4 with King Hussein and other Jordanian officials. The secretary general also toured the Jordanian-Israeli cease-fire line by helicopter and met with Palestinian refugees.

Before departing from Amman, Waldheim said Sept. 4 that he was encouraged by his discussions with the leaders of the region, that the "visit has shown me there exists a general desire for peace in the area."

Kissinger sees no 'miracles.' Henry A. Kissinger, the U.S.' new secretary of state, gave a luncheon for Arab diplomats at the U.N. Sept. 25.

Kissinger asserted that while the U.S. was ready to assist in seeking a solution to the Arab-Israeli question, none of the parties should expect "miracles." He emphasized that "practical means" had to be found to achieve a "situation with which you can all live."

Mahmoud Riad, Arab League secretary and spokesman for the Arab diplomats, broke no new ground in his reply to Kissinger but said that Kissinger's meeting with all the Arabs in this manner was "a good step."

Libya, Algeria, Yemen, Iraq and Syria boycotted the meeting.

Kissinger Mideast effort reported—The London Times reported Sept. 26 that King Faisal of Saudi Arabia had accepted, as a basis for discussion, a Middle East peace plan put forth by Kissinger. U.S. State Department and Saudi Arabian spokesmen denied existence of such a plan.

According to the Times, the plan contained the following points: Israel would withdraw from the banks of the Suez Canal, giving control of both banks to Egypt; Egypt and Israel would jointly rule Sharm el Sheikh; certain areas of the Sinai Peninsula would be under joint Arab-Israeli control; the West Bank would be returned to Jordan, although Israeli settlements would be allowed to remain; Israel would withdraw from parts of the Golan Heights; and Jerusalem would remain part of Israel, with religious shrines protected by the Vatican and Jordan.

Egypt Prepares for War

Throughout 1972 Egyptian policy, at least insofar as it was proclaimed to Egypt's citizens, was based largely on an assumption that the country must prepare itself to fight Israel.

Egyptian economy on war footing. Premier Aziz Sidky of Egypt announced austerity measures Jan. 23, 1972 to place his country's economy on a war footing in the conflict with Israel.

In a speech to the People's Assembly, Sidky disclosed a 50% increase in customs duties on imported luxuries, an additional tax of 20 Egyptian pounds ($46) annually on each acre, and a ban on the import of radio and television sets, cigarettes and cigars, refrigerators, washing machines, rugs and high-quality cotton cloth. Other austerity measures included a prohibition against trading in foreign goods and restriction of wholesale trade in basic commodities, such as flour, tea, coffee, sugar and soap, to state-owned companies.

Sidky said the object of these restrictive economic measures was "total confrontation" with Israel. "Israel should know that we are determined to win back our lands. If Israel thinks it can intimidate us with military superiority, it is mistaken. We are ready for any confrontation."

The premier denounced the U.S. for its attempts "to eliminate the Arab revolutionary forces and to strike at the progressive regimes which obstruct their attempts to subject the Arab region." Hinting at possible action against

American oil companies, Sidky warned the U.S. "should realize its interests in the area are in jeopardy." (He had negotiated Egypt's contracts with two U.S. firms—Amoco-Egypt and Phillips.)

Cairo students demand war. Cairo University students demonstrated Jan. 16–25 to back demands for immediate war with Israel as the only means of resolving the Middle East crisis. The student outbursts were in reaction to President Anwar Sadat's disclosure Jan. 13 that Egypt had reversed a decision to go to war against Israel in December 1971 because of the outbreak of the conflict between India and Pakistan.

The conflict there had disrupted the balance of power in the Middle East because of Soviet commitments to India and U.S. backing of Pakistan, Sadat explained. He added, "I gave orders to Gen. Mohammed Sadek, the minister of war, and told him to wait. We had to make our reassessment of the situation. Our battle cannot be separated from the balance between the big powers." Sadat said consultations with the Soviet Union were continuing.

Several thousand students staged a sit-in at Cairo University Jan. 18 after adoption of a resolution outlining the protestors' demands. The statement called for a war policy against Israel, nationalization of American oil interests in Egypt, a two-month closure of universities to permit students to obtain military training and a fixed date for the "arming of the masses." The statement opposed resumption of peace talks under the guidance of U.N. mediator Gunnar V. Jarring.

President Sadat declared after meeting with his top ministers Jan. 19 that he would not bow to the students' demands. He warned that student discussions must be "conducted within the law." He said "the political situation must be made clear to the people that all fronts will be prepared to cope with the new dimensions of the battle."

Another student rally held Jan. 20 called for a "real government of mobilization" and assailed the Soviet Union as Egypt's "questionable ally."

Sadat and his leading ministers conferred with a student delegation Jan. 22 in an unsuccessful attempt to win an end to the sit-in at the university. Police finally moved into the university Jan. 24 to break up the sit-in. Clashing with demonstrating students in other parts of Cairo later in the day, police used tear gas to stop a march on the center of the city.

In defiance of the ban on demonstrations, students marched through Cairo Jan. 25, shouting their demands and hurling stones at police. Police dispersed the crowds with tear-gas.

Sadat charged in a radio address Jan. 25 that the student rioting had been "concocted" by "outside elements" to split the Egyptian home front.

The president disclosed that he was seeking more arms from the Soviet Union and would go to Moscow if necessary "to complete these negotiations."

In a meeting later Jan. 25 with representatives of various segments of Egyptian society, Sadat rejected student criticism that his policy against Israel was not militant enough. His pledge to go to war against Israel, he said, "was not mere talk but a reality." Egypt's new Cabinet, formed Jan. 17, would "dedicate all its resources and efforts for the sake of the battle," Sadat declared. He denied that his Jan. 13 disclosure of the December 1971 decision to cancel plans for war with Israel meant a military confrontation had been ruled out. For Egypt, he insisted, "there is no other path than the battle." Answering student criticism of his political efforts to solve the Middle East crisis through U.S. mediation, Sadat assured them that "all my discussions, all contacts and anything whatsoever with the United States have been severed."

Sadat charged Feb. 17 that Israeli agents had instigated the student demonstrations.

He said three persons—two Belgians and a Frenchman—had been arrested and admitted distributing subversive literature for Israel. The leaflets, attributed to a secret group called the Egyptian National Front and containing anti-Soviet messages, had been circulated in Cairo in September 1971. Later tracts attacked Sadat and his government.

Sadat delivered the accusation at a closed meeting of the National Congress of the Arab Socialist Union, convened to review policy in the wake of the student unrest.

The three Europeans arrested were identified by the government Feb. 20 as Jacques Pierre Herran and his son Pierre, 18, both Belgians, and Jean Marc Vouaux, a French student. Salah Nasser, state security prosecutor, said the three had "confessed immediately" when confronted with copies of the leaflets. Nasser said Vouaux had admitted being recruited in 1971 by Israeli intelligence agents in Cologne, West Germany. The elder Herran said he had been enrolled by the Israelis in 1968, Nasser said.

Sadat wins confidence vote. The National Congress of the Arab Socialist Union, Egypt's only political party, concluded a three-day special session Feb. 18 by unanimously affirming confidence in the leadership of President Anwar Sadat. Prior to the balloting of the 1,500 delegates, Sadat had declared that Egypt must concentrate on economic and social development but at the same time must prepare "for the battle" to recover the Arab territories occupied by Israel.

At the congress' opening session Feb. 16, Sadat had pledged to resign if the Egyptians lost confidence in his leadership during the "long political and military struggle" to regain the Arab lands. "Changing circumstances," Sadat conceded, had forced Egypt to delay taking immediate military action against Israel. He cited the U.S. decision to sell Israel more warplanes and to strengthen the U.S. Mediterranean fleet. Sadat said Washington had upgraded its commitment to Israel to offset the prestige it had lost during the 1971 Indian-Pakistani war.

A resolution adopted by the congress Feb. 18 charged that Washington's military, political and economic support of Israel had "rendered the proposed peaceful solutions offered by the United States as mere false screens to hide plans to liquidate the Middle East issue, do away with Arab rights and to achieve the ends of Zionist expansion."

Egypt to produce arms. President Anwar Sadat said March 16 that Egypt was producing its own advanced military weapons. According to Egypt's Middle East News Agency, Sadat told a group of Sudanese army officers during a one-day visit to Khartoum: "If the enemy is producing advanced equipment in Israel, we too are producing and are on our way to producing all advanced war equipment in our land."

(Libyan President Muammar el-Qaddafi disclosed March 28 that other Arab states also would soon be capable of manufacturing advanced weapons on their soil. A Beirut newspaper had reported March 6 that Libya and the Soviet Union had concluded an arms agreement under which the Tripoli government was to purchase Soviet weapons for eventual transshipment to Egypt. The newspaper said the deal, to include MiG-23 jets and grount-to-ground missiles, had been negotiated the previous weekend in a meeting in Moscow between Soviet Communist Party General Secretary Leonid I. Brezhnev and Libyan Deputy Premier Abdel Salam Jalloud.)

Sadat calls war inevitable. President Anwar Sadat said March 30 that war with Israel was inevitable. During a visit to an air base in the Nile Delta, the Egyptian leader told airmen that "we cannot liberate our land without a war." Asserting that he was preparing the country for the "zero hour," Sadat added: "I will never throw you into a war just to show the world that we are doing something. We will enter the war with full preparation and clear objectives."

In a Cairo address April 25 marking the anniversary of the eve of the birth of the prophet Mohammed, Sadat vowed that by the same time in 1973 all Arab lands held by Israel would be recovered. Sadat also reportedly promised never to negotiate directly with Israel.

Soviet Relations & Military Aid

Iraqi mission to Moscow. A high-ranking Iraqi military and civilian delegation conferred with Soviet leaders in Moscow Feb. 10–17, 1972.

A communiqué made public Feb. 17 said the Soviet Union would provide Baghdad with more military and economic assistance and that regular ties would be established between the Soviet Communist party and the governing Baath party of Iraq.

Soviet military aide in Cairo. Soviet Defense Minister Marshal Andrei Grechko conferred with War Minister Gen. Mohammed Sadek and other Egyptian military leaders in Cairo Feb. 18–20.

A joint communiqué issued Feb. 21 said the talks had dealt with the question of developing and improving "Egypt's combat capabilities." Grechko's visit, the statement said, had "contributed markedly to developing friendly relations between the two countries and their armed forces."

Grechko said on leaving for Moscow Feb. 21 that he was satisfied with "the standard of training and efficiency of the Egyptian combat forces."

President Anwar Sadat had said Feb. 17 that his meetings with Soviet officials in Moscow Feb. 3–4 had been "a great success," but that discussion of details of more Soviet military assistance to Egypt would be left for the Grechko visit.

(Egypt was reported Feb. 16 to have expelled the chief Soviet military adviser to Gen. Sadek for criticizing the Egyptian armed forces. The Soviet officer, who was not identified, was said to have questioned the military capabilities of the Egyptians before a group of officers that included Gen. Saad Hussein al-Shazli, Egyptian chief of staff.)

Syria to get more Soviet arms. The Soviet Union agreed to supply Syria with more defensive arms, according to a joint communiqué issued Feb. 26 on the conclusion of a six-day visit to Syria by a Soviet economic and military delegation headed by First Deputy Premier Kirill T. Mazurov.

The joint statement said: "Due to the provocative and adventurous policy pursued by Israel, and the consequent grave situation in the Middle East, practical steps have been taken to increase the defense capacity" of Syria.

A protocol signed Feb. 25 by Mazurov and Premier Abd al-Rahman Khulayfawi provided for Soviet cooperation in carrying out Syria's economic development program.

Under an agreement signed in Damascus May 13, the U.S.S.R. was to send additional arms to Syria. The accord was signed by Soviet Defense Minister Andrei A. Grechko and Syrian Defense Minister Mustafa Tlas.

More Soviet economic and military aid was promised later, according to a joint communiqué released in Moscow July 8. The statement was made public following the conclusion of a three-day visit to Moscow by Syrian President Hafez al-Assad.

The communique also pledged closer relations between the Communist party of the Soviet Union and the Socialist Baath party of Syria.

An agreement on economic and technical cooperation and a second pact establishing a joint commission in these fields were signed earlier July 8 by Soviet Premier Aleksei Kosygin and Syrian Premier Abd al-Rahman Khulayfawi.

Sadat visits Moscow. Egyptian President Anwar Sadat, accompanied by the commander of the Egyptian air force, ended a three-day visit to the Soviet Union April 29, 1972.

Sadat had talks April 28–29 with Leonid I. Brezhnev, Communist party general secretary, and was seen off at the airport by Premier Aleksei N. Kosygin. A joint communique said the two sides had "reached agreement on further strengthening of military cooperation" and had taken unspecified "appropriate measures in that direction." The dispatch also said that because of the continuing political deadlock in the Middle East "the Arab states had every reason to use other means, too, to regain the Arab lands captured by Israel."

Soviet military aid to Egypt thus far totaled $5 billion, the Cairo newspaper Al Ahram reported March 30. The figure had been disclosed at a recent conference in Cairo of Soviet and Arab historians, scholars and political commentators. The Arabs included representatives of Egypt, Lebanon and Iraq and Palestinian guerrillas.

Soviet-Egyptian arms pact. Egypt and the Soviet Union signed a new agreement under which Moscow was to provide Cairo with more arms, the newspaper Al Ahram reported May 18. The pact was signed in Alexandria by Soviet Defense Minister Marshal Andrei A. Grechko and Egyptian War Minister Mohammed Sadek.

Soviet MiGs fly over Sinai. Two Soviet-made MiG-23 jet fighters, presumably piloted by Russians, flew over Israeli positions in the Sinai Peninsula March 10. Israeli military authorities said the aircraft had crossed the Suez Canal north of Ismailia and penetrated 10 miles inside Sinai, then flew southeast over Israeli-occupied Sharm el-Sheik before heading back toward Egypt. Pursuing Israeli interceptors made no contact with the Soviet aircraft.

Israel reported that two MiG-23s again flew over the Sinai May 16. It was not known whether the planes were piloted by Egyptians or Russians.

According to the Israelis, the MiGs flew along the eastern bank of the Suez Canal from Port Said to Sharm el Sheik, a distance of 210 miles.

Israel filed a complaint with the U.N. Truce Supervision Organization in Jerusalem, charging that the overflight was a violation of the Suez Canal ceasefire.

The Israeli radio said the purpose of the intrusion was "to update the maps Egyptian intelligence already has of the Israeli military deployment in the area."

Reports of the violation of the Israeli airspace followed an Egyptian aerial display May 15 staged for the benefit of Soviet Defense Minister Andrei A. Grechko, who had arrived in Cairo May 14, following a four-day visit to Damascus.

Libya criticizes Soviet on arms aid. Libyan Premier Muammar el-Qaddafi charged June 4 that the Soviet Union was responsible for the "deathly conditions" in which Arabs lived because it had failed to live up to promises of military aid.

Qadaffi asserted that the Arabs should renew their fight with Israel immediately but asserted that the Kremlin was holding back the necessary arms.

Soviets caution Arabs against war. Soviet military officials were reported June 29, 1972 to have warned that the full forces of Egypt and Syria were not yet capable of defeating Israel and that another war could lead to an Arab defeat as in 1967.

The assessment had been disclosed by Soviet Communist party officials at a recent meeting in Moscow with Syrian Communist party leaders. A text of the statements was published by the Beirut leftist weekly Al Rayah. Among other points made by the Soviet representatives, according to the journal: The Soviet Union was not ready to risk a confrontation with the U.S. in the Middle East that could lead to World War III. The Soviet Union supported a peaceful solution of the Middle East dispute on the basis of the 1967 U.N. Security Council resolution. The Soviet Union opposed the Arab slogan calling for the destruction of Israel. "Neither the Soviet Union nor any friend of the Arabs will support such a slogan," the officials said. The Soviet Union advocated the reopening of the Suez Canal because it would "lead to increasing the contradictions among the imperialist states."

The Arabs' military ability was further questioned by Soviet President Nikolai Podgorny at a meeting in Moscow in June with Lebanese Parliament Speaker Kamel Assad. The Beirut newspaper An Nahar reported July 10 that in reply to Assad's question as to why Soviet military supplies to the Arabs did not match American military aid to Israel, Podgorny said the Arabs were not capable of handling the modern equipment given them by the Soviet Union. In the case of Egypt, for example, it had "only one third of the pilots required for the planes in her possession," Podgorny was quoted as saying.

Russians arm commandos. A New York Times dispatch from Geneva Sept. 17 reported that the Soviet Union for the first time had begun sending arms directly to Al Fatah, the chief Palestinian guerrilla organization. Sources in the Swiss city said the first shipment had arrived within the last few weeks. The Soviet Union was said to have pledged the weapons during talks in Moscow in July with a delegation of commando groups led by Yasir Arafat, Al Fatah head.

The Soviet arms shipment was confirmed by pro-commando sources in Beirut Sept. 21. Its destination, according to the sources, was Syria where Al Fatah maintained its military headquarters. One Arab informant was quoted as saying that the Russians had sent "only light weapons this time—but there will be more deliveries."

Other Arms Suppliers

Lebanon gets French arms. France agreed to sell Lebanon military equipment under an agreement signed in Beirut Jan. 21, 1972. It was signed by Premier Saeb Salam and French Ambassador Bernard Dufornier.

Lebanon announced Feb. 3 that the U.S. had said it was anxious to "safeguard Lebanon's independence and territorial integrity." The statement said that President Suleiman Franjieh had received these assurances in response to his appeal to the U.S., Britain, France and the Soviet Union following Israel's alleged threat in February to occupy parts of southern Lebanon to neutralize attacks by Palestinian commandos.

Jordan to get U.S. jets. The U.S. agreed to sell Jordan 12–24 F-5 jet fighter planes over the next two years, it was reported by diplomatic and military sources in Washington March 31. The agreement was said to have been reached in meetings in Washington March 28–29 between King Hussein and U.S. officials. Jordanian and Defense Department officials were said to

be negotiating to determine the exact number of planes to be sent and the delivery schedule.

U.S. government analysts contended that Jordan's acquisition of additional aircraft would not upset the balance of power in the Middle East. They said Amman had only about 35 planes while the Israeli air force consisted of about 400 aircraft.

Hussein Seeks Federation of Jordan & West Bank

Jordan proposes West Bank merger. King Hussein of Jordan proposed March 15, 1972 the creation of a federated Arab state comprising two autonomous regions—Jordan and Jordan's former West Bank, occupied by Israel since the 1967 war.

East Jerusalem would be the capital of the West Bank region while Amman would be the capital of the entire new nation as well as of the Jordan region. Hussein said the federation, to be known as the United Arab Kingdom (name changed from the Hashemite Kingdom of Jordan), would also include "any other Palestinian territories to be liberated," an apparent allusion to the Gaza Strip, also occupied by Israel.

Hussein's plan was rejected by Israel and the Palestinian commando organizations.

Among other aspects of Hussein's proposal:

The king would be head of state and would assume the central executive authority with the aid of a council of ministers. Legislative authority would be held by the king and a national assembly in which each region would have an equal number of members.

Hussein announced his proposal to an audience of Jordanian and Palestinian dignitaries in the royal palace at Amman.

Hussein had communicated key elements of his plan March 13 to the other Arab states and to the Soviet Union, Britain, the U.S. and France. U.S. officials said March 15 that Hussein would visit Washington at the end of March to discuss his proposal with President Nixon.

The first indication that the Jordanian leader had drawn up the plan came from Baghdad radio March 14. The Iraqi broadcast also said the proposal envisioned a political settlement between Jordan and Israel. Israel, however, denied it had entered into any secret negotiations with Jordan and Hussein gave no indication that his proposal had been preceded by any dealings with Israel.

In a further explanation of his plan, King Hussein said March 16 that it would be carried out only "after the occupation had been eliminated and our people there liberated." The monarch's position was elaborated in a cablegram sent to Mustafa Doudin, secretary general of the Jordanian National Union, the country's only legal political organization. The projected federation "is a new step in the direction of liberation" and its purpose was "to foil the enemy's designs" in the occupied areas, he said.

Israeli & Arab reaction—Israeli Premier Golda Meir denounced King Hussein's federation plan in parliament March 16. She asserted that Hussein "is treating as his own property territories which are not his and are not under his control." He "envisions himself as the ruler of larger territories than were under his control prior" to the 1967 war, she said.

Mrs. Meir deplored Hussein's failure to mention the word "peace" in his proposal, which she contended was "based on the assumption that he is capable of reaching a solution of the controversial problems" without a negotiated agreement with Israel. She urged Hussein to enter "serious negotiations for a peaceful solution."

Mrs. Meir's statement precipitated a two-hour debate in parliament in which opposition spokesmen complained that the government's reaction to the Hussein plan was too mild. One opposition leader, Menahem Begin, of the right-wing Gahal party, called for outright Israeli annexation of the West Bank.

In an initial reaction to the proposed West Bank-Jordan merger, a spokesman for Mrs. Meir's office had said March 15 that it "negates the cause of peace." Israel, the spokesman said, "is ready at any time to enter into negotiations with Jordan without prior conditions on a peace treaty."

Iraq March 15 called the proposal a threat to Arab unity and proposed a merger of Iraq, Egypt and Syria to prevent such a breakup. A government statement broadcast by Baghdad radio called Hussein's plan "a defeatist idea advanced by a hireling regime."

Although Egypt remained silent on Hussein's proposal, the newspaper Al Ahram, which reflected the government's views, denounced it March 15 as a Jordanian-Israeli collusion against the Arab cause. Its ultimate aim, the newspaper said, was to eliminate the Palestine issue.

At the conclusion of three days of meetings in Beirut on Hussein's proposal, the 13-member executive committee of the Palestine Liberation Organization issued a statement March 16 rejecting it "categorically and conclusively" and urged all Arabs "to join hands in foiling the scheme." Israel had colluded with Amman to give Jordan a share in ruling the West Bank, the statement said: According to the PLO, Palestinians in the West Bank and the Gaza Strip were questioned by organization representatives and "they all rejected the plan."

The Syrian-supported As Saiqa commando group called the proposal March 16 "the most dangerous scheme for liquidating the Palestine cause" and for extending Arab recognition of Israel.

Hussein's plan was denounced March 18 by the Presidential Council of the three-nation Federation of Arab Republics. The council called on other Arab states to reject the proposal, charging that the U.S. "is behind this plan to shatter our forces further and to obstruct every effort for a unified Arab stand against aggression."

Al Fatah, the Palestinian guerrilla group, issued a statement after a meeting in Beirut March 17 calling for "the removal of the Jordanian regime and the Hashemite dynasty in Amman" because of Hussein's proposal. Al Fatah described it as "the start of a large-scale conspiritorial chain that seeks to strike at the Arab liberation movement."

After a three-day meeting in Baghdad, Al Fatah leader Yasir Arafat and Iraqi officials announced agreement March 20 on undisclosed "practical steps" to combat Hussein's plan.

Arafat flew to Kuwait later March 20 on his continuing tour of Arab states to enlist their support against Hussein. He claimed that Jordan had reached an agreement with Israel on the proposed East-West Bank merger and that Hussein had recently met with Premier Golda Meir at the Jordanian port of Aqaba. Arafat said the king had been accompanied by a Jordanian officer, who later defected to Cairo and told about the meeting.

Israel and Jordan reiterated denials of bilateral discussions before Hussein had made his proposal. Mrs. Meir March 21 described Arafat's account of her meeting with Hussein as "fanciful." She said she "would be perfectly happy to go to Amman at any time if Hussein says he would like to meet me."

Jordanian Foreign Minister Abdullah Salah denied March 17 that Hussein was seeking a unilateral peace agreement with Israel. In an interview published in a Beirut newspaper, Salah said "certain Arab quarters want to see Jordan take this step because they themselves want such a settlement." Alluding to the Palestinian commandos, Salah said the king's proposal was aimed at the Palestinian "silent majority" so that it might decide its own future without domination by "a minority which claims without any right to speak for the Palestinian people."

Amman radio reported March 19 that Hussein had received dozens of messages of support, including those from 10 West Bank Palestinian leaders.

A Saudi Arabian newspaper, which reflected the government's views, supported the Jordanian monarch March 18 by assailing Arab critics of his plan. The newspaper said the federation proposal was better than permitting the West Bank Arabs to "become the victims of municipal elections" which Israel was planning to hold the following week.

Chinese Foreign Minister Chi Peng-fei denounced Hussein's plan March 18 as a "plot aimed at splitting the unity of the Palestinian and other Arab peoples." Chi made the remark at a meeting in Peking with a group of Arab diplomats. The plan was also denounced March 22 by Deputy Premier Li Hsien-nien. He said it could not be successful "in the face of 100 million awakened and militant Arabs." Li spoke at a banquet in honor of Mahmoud Riad, foreign affairs adviser to President Anwar Sadat of Egypt.

In an effort to soften Arab criticism of his plan for the West Bank, Hussein explained at an Amman news conference March 23 that the plan "was for the future." Its implementation, he said, would not be sought until there was a permanent Arab-Israeli peace settlement and the Arab lands occupied by Israel were recovered. The king added: "There is nothing immediate concerning the steps we take. We are just putting the plan in its right context."

Israeli Deputy Premier Yigal Allon said March 24 that he had no quarrel with the basic concept of Hussein's proposal. "It may be easier to find a solution to what is called the Palestinian problem in the framework of a federation than in other ways," Allon said. The Israeli leader, however, rejected Hussein's proposal for the future frontier between Israel and the proposed federation, which envisioned total Israeli withdrawal from the West Bank.

Joint Jerusalem rule urged—King Hussein proposed March 29 that a final settlement provide for joint administration by Jordan and Israel of Jerusalem as "a unified, open city—a meeting place for the three great religions of the world." Hussein advanced the proposal in an interview in Washington, where he had conferred with President Nixon March 28.

Hussein insisted that the eastern part of Jerusalem taken by Israel in the 1967 war should be returned to Jordan. He proposed that the city become "the capital of Israel and the capital of the Palestine portion of Jordan." (Under the 1947 U.N. partition plan for Palestine, Jerusalem had been set aside as an internationalized city, but Jordan had seized the eastern sector in the fighting that followed in 1948 and held it until 1967.) In the interview, Hussein rejected any return to internationalization of Jerusalem, saying "the Arabs and the Israelis should do it themselves." He said as part of a peace agreement, Israel must accept the principle of Arab sovereignty over eastern Jerusalem. This would be "a point of departure for creating an entirely new situation," the king asserted.

In his meeting with Nixon March 28, Hussein had discussed his plan for a federated kingdom on the East and West Banks of the Jordan River under his leadership and Jordan's need for continued American economic and military assistance.

At a news briefing on the Hussein-Nixon talks, White House Press Secretary Ronald L. Ziegler said the monarch's proposal for a federation was "essentially a plan for reorganization within Jordan when there is a peace settlement. If there is to be a lasting settlement in the Middle East, the legitimate aspirations of the Palestinians will have to be met."

Egypt cuts ties with Jordan. Egypt severed diplomatic relations with Jordan April 6 in opposition to King Hussein's proposal for a federation of the occupied-West Bank and Jordan. The decision was announced at a Cabinet meeting presided over by President Anwar Sadat.

In making the announcement, Information Minister Abdel Kader Hatem said Cairo had decided to break its ties with Amman after it had become clear that Hussein's plan was identical with that of Israeli Deputy Premier Yigal Allon which was aimed at "implementing an imperialist plot in the area." Allon had proposed after the 1967 war that a demilitarized, autonomous West Bank be established with an Israeli security belt along the Jordan River facing Jordan.

Egypt's decision was announced a few hours before the Palestinian National Council, the "parliament-in-exile" of the Palestinians, opened a four-day meeting in Cairo to discuss Hussein's plan.

Addressing the council, Sadat declared that "Egypt will not allow anyone to liquidate the rights of the Palestinian people. Palestine will not be lost and the political rights of the Palestinian people will not be a point of bargaining." The Egyptians and Palestinians, Sadat said, "must make it clear that we will fight in defense of the rights of our nation."

Commandos kill Jordanians. A Jordanian soldier and three civilians were killed when their vehicle struck a mine near the Syrian border March 31. Al Fatah claimed responsibility for the incident April 1, saying that it was the first commando blow in a new campaign launched March 27 to overthrow King Hussein of Jordan for his plan to federate the East and West Banks of the Jordan River under his sovereignty.

The Fatah statement, issued in Beirut, also called on Arab countries which had rejected the king's proposal "to transform their refusal and condemnation into drastic sanctions that would disqualify King Hussein from talking to any international quarter on behalf of the Palestinians or Arabs."

Plot against Hussein crushed. King Hussein confirmed in late November that his government had thwarted a Libyan-backed Palestinian commando plot to assassinate him, overthrow his regime and proclaim a republic. Reports of a coup had first been broadcast by Damascus radio Nov. 15.

In an interview published Nov. 27 in the Beirut newspaper An Nahar, Hussein said commando leader Yasir Arafat had taken part in the conspiracy and that Arafat's deputy, Salah Khalef, had made the contacts with the Jordanian plotters. According to the monarch, Maj. Rafeh Hindawi, commander of Jordan's 4th Armored Brigade, was the only military man arrested and confessed that Khalef had given him $60,000 to finance the uprising.

Hussein said Hindawi had quoted Khalef as saying that when the time came to launch the coup, Libyan leader Col. Muammar el-Qaddafi was to arrive in Damascus to put pressure on the Syrian and Iraqi governments to send planes to bomb the royal palace, radio station and military installations in Amman. Qaddafi, Egyptian President Anwar Sadat and Syrian President Hafez al-Assad had agreed in October to delay discussing rapprochement with the Jordanian government after Arafat informed them he was working on an "operation" against Jordan, Hussein said.

Another Beirut newspaper, Al Moharrer, said the coup had been engineered by 300 dissident Jordanian air force and army officers who had been arrested and that Said Dajani had financed the attempt with $20,000 recieved from Qaddafi.

East Bank development pressed. Jordan was reported Nov. 14 to be pressing plans for the development of its East Bank without waiting for a settlement with Israel on the disposition of its former West Bank lost in the 1967 war. The coordinator of a three-year development program was Prince Hassan Ibn Talal, King Hussein's brother, who said "We are not forgetting the West Bank in our plans, but we must get on with what we can do."

Plans called for obtaining $148 million in foreign loans to finance a number of projects, including housing, agriculture and irrigation. Most of the projects would be carried out along the Jordan River. The plans were outlined at a major conference earlier in the week of foreign lenders and international agencies. The 150 participants included representatives of the U.S. Agency for International Development, which was providing $50 million.

Syria to reopen Jordan border. Syria announced Nov. 30 that it would reopen its border with Jordan that had been closed since Damascus ended relations with the Amman government in July 1971.

A Syrian spokesman said his government had decided to take the action to "lighten the difficulties" encountered by the Jordanians in the border closing and to enable the Jordanian army to "fulfill its role in the confrontation" against Israel.

Egypt Expels Soviet Advisers

Sudden withdrawal begun. President Anwar Sadat said July 18, 1972 that he had ordered the immediate withdrawal of Soviet "military advisers and ex-

perts" from Egypt. This force reportedly totaled about 5,000 men. Sadat also directed that Soviet bases and equipment in the country be placed under exclusive control of the Egyptian forces. He indicated that his decision was based on difficulties Egypt encountered in getting all the Soviet arms it wanted for its confrontation with Israel.

A Soviet government statement July 19 confirmed Sadat's surprise announcement but said the Russian soldiers were being taken out of Egypt by mutual agreement with Cairo.

Neither the Egyptian nor Soviet statement made clear whether Sadat also was demanding the exit of an estimated 10,000–15,000 Soviet combat personnel who operated anti-aircraft missiles and performed other air-defense duties and the 200 airmen who piloted MiG-23 jets.

Sadat's announcement was contained in a 90-minute speech to the Central Committee of the Arab Socialist Union, Egypt's only political party. The Egyptian leader recalled Cairo's repeated failure to obtain the Soviet offensive weapons necessary to implement his plans to invade Israeli territory by the end of 1971. "These arms did not arrive on the agreed dates and that is what made me say then we need to re-evaluate our position." Sadat complained of conditions the Soviets had attempted to impose on the use of their equipment, presumably to prevent Egypt from launching any attack. He said he had refused "to place any restrictions on the use of arms, whatever their kind, based on Egypt's principle that any political decision must be made in Egypt by its political leadership without having to seek permission from any quarters, whatsoever its status." Sadat said he had raised these objections in his meetings with Soviet leaders in Moscow in February and April.

Sadat suggested that President Nixon's talks with Soviet leaders in May had influenced his decision to reduce the Soviet presence in Egypt. "After receiving Soviet explanations to the Moscow talks with President Nixon I felt the need to review the situation," and "after reviewing the situation, . . . I found it necessary "to demand the withdrawal of the Soviet "advisers and military experts," Sadat said.

Sadat also proposed "a Soviet-Egyptian meeting, at a level to be agreed upon, to hold consultations to decide the next phase of operations." He insisted that his decision would not postpone "our battle against Israel, since it was never our intention to make our friendly Soviet experts fight with us."

Sadat's announcement had been preceded by reports from Cairo about a major development in Soviet-Egyptian relations. One report linked the diplomatic shift to Egyptian Premier Aziz Sidky's visit to Moscow July 13 to press Cairo's demands for offensive weapons. After receiving Moscow's rejection of Cairo's plea, Sidky reportedly informed the Russians of his government's decision to reduce the Soviet force in Egypt.

Soviet statement on withdrawal—Moscow's July 19 statement on the troop withdrawal, as reported by Tass, said that since the Soviet military men had completed their training of Egyptian forces both "sides deemed it expedient after an exchange of views to bring back to the Soviet Union the military personnel that had been sent to Egypt for a limited period."

The Soviet forces, the statement emphasized, had been in Egypt on temporary "assignment in accordance with the requests of the leadership of Egypt for help in insuring its defense potential in the face of Israeli aggression. Both sides have many times expressed their satisfaction with the effectiveness of such measures." The statement quoted Sadat as saying that the move "in no way affects the foundations of Egypt-Soviet friendship." It was the first time that Moscow had publicly stated in such forthright manner the scope of its military assistance to Egypt.

Many of the Soviet military advisers and technical experts were reported leaving Egypt July 19. Egyptian military units were said to have taken over the installations and sites of the SAM-2 and SAM-3 missiles from Soviet personnel.

Egypt blames Soviets for troop exit. President Anwar Sadat declared July 24 that the Soviet Union's "excessive caution" in providing Egypt with military support against Israel had prompted him to request the departure of Soviet military advisers from his country. Sadat's statement was made in a speech to the Central Committee of the Arab Socialist Union.

In his speech Sadat contrasted what he described as the Soviet Union's hesitant support of Egypt with the U.S.' wholehearted backing of Israel. The U.S., he said, was committed "to maintain Israel's military superiority in all circumstances" and was determined to prevent the start of peace negotiations except on conditions approved by Israel. The Soviet Union, on the other hand, "is not engaged to do for us what the United States does for Israel," Sadat said.

The Egyptian leader said his differences with the Soviet Union first emerged after his trip to Moscow March 1, 1971. The Kremlin, he said, regarded the Middle East "as problem number three or four in the world, while we view it as number one, as everything." After the signing of a 15-year friendship and cooperation pact in May 1971, President Nikolai Podgorny assured him that Egyptian-Soviet differences "would be solved four days after he returned to Moscow," Sadat said. Sadat complained that in subsequent contacts with Soviet officials through the remainder of 1971 and in meetings with them in Moscow in February and April 1972, the Russians had failed to give him assurances they would implement their pledge "to help liquidate Israeli aggression."

Sadat said the Soviet Union's explanation of its talks with President Nixon in Moscow in May ended his doubts about the Kremlin's promise to aid Egypt. He recalled that in anticipation of those summit meetings he had warned the Russians in April not to agree to a U.S.-Soviet embargo of arms to the Middle East as long as Israel occupied Arab territories and not to discuss borders because the Arabs would not surrender any of the occupied areas. The Soviet response, Sadat said, was "yes, yes, yes to make things easy for us, but then we were caught in a whirlwind."

Despite Egyptian-Soviet differences, Sadat said he would not permit a total rupture with Moscow. But he said "we shall stand alone on the battlefield if need be."

Egypt's ambassador to the Soviet Union Yehia Abdel Kader, had praised relations between the two countries in a television broadcast in Moscow July 21. Without mentioning the rift, Kader said "I want to take this opportunity to convey to the great Soviet people the assurances of feelings of love and friendship on the part of the people" of Egypt.

Israel's Meir urges peace move. Premier Golda Meir July 26 seized on the departure of Soviet military advisers from Egypt as a fresh opportunity for Egypt and Israel to negotiate their differences. "It would seem that this hour in the history of Egypt can, indeed should, be the appropriate hour for change—and if it truly is the hour for change, let it not be missed," she said.

In an address to the Israeli parliament, Mrs. Meir reiterated her government's position on peace talks, that both sides must agree to negotiate without prior conditions. She said: "We have not declared permanent borders, we have not drawn up an ultimate map, we have not demanded prior commitments on matters which must be clarified by means of negotiations. We do not intend to perpetuate the cease-fire lines between us, or to freeze the existing situation."

The Israeli premier cautioned that although the withdrawal of the Soviet advisers constituted "a significant fact," there was no indication of "the cessation of the Soviet Union's role in Egypt." She then cited these figures: "The Soviet Union stationed in Egypt more than 7,000 advisers, experts and instructors in all the armed forces, and close to 10,000 additional military personnel to operate squadrons of MiG-21 and other aircraft, SAM-3 and SAM-6 battalion batteries and personnel in various command formations." Mrs. Meir stressed that Egypt's order for the removal of Soviet advisers did not apply to the instructors, who "will continue to function." She noted, however, that "the demand for the evacua-

tion also affects the Soviet operational units, which are integrated in the Egyptian air defense system."

A Reuters report from Cairo July 26 said that Egypt had rejected Mrs. Meir's proposal for direct talks. The semi-official newspaper Al Ahram was quoted as saying that her bid for talks to reopen the Suez Canal was "also rejected by Cairo because the reopening of the canal is not an end in itself."

President Sadat confirmed the Egyptian stand July 27.

In a speech at Alexandria, Sadat, making no direct mention of Mrs. Meir's bid, was quoted as saying: "Can anyone accept to negotiate while his land is occupied? Did the United States negotiate with Japan after Pearl Harbor?"

Sadat had denounced Mrs. Meir's statement as "propaganda" and set down conditions for any negotiations with the Israelis, a member of the French parliament said Aug. 1. Claude-Gerard Marcus, who had visited the Egyptian leader in Cairo the previous week with other French parliament members, said Sadat had insisted that any Egyptian-Israeli discussions must be held in the presence of representatives of the U.S., Britain, France and the Soviet Union, who were not to act as mere "observers."

Soviet plane withdrawal seen. U.S. intelligence sources in Washington said there were "strong indications" that the Soviet Union was withdrawing from Egypt most of its planes assigned with Soviet crews to the Egyptian air defense, the New York Times reported July 26. It was said the aircraft being pulled out included most of the 18 TU-16 reconnaissance bombers, about 70 MiG-21 jet fighter-bombers, and about six advanced MiG-23s. Egypt, according to the report, would keep more than 200 older MiG-19s, MiG-21s and Sukhoi-7 bombers and surface-to-air missiles, all operated and controlled by Egyptian personnel.

Other reported assessments of the U.S. intelligence: The 10,000 Soviet combat troops in Egypt would eventually be pulled out. No more than 200-300 Soviet technicians would remain to assist Egyptians in operating advanced surface-to-air missiles in the Cairo-Alex-andria area and around the Aswan Dam on the Upper Nile. The Russians would be permitted to retain their naval facilities in Alexandria, Mersa Matruh, Port Said and Sollum, as well as some navy personnel.

Israel downed Soviet pilots in '70. An associate of President Anwar Sadat said Aug. 11 that five Soviet-piloted planes had been shot down in less than a minute by Israeli jet Phantoms over Egypt in June 1970. Writing in the Cairo newspaper Al Ahram, commentator Mohammed Hassanien Heykal made the disclosure in discussing his government's decision to request the departure of Soviet military forces from Egypt.

Heykal said the late President Gamal Abdel Nasser had informed him of the incident in a telephone call at the end of June 1970. He quoted Nasser as saying "that something strange happened today. Five Soviet planes with their crews have been shot down by the Israelis."

There had been widespread but unconfirmed reports of Soviet pilots being shot down by the Israelis, but this was the first time that such an encounter had been confirmed by the Egyptians. The Israeli press had reported July 30, 1970 the downing of four Soviet-piloted planes by Israeli jets.

Russia completes exit from Egypt. The Soviet military withdrawal from Egypt, which had begun in mid-July, was complete, Egyptian and Soviet officials announced Aug. 6. The force, consisting of military advisers, pilots and missile crews, was said to have totaled 15,000–20,000 men. Fewer than 3,000 Soviet missile technicians and other instructors reportedly remained in Egypt. The initial report on the Soviet pullout in July had indicated that only 5,000 men were involved in the withdrawal.

Israel may redeploy Suez force. Defense Minister Moshe Dayan said Aug. 11 that Cairo's decision to expel Soviet military forces and advisers from Egypt would ease Israel's military needs, making possible redeployment of forces along the Suez Canal and a reduction in call-ups of reservists for active duty.

Interviewed on state television, Dayan said he hoped the easing of tension would enable Israel and Egypt to reach a partial or interim settlement "in the not too distant future." He said the Russian ouster was not so much a "de-Sovietization of Egypt as a de-Sovietization of the war." At the same time, the Israeli military leader cautioned against "ignoring the acute dangers facing us along" the western bank of the Suez Canal, where, he said, 800,000 Egyptian troops remained stationed. In view of this, Dayan said Israel's strategy must continue to be based on "adequate and considerable" power in case of any emergency.

Soviet-Egyptian Tie Restored, Preparations for War Continue

The Soviet-Egyptian rupture did not last long and, with Syrian mediation, appeared to have been healed during 1972 within a matter of three or four months. The divided Arabs continued efforts to unite in the interest of defeating Israel.

The Cairo newspaper Al Ahram reported Aug. 7 that Soviet Communist party General Secretary Leonid Brezhnev had sent a message to President Anwar Sadat requesting a high-level meeting to improve their strained relations.

Soviet President Nikolai V. Podgorny had met with a visiting Egyptian parliamentary delegation Aug. 5 and told them he was certain that "friendly Soviet-Egyptian relations would go on developing."

Egyptian premier in Moscow. Egyptian Premier Aziz Sidky conferred with Soviet officials in Moscow Oct. 16–18 on bilateral relations and the Middle East situation.

A joint communiqué issued at the conclusion of the talks Oct. 18 did not mention a Soviet pledge to Egypt of military aid or other assistance. Sidky reportedly had been seeking assurances that the Soviet Union would continue economic help to Egypt and provide it with spare parts for the military equipment already sent to Egypt.

On the eve of Sidky's departure from Moscow Oct. 15, President Anwar Sadat had told the People's Assembly (parliament) that he would seek to improve the tense relations with the Soviet Union that resulted from the ouster of Russian military personnel from Egypt.

Sadat's decision to send Sidky to Moscow had been made following a meeting between Sadat and Syrian President Hafez al-Assad in Cairo Sept. 29. Assad had arrived from Moscow where he sought to mediate the Soviet-Egyptian dispute.

In a Beirut newspaper interview published Oct. 5, Sadat declared that he "would have accepted a peaceful settlement" in the Middle East if the Soviet Union had provided Egypt with advanced military equipment to counter Israeli power. Sadat told the weekly Al Hawadess that Soviet refusal to give Egypt MiG-23 fighter-bombers, capable of "striking in depth" against Israel, made it impossible to meet the Soviet requirement for "a peaceful settlement."

Sadat's moves to bring about a Soviet reconciliation were later endorsed at a meeting Oct. 25 of 600 party leaders and members of parliament.

Egyptian military shakeup. Two top Egyptian military commanders reportedly opposed to President Anwar Sadat's efforts to improve strained relations with the Soviet Union resigned Oct. 26 and 28.

Gen. Mohammed Sadek resigned Oct. 26 as vice premier, war minister, armed forces commander in chief and minister of war production. Maj. Gen. Ahmed Ismail, 54, chief of intelligence, was appointed by Sadat as war minister and commander in chief. Ismail was promoted to the rank of general.

No official reason was given for Sadek's resignation, but a correspondent close to Sadat said Oct. 29 that the minister was dropped for insubordination. Ihsan Abdel Kuddous, writing in the newspaper Al Akhbar, said Sadat had discovered Oct. 24 that at a meeting of the Armed Forces Supreme Council "some directives to Gen. Sadek had not reached

the various commands, while others had not been implemented." Other Egyptian sources said Sadek had failed to pass on to senior officers under him the results of Premier Aziz Sidky's visit to Moscow Oct. 16–18.

In the second military shift, Sadat announced Oct. 28 that he had named Vice Adm. Fuad Zikry to replace Rear Adm. Mahmoud Abdel Rahman Fahmy as navy commander. Fahmy was a close friend of Sadek.

Anti-Sadat plot reported crushed. A rightwing military coup aimed at overthrowing President Sadat was crushed Nov. 11, according to reports in the Arab and Western press. Cairo officially denied the accounts Nov. 19.

A New York Times dispatch Dec. 4 said on the basis of its reports, the conspirators, led mostly by anti-Soviet colonels, had planned to oust Sadat Nov. 15 and form a military junta with Gen. Mohammed Sadek as a figurehead. The uprising was thwarted with the arrest of 25–30 officers, including Gen. Mustafa Mehrez, chief of military intelligence, the Times said. The attempted coup reportedly had been set to start before the ouster of Soviet military experts in July, then was delayed and revived about the time of Premier Aziz Sidky's visit to Moscow in mid-October.

Sadik and Libyan leader Muammar el-Qaddafi were said by Arab sources to have planned to overthrow Sadat

Egyptian Assembly backs war policy. Egypt's National Assembly (parliament) Dec. 12 unanimously approved the government's foreign and defense policies following two days of debate in which a major policy statement by Premier Aziz Sidky had come in for unusual criticism.

The Assembly was particularly critical of the remark in Sidky's annual report delivered Nov. 27 that Egypt had drawn up a plan for a military solution to the confrontation with Israel. The Assembly's policy committee issued a reply to Sidky Dec. 10, asserting that it had heard that war preparations had been completed "without being convinced that such a plan had in fact been realized."

In reply to attacks on his policies, Premier Sidky told the Assembly Dec. 12 that it was "not in the interest of the nation to discuss matters of war" at a plenary session of the legislative body. He did disclose, however, that Egypt had spent $225 million in the past four years in preparation for war with Israel. Sidky said there was no alternative to a military struggle with Israel.

"We have tried every method to restore our rights through a just settlement of our cause, but Israel—backed by the United States—is challenging the whole world and continues to occupy our land," Sidky said.

Meanwhile, chiefs of staff of 18 Arab armies met in Cairo Dec. 12–14 to effect a joint military plan against Israel. Lt. Gen. Saad Hussein al-Shazli, Egypt's chief of staff, told the opening session of the three-day conference, "There is no other way to regain our land except with plenty of blood and sacrifice."

Premier Golda Meir had warned Israelis Dec. 7 to prepare for a new round of fighting on their borders. She said new shipments of arms to the Arabs and Egyptian President Anwar Sadat's domestic problems made renewal of war a possibility.

Sadat announces plans for war. President Anwar Sadat declared Dec. 28 that he had instructed the Egyptian Cabinet to "prepare for a resumption of fighting at any moment."

Addressing the People's Assembly, Sadat said Egypt had worked out a plan of action with Syria and Libya, its partners in the Federation of Arab Republics, for a long-term conflict with Israel. A "high council of battle" was to be established in each of Egypt's 23 governates, Sadat said. The councils were to include the secretary of the Arab Socialist Union, the country's only political party, a military adviser and a security director. The councils were to be under the jurisdiction of a permanent committee headed by Sadat.

Soviet military aid to Syria. Plans to provide the Soviet Union with naval facilities in Syria and an airlift of Soviet men and military supplies to Syria were reported by American officials Sept. 13 and 24, 1972.

U.S. Administration officials said Sept. 13 that both countries had recently negotiated a security arrangement for construction of naval facilities at the Syrian ports of Latakia and Tartus for use by Soviet warships. In exchange Damascus would receive Soviet supplies of advanced air defense missiles and jet fighter planes. Soviet ships were currently operating from the Egyptian ports of Alexandria, Mersa Matruh and Port Said, but the Russians reportedly were under orders to withdraw their naval personnel from repair facilities and spare parts warehouses in Egypt.

The Soviet airlift to Syria was disclosed Sept. 24 by U.S. Defense Secretary Melvin R. Laird, who expressed concern over the developments. It also was confirmed in a dispatch from Beirut, which quoted Damascus sources.

Syria to get Egyptian MiGs—Syria was to get MiGs from Egypt to bolster its air force as the result of one of several anti-Israeli measures decided at a meeting of representatives of the 12 Arab League countries and a delegation of Palestinians in Kuwait Nov. 15–18. The decision formalized the plane transfer which had been arranged during a recent visit to Damascus by Egyptian War Minister Gen. Ahmed Ismail. Ismail also reportedly promised that Egyptian artillery would resume shelling Israeli positions along the Suez Canal if Israel launched a major assault against Syria.

In opening the conference Nov. 15, Arab League Secretary General Mahmoud Riad of Egypt had called for adoption of "a collective Arab plan of action against Israeli aggression." He said "it is now clear that no one Arab state can resist aggression, liberate our Arab lands or prevent more occupation."

President Hafez al-Assad was reported Nov. 25 to have urged the Soviet Union to consider a Syrian request for SAM-3 antiaircraft missiles, which were effective against low-flying planes.

The Washington Post Jan. 10, 1973 quoted diplomats as saying that the Soviet

Union had completed a massive arms airlift to Syria in late 1972. The shipment was said to have included 18 Soviet MiG-21s to replace losses suffered in clashes with Israel. The equipment was said to have been brought by 40 Soviet transport planes during November–December. A previous Soviet airlift of military supplies to Syria was reported to have been carried out in September–October and included about 150 Soviet military advisers.

Palestine exile regime proposed. President Anwar Sadat of Egypt proposed Sept. 28, 1972 that the Palestinians form a government in exile, which, he said would receive immediate recognition from Cairo. The Palestine Liberation Organization (PLO), representing various commando groups, indirectly rejected the proposal Oct. 2.

PLO spokesman Kamal Nasser said the organization's executive committee had decided that their cause would be best served by "consolidating the existing organization."

Amman radio in Jordan Sept. 28 denounced Sadat's proposal as an Egyptian attempt to avoid responsibility for the Palestinian cause.

New front formed for Palestinians. The formation of a new organization aimed at assisting the cause of the Palestinian commandos was agreed upon at a meeting of leftists and Communists of the Arab world and the eastern European bloc in Beirut Nov. 27–28.

The new group was called the Arab Front for Participation in the Palestinian Resistance. It was said to have a 12-member secretariat headed by Kamal Jumblat as secretary general. Jumblat was a member of the Lebanese parliament and leader of the Progressive Socialist party. The other 11 members included representatives from the ruling parties in Algeria, Syria and Iraq, the Communist party in Lebanon and Al Fatah.

The Beirut meeting was designated the Arab People's Conference for the Support of the Palestinian Revolution. It was attended by delegates of the Communist parties in the Soviet Union, Hungary, Poland, East Germany, Bul-

garia, Rumania and representatives of the Viet Cong and Uruguay's Tupamaro guerrillas. In addition to CP leaders from Arab countries, the conference was also attended by officials of the ruling Baath party of Syria and Iraq and of the ruling National Liberation Front of Southern Yemen.

Arabs coordinate military efforts. Egyptian War Minister Ahmed Ismail was given command of the Egyptian, Syrian, Libyan and Jordanian armed forces early in 1973 as a step toward coordinating Arab military power for the coming war with Israel.

The Cairo newspaper Al Ahram reported Jan. 21 that Ismail's appointment as commander was made in decrees issued by Syrian President Hafez al-Assad and Libyan leader Muammar el-Qaddafi.

The decision to place Jordan's forces under Ismail's command had been taken by the 18-nation Arab Joint Defense Council, composed of foreign and defense ministers, it was announced Jan. 28. Jordan was reported Jan. 29 to have agreed to reactivate the Arab's eastern military front against Israel from which it had withdrawn following its crackdown against Palestinian commandos in Jordan in 1970. Jordanian Foreign Minister Saleh Abu Zaid was said to have given Amman's assent at a meeting of the council, which had opened in Cairo Jan. 27. Jordan, however, insisted that it would permit commando units to return to its territory for action against Israel only if they remained under the control of the Jordanian army and were confined to an area east and north of Aqaba in southern Jordan.

The leader of the Palestinian delegation to the Defense Council conference walked out of the Jan. 29 session after denouncing Jordan's agreement to rejoin the eastern front as a sham. Abu Yussef said the commandos would not agree to come under a unified Egyptian command unless Jordan agreed to a full-scale resumption of guerrilla warfare against Israel.

Syria had expressed doubts about joint Arab military action against Israel prior to the opening of the council conference. The Lebanese newspaper Al Anwar Jan. 23 quoted Foreign Minister Abdel Halim

Khaddam as saying "There is no plan—not even a conception of a plan" and that Syria "had no confidence in the effectiveness of such meetings."

Egypt announces 'war budget.' Egyptian Premier Aziz Sidky announced Feb. 11 that his government had decided to adopt a "war budget" in preparation for the "battle with Israel."

Sidky said "the present explosive situation makes it imperative for us to start the immediate mobilization of our entire economy to finance the growing needs of the armed forces and meet the requirements of national security." The war budget was being adopted, the premier declared, because of Israeli refusal to relinquish occupied Arab territory.

Under the new austerity program, Egypt was abandoning some of its long-range industrial and agricultural projects outlined in a previous budget and adopting new measures that would include a freeze of government salaries, reducing imports of consumer goods and "postponement or rescheduling" of payments on some of Egypt's foreign debts due in 1973.

Sadat amplifies his power. The Egyptian government underwent a major shakeup with the forced resignation of Premier Aziz Sidky and his Cabinet March 24, 1973. President Anwar Sadat assumed the premiership himself March 26 and formed a new Cabinet March 27.

Sadat had asked for Sidky's dismissal so that he could take personal charge of government operation in the additional post of premier. In his March 26 announcement, Sadat spoke of "internal contradictions and confusions." He added that the government shift also was aimed at preparing Egypt for "total confrontation" with Israel on either the military or diplomatic front. He charged that a U.S. decision to sell Israel more war planes "creates a very dangerous situation, for which the United States must bear full responsibility."

Sadat said that the Middle East situation "has become very explosive, and could explode at any moment." Sadat reiterated his diplomatic stance against Israel, saying he was opposed to a partial settlement that did not provide for total Israeli withdrawal from all Arab lands, that he was against demilitarization of the Sinai and that he would not enter into direct negotiations with Israel.

Sadat March 28 proclaimed himself military governor of Egypt with power to declare martial law. Sadat acquired the additional post by issuing a decree which also named Interior Minister Mamdouh Salem deputy military governor general.

In a move aimed at backing his claim that he was preparing Egypt for "total confrontation" with Israel, Sadat announced plans to form a People's Militia to support the armed forces, it was reported April 25. The announcement said Maj. Gen. Ahmed Fathi Abdul Ghani, assistant to the war minister, would be in charge of establishing training camps and recruitment. Volunteers were urged to enlist to receive three weeks' training in firearms and guerrilla tactics.

According to another "war measure" announced in Cairo April 26, "all public utilities and state institutions will be placed at the disposal of the armed forces."

Sadat urged the Soviet Union May 1 to reject American proposals for reopening the Suez Canal as part of an interim peace agreement. Speaking at a May Day rally, Sadat said this kind of a settlement was a fraud. He charged that the U.S. and Israel did not want peace but a continuation of the truce to enable Israel to safely colonize the Arab territories it occupied.

Egypt-Libya merger plan. Col. Muammar el-Qaddafi, the Libyan leader, and Egyptian President Sadat agreed Aug. 2, 1972 to establish by Sept. 1, 1973 a "unified political leadership" over a union of their two countries, which would constitute the largest state in Africa.

Before the declaration was read over Cairo radio, the announcer revealed that Sadat and Qaddafi had telephoned Syrian President Hafez al-Assad to tell him about the agreement. (Syria, Libya and Egypt formed the Federation of Arab Republics.)

In a speech in Ziwarah April 15, 1973, Qaddafi accused Egypt and Syria of abandoning the Palestinian cause by concentrating on efforts to regain their territories lost to Israel in the 1967 war. He assailed both states for spurning his plan for coordinated military action against Israel after the Israeli downing of a Libyan airliner in February. Qaddafi criticized Lebanon for refusing to let Libya send Arab volunteers to its territory to fight Israel. The Libyan leader also scorned the Palestinian commandos, saying their resistance movement "is non-existent. It exists in broadcasts from Tripoli, Algeria, Cairo and Baghdad . . . it has been destroyed by the Arabs in cooperation with Israel."

About 30,000 Libyans began a 1,500-mile journey to Cairo July 18 to press for the immediate merger of Egypt and Libya. A 1,000-vehicle caravan reached Egyptian territory July 20 but began heading back to Libya July 21 on orders from Col. Qadaffi following complaints from the Egyptian government.

In another development related to the unity plan, Qaddafi resigned July 11, but announced July 23 that he was retracting his decision and would stay at his post until union with Egypt was carried out.

The Libyan trek to Egypt was launched after an apparent breakdown in unity talks between Qaddafi and Sadat in Cairo June 23–July 9. The Egyptian government July 19 made public three Cairo proposals for unity that were short of Qaddafi's demand for a merger by Sept. 1. The two finally agreed on one of the plans. The plan called for "a constitutional declaration of unity between Egypt and Libya." A Constituent Assembly composed of 100 members from each country would be set up, and a referendum was proposed for both countries Sept. 1 on a constitution for the projected union.

The other two proposals called for prior agreement on a unified foreign policy and on a confrontation with Israel before a merger took effect and the establishment of a centralized federation with separate legislative councils, a vice president of the union who would be Libya's chief executive and regional representation in the federal government.

Qaddafi announced his decision to withdraw his resignation in a speech in Benghazi July 23.

In an address earlier July 23, Sadat had called on Qaddafi to withdraw his resignation and warned that Cairo would not conclude the merger "contract" with Libya unless the colonel and his ministers remained in office.

Sadat suggested that the "huge Arab potential" of oil should be used in the confrontation with Israel. He said Cairo was ready to negotiate with Israel in the U.N. if it withdrew its forces to the boundaries that existed before the 1967 war.

Jordan severs ties with Tunisia. Jordan severed diplomatic relations with Tunisia July 17. The decision was in reaction to a statement made by President Habib Bourguiba the previous week in an interview in the Lebanese newspaper Al Nahar.

Bourguiba had called for the abdication of King Hussein to permit creation of a Palestinian state on the east and west banks of the Jordan River. Bourguiba described Jordan, originally created by the British as Trans-Jordan, as an "artifical entity." The Tunisian leader also called for the application of the 1947 U.N. partition plan, which had created a Jewish and Palestinian state.

Amman's decision to end relations with Tunisia followed the recall of Ambassador Wajih Kailani from Tunis July 16. Kailani had held an angry meeting with Bourguiba in which the president had rejected a Jordanian request for an explanation of the statements made in the interview.

Jordan had begun work in May on a $100 million plan to resettle the east bank of the Jordan River.

The newly-formed Jordan Valley Authority planned to resettle farmers, including Palestinian refugees, in 38 settlements along the river.

Egypt resumes ties with Jordan. Egypt announced Sept. 12 resumption of diplomatic relations with Jordan. The agreement was reached in talks held in Cairo Sept. 10–12 by King Hussein of Jordan and Presidents Anwar Sadat of Egypt and Hafez al-Assad of Syria.

A joint declaration issued after the talks did not mention the two principal topics reportedly discussed—reactivation of the eastern front against Israel and return of some Palestinian guerrillas to Jordan. The eastern front consisting of the forces of Jordan, Syria and Iraq collapsed in 1970 following Jordan's war with the Palestinian commandos.

Egypt had broken relations with Jordan in April 1972 in protest against Hussein's proposal for a federation of the occupied-West Bank and Jordan. Syria had severed ties with Amman in August 1971 following a border clash linked to Jordan's suppression of the commandos.

Commenting on the Cairo talks, the Palestine Liberation Organization (PLO) had charged Sept. 10 that Egypt and Syria were more interested in seeking reconciliation with Jordan than in supporting the Palestinian cause against Israel. The PLO said that although Hussein was interested in reestablishing the eastern front against Israel, Jordan had no inclination to fight.

King Hussein later declared an amnesty Sept. 18 for about 1,500 political prisoners, including 754 Palestinian commandos imprisoned after fighting with Jordanian forces in 1970 and 1971. The king's decision was regarded as a peace gesture toward the Palestinian movement that grew out of his reconciliation with Egypt and Syria.

Hussein said his amnesty covered "all convicts, detainees and wanted people within and outside the kingdom who had committed political crimes against state security with the exception of murder and espionage." He said the move was taken in the interest of, national unity "now that life has returned to stability and normality" in Jordan. (The amnesty also applied to 2,500 commandos outside Jordan who had been sentenced in absentia or were wanted for trial.)

Jordanian officials had said Sept. 16 that the main result of Hussein's talks with Sadat and Assad was an agreement that their three nations would adopt a common position on political issues concerning the Middle East at the United Nations in the event of a possible new U.S. peace initiative.

The PLO's executive committee approved the reconciliation of Egypt and Syria with Jordan during a top-level meeting in Beirut Sept. 21-22.

A committee statement issued at the conclusion of the discussions also called for the reopening of a "fighting eastern front" along the Jordan River against Israel. The statement said the commandos would not accept reconciliation with Hussein unless he permitted the guerrillas to return to Jordan with "full freedom to carry out fighting against Israel."

Hussein declared in a statement made public Sept. 23 that he would refuse commando permission to return to Jordan in force.

Soviet-Egyptian talks. Hafez Ismail, national security adviser to Egyptian President Anwar Sadat, held high-level talks on the Middle East situation with Soviet officials in Moscow Feb. 7-10, Feb. 27-March 2 and July 11-13, 1973.

A statement Feb. 10 said the Soviet Union expressed "full understanding" of Egypt's declared intention "to press for a general settlement of the Middle East problem and its rejection of any plans for a settlement on the basis of a so-called partial solution." (The term partial solution referred to proposals under which Egypt would reopen the Suez Canal without guarantees of regaining the Sinai Peninsula occupied by Israel since the 1967 war.) The statement said the U.S.S.R. pledged to "facilitate the strengthening" of Egypt's "military potential" and reaffirmed the right of Arab countries "to use any forms of struggle against Israel" in principle. It "confirmed the importance of the practice of holding regular contacts between leaders" of Egypt and the Soviet Union.

Ismail had conferred with Soviet Foreign Minister Andrei A. Gromyko and Communist party General Secretary Leonid I. Brezhnev. Sadat's envoy held an unannounced meeting Feb. 9 in Moscow with Gunnar V. Jarring, U.N. representative for the Middle East and Sweden's ambassador to the Soviet Union.

Following his July trip to Moscow, Ismail said in Cairo July 14 that the U.S.S.R. and Egypt were "in total accord in their assessment of the Middle East situation."

Ismail added that the Soviet Union was "determined to strengthen the Egyptian and Arab capability to confront the Zionist occupation, . . . until this aggression is liquidated and the aspirations of the Palestinian people are realized."

North Koreans pilot Egyptian jets. The Israeli military command reported Aug. 15 that 10–20 North Korean pilots had arrived in Egypt several weeks ago and were flying jet fighters for the Egyptian air force.

The U.S. State Department corroborated the Israeli report and estimated that as many as 30 North Korean pilots were involved.

'Third World' support. The 41-member Organization of African Unity (OAU), celebrating its 10th anniversary, held its annual summit conference in Addis Ababa, Ethiopia May 24–29.

After an intensive lobbying effort by Arab delegations, especially the Libyan representatives, the summit conference passed a resolution May 29 warning Israel that OAU members might "take, at the African level, individually or collectively, political and economic measures" against it if it "persists in its refusal to evacuate territories of countries which have been the victims of this aggression." A Libyan proposal to hold future OAU meetings in Cairo rather than Addis Ababa was defeated by the ministerial council. Libya's May 26 charge that Ethiopian Emperor Haile Selassie supported "Zionists and colonialists" because he maintained diplomatic relations with Israel reportedly antagonized some black African leaders and contributed to Arab-black tensions within the group.

The fourth conference of nonaligned nations was held in Algiers Sept. 5–9, with leaders of 76 Asian, African and Latin American member nations and nine observer nations attending.

Among the resolutions passed by the conference at its closing session was one stating that the nonaligned countries would take "individual and collective measures" to help Arab countries oust Israeli forces from territory occupied in the 1967 war. The Arab nations had hoped for a declaration calling for the severance of diplomatic relations with Israel, but opposition or indifference among Asian and Latin American delegations forced a more moderate resolution. But in a surprise move, Cuban Premier Fidel Castro announced that his country would sever relations with Israel.

Arab report on boycott of Israel. The Arab organization that conducted an economic boycott of Israel reported June 25 that more than 100 foreign firms had notified the Arab League that they had broken off all transactions with Israel. The report was issued by Mohammed Mahjoub, secretary general of the league's Central Boycott Office, based in Damascus, Syria.

Mahjoub disclosed the information in Cairo, where boycott liaison officers were holding a conference. He said "more than 90% of the 140 companies, whose status is being discussed by the conference, have responded to the boycott rules and submitted documents proving that they have ended their dealings with Israel."

Arming the Arabs. King Faisal of Saudi Arabia visited France May 14–18. He conferred with President Georges Pompidou May 15 and 17, 1973. The Saudi desire to purchase French military planes, particularly the Mirage, figured prominently in the discussions. It was the first official visit by a Saudi ruler to France.

Israel had said April 22 that it had proof that Libya had sent French Mirage jets to Egypt. The Israelis reminded France that it had pledged to cut off the supply of the planes, which it had sold to Libya in 1970, if any were handed over to Egypt. Israel disclosed that Foreign Minister Abba Eban had summoned French Ambassador Francois Hure and furnished him "with data" on the plane transfer. Eban asserted that the transshipment influenced the balance of power in the Middle East. The French government said April 22 that Israel had not given it convincing evidence.

Israeli sources had reported April 10 that Libya was transferring about 60 Mirages to Egypt and that another 44, on order from France, were to be sent on to Cairo. According to the report, 50 Egyptian cargo planes had been carrying electronic equipment for the Mirages from Libya to Cairo since April 6.

Israel's chief of staff, Lt. Gen. David Elazar, said April 19 that the transfer of the Mirages "verifies our warnings that the planes were meant to strengthen the Egyptian air force for a possible war." Elazar said Egypt also had received

British-built Hawker Hunter planes from Iraq the previous week. The jet shipments, Elazar said, would not dramatically affect the Middle East situation, but might encourage Egypt "to start the battle" again.

Foreign Minister Abba Eban called on France April 26 to stop future deliveries of the planes to Libya "or to tell us" that its official policy on banning transfer of the aircraft to any third country "has been changed." Eban said Libya had given Egypt 18 Mirages in early April. Their delivery, he said, might "increase the possibility of a hit and run attack" against Israel by Egypt since the Mirages had "a longer range than the MiGs" in the Egyptian air force.

At a press conference later in the day the foreign minister said Israel had provided France with "incontestable evidence" on the dates and times that "about 20" Mirages left Libya and arrived in Egypt and the present locations of the planes in Egypt. Eban noted that "other countries with military attaches" in the area could substantiate these claims.

France again denied the Israeli charges April 26. A Cabinet statement following a meeting presided over by President Georges Pompidou said, "We have asked the Egyptian and Libyan governments for information on the subject and we received a denial." The statement added: "We have no confirmation so far of rumors circulating on this subject nor have we received evidence for the concern being expressed."

A New York Times report from Beirut April 30 quoted diplomatic sources there as saying that ground equipment had been installed at some Egyptian bases to handle the Libyan jets. The report said the Egyptian equipment also had been tested for British-built planes flown from Saudi Arabia, Kuwait and Abu Dhabi.

France conceded May 2 that there was a possibility that some of the Mirage jets it had sold to Libya might have made occasional flying visits to Egypt. But Foreign Minister Michel Jobert told the National Assembly that it did not constitute a violation of the Libyan-French agreement barring transfer of the aircraft to a third country.

Jobert said the jets France sold to Tripoli "are of course not meant to remain on the ground nor to fly on the same circuit around a fixed base." The minister repeated Paris' assertion that after it had "approached the Libyan and Egypt governments" about the alleged transshipments of the jets to Cairo, "nothing permits the conclusion that the accord was violated."

A senior official for the Israeli government said May 3 that his government expected the 18 Libyan jets flown to Egypt to be returned secretly to Libya. The official said Israel "tended" to accept reports from Paris and Arab capitals that France was pressing Libya to return the Mirages from Cairo.

A Paris souce reported May 5 that France would complete the sale of the 110 jets to Libya by 1974 as scheduled. Thus far Libya had received 60 of the Mirages ordered in 1969.

Egypt was constructing an air defense system for Libya with Soviet-supplied air-to-surface missiles, according to the Washington Post May 2. The sites were said to be located around Tripoli and Tobruk.

U.S. Defense Department sources had reported April 20 that the Soviet Union had delivered 40 MIGs to Syria since January 1973. Other Russian military equipment recently sent to Syria, according to the sources, included two minesweepers and an unspecified number of SAM-2 and SAM-3 missiles for Syrian air defenses. At the same time the Soviets were said to have supplied Iraq with rocket launchers and helicopters.

The French newspaper Le Monde reported April 21 that two Soviet warships had transported a large contingent of Moroccan troops to Syria the previous week to be deployed against Israel. The soldiers were said to have embarked at a port near Oran, Algeria after crossing the border by land from Morocco.

An accord announced May 10 provided for Britain to modernize Saudi Arabia's air defenses. The deal was said to total $625 million and was to cover a five-year period. In making the announcement, Ian Gilmour, British minister of state for defense, said the British Aircraft Corp. would employ 2,000 experts to train Saudi Arabian air personnel and maintain equipment and airfields. It was reported that no offensive weapons were involved.

The Israeli ambassador to the U.S. was informed of American arms negotiations with Saudi Arabia and Kuwait May 24 by Assistant Secretary of State Joseph Sisco. U.S. Defense Department officials confirmed May 26 that discussions were in progress for providing the two nations with $500 million each in American military equipment.

State Department spokesman Paul Hare had said May 23 that the U.S. had "important interest in the Gulf area." Now that Britain had ended its protective role in the region, it was U.S. policy to help those Persian Gulf states "to take greater responsibility for their protection" by selling them "reasonable quantities of military equipment and services," Hare said.

Foreign Minister Eban May 28 emphasized to the Israeli Knesset the mutual trust between Israel and the U.S., but he confirmed that his government had voiced its apprehension over the proposed sale of arms to the Arab states.

Eban said Israel appreciated the need for a military balance in the Persian Gulf area, but he called it also "important to understand that even those Arab states which are at loggerheads with each other on political matters or international issues are united in a posture of hostility toward Israel."

The U.S. State Department May 31 again confirmed that the U.S. was willing to sell Saudi Arabia a "limited number" of Phantoms. The figure was said to be between 24 and 30. Kuwait was believed interested in buying about 16 Phantoms. Formal negotiations with the Saudis had not yet begun, but U.S. officials estimated it would take them three–five years after delivery to turn their Phantom force into an effective air arm. Discussions with Kuwait were described as less advanced.

The U.S. State Department attempted to allay Israeli apprehensions in a policy statement May 31. It said that any military sales to Saudi Arabia and Kuwait would take "fully into account our long-standing policy of support of Israeli security. Obviously we will not make any military sales that would put Israeli security in jeopardy."

Israeli Foreign Minister Abba Eban said May 31 that the pending arms sale to the two Arab states "will definitely influence the balance of power in the Middle East." Defense Minister Moshe Dayan said if the arms deal were carried through "in the next 10 years we will be surrounded by a new and different military situation."

Ambassador Simcha Dinitz discussed the matter in Washington June 2 with Henry A. Kissinger, President Nixon's national security adviser. The ambassador also had met with Assistant Secretary of State Joseph J. Sisco. Dinitz and other Israeli officials were said to accept Washington's argument that the projected arms deal with Kuwait and Saudi Arabia was aimed at improving the military capacity of the Persian Gulf states to protect their oil resources. But the Israelis feared that the U.S. could not enforce its ban on shipment of the arms to a third Arab country for use against Israel or prevent the Saudis themselves from employing the planes against Israel.

The Israelis were further apprehensive that the projected sale of 19 U.S. warships to Saudi Arabia could pose a threat to Israel's freedom of naval action in the Red Sea.

Kuwaiti Foreign Minister Sheik Sabah al-Ahmad al-Jaber said June 4 that the arms his country was planning to purchase from the U.S. "is not for use against anybody and is for our own defense." Other Kuwait officials scoffed at Israeli fears that the arms would upset the Middle East balance, citing Israel's superiority in planes and tanks.

U.S. Secretary of State William P. Rogers June 5 defended the proposed sale of warplanes to Saudi Arabia on the ground they were necessary for self-defense and would pose no threat to Israel.

Testifying before the U.S. Senate Foreign Relations Committee, Rogers said the purpose of the projected sale of planes to Saudi Arabia, as well as to Kuwait and Iran, also would be to show support for their moderate governments and offset the influence of Syria, Iraq and Libya. If the U.S. did not sell these aircraft, some other country would, Rogers said.

Joseph J. Sisco told a House Foreign Affairs subcommittee June 6 that the Saudis had first approached Washington about buying Phantom jets two months ago. He said the U.S. three weeks ago had "indicated a willingness to supply a limited number" of the planes, but there had been no further response from the Saudis.

Sisco also said the Saudis, Iranians and Kuwaitis wanted U.S. planes advanced enough to cope with Soviet MiG-21s which he claimed were being sent to Iraq.

A U.S. official in Washington was reported June 7 to have said that Egypt was urging Saudi Arabia to purchase Mirage fighter-bombers from France rather than U.S. Phantoms. Cairo's suggestion, it was said, was based on the belief that in the event of a new Arab-Israeli war, Saudi Arabia's air force would be compatible with Libya's, which had 40 Mirages.

U.S. officials reported Sept. 13 that Libya had purchased a new French anti-aircraft missile system and had begun to deploy the weapons.

Pentagon officials reportedly were concerned about Libya's operation of the missile since the U.S. also was interested in purchasing it. The Soviet Union could gather information on the Crotale from the Libyans and thus reduce its effectiveness in the hands of the U.S. Army, according to U.S. officials.

Saudi Arabia also was interested in buying the Crotale, French Defense Minister Robert Galley said in Paris after returning Sept. 16 from a five-day official visit to that country. Galley's return was coupled with an official announcement of a Saudi-French military cooperation agreement. Paris sources said Sept. 17 that France was negotiating to sell the Saudis 34–38 Mirage III-E deep-penetration bombers.

Saudi Defense Minister Sultan Ibn Abdul Aziz had said Sept. 6 that his country would refuse to accept any restrictions on arms it might buy from the U.S. His statement was in contrast to a report that the U.S. would insist on placing curbs on planes sold to the Saudis to prevent their use against Israel.

Occupied Areas & Israeli Arabs

Arab spokesmen and other supporters of the Arab cause accused Israel repeatedly of violating the rights of Arabs both in Israel and in the areas Israel had seized during the 1967 war.

U.N. scores Israeli occupation. The U.N. Human Rights Commission March 22, 1972 adopted a resolution accusing Israel of "war crimes" in the occupied Arab territories. It was approved by a 15–4 vote with 11 abstentions. Voting against were the U.S., the Netherlands, Guatemala and Zaire. The resolution was sponsored by Egypt, Lebanon, Tanzania, India and Pakistan.

The resolution called on Israel to rescind and desist from all practices affecting the population composition and physical character of the occupied Arab areas and the rights of their inhabitants.

Israeli representative Jacob Doron was critical of the resolution's invocation of the war-crimes provisions of the charter of the Nuremberg military tribunal. He called it "an affront to the memory of the 6,000,000 Jews who lost their lives in the holocaust in Europe."

A three-nation U.N. inquiry committee (Yugoslavia, Somalia and Sri Lanka) accused Israel Oct. 18 of continued violations of Arab rights in the territories occupied since the 1967 war.

The committee, formed by the General Assembly in 1968, charged in a report that Israel had displaced 11,000 Arabs in 1972, particularly in Gaza and the Sinai Peninsula, and that Israel had established 43 settlements in the territories since the war. The committee warned that Israel would "make the occupied territories socially, economically, politically and juridically part of Israel unless some form of supervision of the occupation is put into effect immediately to arrest such a trend."

The U.N. report conceded that Israel had relaxed security measures in the last year, but it said prisons were overcrowded and interrogation procedures "very frequently involved physical violence."

Israel dismissed the report as "grist for the Arab propaganda machine." It said the residents of the occupied areas "enjoy tranquility, prosperity and respect for their human rights unknown there before 1967 and unknown in most Arab countries."

Gaza Arabs may enter Israel. The 350,000 Arabs living in the Israeli-occupied Gaza Strip were allowed to enter Israel without permits for the first time starting April 30.

The Israeli Cabinet had approved the free movement plan of Defense Minister Moshe Dayan April 23. During a visit to Gaza city April 25, Dayan declared that Israel considered itself the only authority in the strip "and must therefore treat the local residents as Israelis." He insisted that Israel was not annexing the territory but was creating "a new reality which the people of Gaza will not oppose."

West Bank elections. Arabs voted March 28, 1972 to elect municipal councils in 10 towns in the Israeli-occupied West Bank. Defying demands by King Hussein of Jordan and the Palestinian commandos for a boycott of the balloting, 84% of the 16,000 eligible voters went to the polls. It was the first election held in the West Bank since the 1967 war.

According to final results announced March 29, incumbent leaders in five towns, including Nablus, were re-elected. They had been committed to continued union with Jordan. Five new leaders opposed to Hussein and in favor of an independent Palestinian state were elected in Jericho, Jenin, Qalquilyah, Yabed and Tubas.

Anti-election agitation had centered largely in Nablus, where eight candidates, including former Mayor Hamidi Kanan, had withdrawn from the race following pressures from Jordan and death threats from the commandos. Israeli Defense Minister Moshe Dayan summoned Nablus Mayor Haj Mazuz el-Masri to Jerusalem March 20 and warned that the Israeli army would take control of the town if order was not restored and new city officials elected as scheduled. Kanan did not reenter the race, but Masri and the nine other incumbent members of the town council submitted their candidacies.

A second round of local West Bank elections was held May 2.

According to results released May 3, 80 new candidates won in 107 council and mayoral contests held in 12 towns and villages. Of the 10 incumbent mayors, only three were re-elected.

Israel to tighten army control. Defense Minister Moshe Dayan pledged July 9, 1972 to tighten controls on the military after receiving complaints of Premier Golda Meir at a Cabinet meeting that day of "painful irregularities" by Israeli army authorities in the occupied Arab territories.

In a recent incident, Israeli troops had sprayed poison chemicals on a 125-acre plot of Arab farmland on the West Bank of the Jordan River. Dayan was said to have told the Cabinet meeting that the area had been designated a military firing range and that the Arabs had been warned not to reoccupy and farm the land there. Dayan admitted the destruction of the crops was a mistake.

In another incident, civilians in Hasbaya, Lebanon suffered heavy casualties as a result of a bombing accident in the course of an Israeli operation against Palestinian commando bases June 21. Fourteen civilians were killed and 25 wounded. Israeli sources acknowledged that bombs dropped by Israeli jets had fallen short of targets and exploded on houses and shops at the edge of a guerrilla camp.

Israel bars Arab villagers' return. The Israeli Cabinet July 23, 1972 rejected a request by Arab residents to return to the ruined villages of Ikrit and Berem in Israel on the Lebanese border. The decision was part of an overall ruling against re-establishment of Arab villages within range of Palestinian commando infiltration areas near the frontier.

The Arabs of Ikrit and Berem, who had sided with Israel in the 1948 war, had been evicted from the villages after the conflict for security reasons and were moved to other parts of Israel. Israeli troops in 1952 blew up stone houses in the communities, presumably to deny their use to infiltrators.

Israeli Jews joined a demonstration in Ikrit and Berem Aug. 5 to support the return of the Arabs.

The spiritual leader of the Greek Catholic community in Israel, the Most Rev. Joseph M. Raya, appealed to Premier Golda Meir to permit the Arabs to return to Ikrit and Berem. Mrs. Meir rejected the plea Aug. 8, asserting that the government had been rehabilitating the villagers "by means of indemnification, the allocation of lands and aid in building new homes."

Israelis settle territories. Israel's minister without portfolio, Israel Galili, said 44 new communities of Israeli settlers had been established since the 1967 war in the occupied territories. It was reported July 24, 1972 that 15 of the settlements were on the Golan Heights, 15 on the West Bank of the Jordan River, and 14 in the Sinai Peninsula and the Gaza Strip.

Israel ousts Gaza city mayor. Israeli officials Oct. 22, 1972 ousted Rashad Shawa as mayor of Gaza city in the occupied Gaza Strip.

The Israeli government radio said the action was taken because of Shawa's refusal to extend municipal services to the nearby Shati Palestinian refugee camp. Shawa had refused the order, contending that to do so would alter the legal standing of the refugees and endanger their status with U.N. relief organizations. An Israeli military official was appointed to administer Gaza city.

Shawa had been under increasing criticism by Gaza Arabs for supporting the inclusion of the Gaza Strip in a federation of the East and West Banks of the Jordan River as proposed by King Hussein of Jordan.

Party debates Dayan policy. Dayan's policies in the occupied Arab territories were questioned by other government officials at a meeting of the central committee of the ruling Labor party in Tel Aviv Nov. 9, 1972.

Deputy Premier Yigal Allon and Finance Minister Pinhas Sapir opposed Dayan's view that Israel must rule as a regular government in the area of the West Bank because an early peace agreement was improbable and because Israel must integrate its economy with that of occupied areas. Allon and Sapir held that the pursuit of these policies could deter an Israeli accord with the Arabs.

Sapir called Israeli rule in the West Bank "creeping annexation" and was critical of Dayan's program of permitting tens of thousands of Arabs in the occupied areas to enter Israel to work. Flooding the Israeli labor market with cheap Arab labor posed moral, social, political and security problems, the minister asserted.

Defending Dayan's policies, Transportation Minister Shimon Peres argued that it had produced tranquility and prosperity in the occupied areas. Dayan's open communications with Jordan represented the first attempt to break traditional Arab hostility and had altered the Arab hard-line stand on Israel, Peres said.

Dayan defends policies—Dayan Dec. 13 defended his administration of the occupied territories in the face of sharp criticism by other members of the Cabinet.

Dayan argued in parliamentary debate that a "tremendous social, economic and technological revolution" was in progress in the Arab areas occupied by Israel in the 1967 war. For the first time he provided figures on Israeli earnings from Egyptian oil wells captured in the Sinai Peninsula. He said since 1967 the government had produced $85 million worth of oil and was currently pumping oil with an annual value of $20 million. Dayan said under Israel's administration the standard of living in the West Bank had risen by 45% and in the Gaza Strip by 58%.

Israel reports on convicted Arabs. The Israeli Defense Ministry reported Dec. 23 that Israel had convicted 1,610 Arabs in the occupied territories on charges of sabotage and working with commando groups since the 1967 war. The ministry said 148 Arabs were being held without trial. The report was aimed at countering a charge made earlier in the week by the British Union of Liberal Students, an offshoot of the Liberal party, that the Israelis had jailed 4,000 Palestinians and held 10,000 in administrative detention without trial since the 1967 war.

Dayan adamant. Dayan Jan. 20, 1973 declared his opposition to any Middle East peace accord that would permit

Arab rule over Israeli settlements established in Arab territory occupied since the 1967 war.

The Israeli Cabinet official said the settlements set up in captured Jordanian, Egyptian and Syrian areas would never be able to survive without the continued protection of Israeli forces.

Dayan dismissed as "just one more Arab statement" the reported Jordanian decision to join a unified military command with Egypt and Syria. He warned Jordan, however, that Israel's attitude would be affected if Jordan permitted Iraqi and Syrian troops on its soil and allowed Arab commandos to resume attacks against Israel from Jordan.

Dayan Feb. 7 reiterated his views on Israeli settlements in Arab territories, particularly those in the West Bank. Any Israeli-Jordanian peace agreement, Dayan said, must include the Israeli right to settle anywhere in the West Bank. Describing this as a "minimum condition" for peace with Jordan, Dayan explained: "The West Bank—I prefer to call it Judea and Samaria—is part of our homeland. Being our homeland, we should have the right to settle everywhere without visas or passports from anyone else. The Israeli government should make sure that any peace agreement it signs includes that right."

Dayan said another prerequisite for a peace agreement should be the right of Israeli troops to remain stationed along the Jordan River and that no other forces should be permitted to cross it.

As controversy grew, Dayan amplified his views March 29 and suggested that individual Israelis be authorized to purchase land from "willing [Arab] sellers" in the West Bank, that new Israeli towns be created at strategic points and that there be greater Israeli investment and fuller integration of the economies of the West Bank and the Gaza Strip.

Premier Golda Meir and Foreign Minister Abba Eban criticized Dayan's proposal, saying they would have the effect of giving private citizens the power to make military and political policy for the government. They also argued that Dayan's plan would impede the government's options in any future peace negotiations with the Arabs.

Dayan countered that since there was no possibility of Arab-Israeli negotiations in the next 10 or 15 years, there was no point in the government's "standing idle" in the occupied areas.

The government decision reaffirmed the existing policy allowing transfers of land only among residents of the occupied areas and to government-approved settlements.

U.N. Secretary General Kurt Waldheim received a joint letter April 7 from the Egyptian, Jordanian and Syrian delegates asking him to prevent the Israelis from carrying out a "largescale expropriation of Arab land and property" in the occupied areas.

Israelis back occupation. An Israeli public opinion poll published April 18, 1973 showed that most Israelis favored keeping land captured in 1967.

According to a survey conducted in October-November 1972 by the Israel Institute for Applied Social Research: 96% were against ceding Sharm el Sheik at the southern tip of the Sinai Peninsula, but 59% expressed willingness for returning part of the peninsula to Egypt for a genuine peace treaty; 58% interviewed opposed giving up any part of the West Bank (compared with 47% in May-July 1972), while 34% said they would favor handing back part of that region in exchange for a peace treaty with Jordan; 93% were adamant on keeping the Golan Heights; and 66% wanted Israel to hold the Gaza Strip.

Israeli Finance Minister Pinhas Sapir expressed opposition April 23 to keeping all the captured Arab territories and incorporating them into Israel. He said Israel should be guided only by security in regard to the Arab areas, not by historical, religious or emotional associations.

Israel expands Arab visits. The Israeli Cabinet decided May 13 to permit Arabs to visit Israeli-occupied areas throughout the year instead of only in the summer. Permits for summer visits had been issued previously almost automatically, except in specific cases involving security. Permits had been granted the rest of the year only for compassionate, health, business or other special reasons.

A Defense Ministry official described the expansion of Israel's "open-bridges" policy as "creeping normalization," saying it contributed to normal relations between Arabs in the occupied territories and their relatives in Arab countries as well as between Arabs and Israelis.

Israel admits Sinai looting. In the months after the June 1967 war, Israelis had looted millions of dollars worth of Egyptian equipment and property in the Sinai Peninsula, according to a report prepared by the Israeli state controller. An account of the report appeared in Israeli newspapers March 22–23, 1973 with the approval of the government.

The press dispatches said individuals and civilian contracting companies involved in road-building and other construction projects in the Sinai had dismantled heavy machinery and equipment of Egyptian mining and oil enterprises before Israeli authorities had established military rule in the area. Some valuable equipment left behind was said to have been vandalized. Much of the material was transported back to Israel for use or sale.

Arms & Military Force

U.S.-Israeli arms pact. State Department officials said Jan. 13, 1972 that the U.S. had signed an "agreement in principle" with Israel Nov. 1, 1971 to assist it in producing "certain U.S.-designed defense equipment." The objective was to make Israel more self-sufficient in the production of its own weapons and less dependent on the U.S.

Department spokesman Charles W. Bray 3rd said "no specific items" had yet been covered by the agreement but they would be discussed in the future "on a case-by-case basis." Israel was reported to have requested permission to manufacture certain components, rather than full weapons systems. The requests were said to include a diesel engine transmission that could be used in improving American and British

tanks or a new tank that Israel was trying to develop, and a nose-wheel steering mechanism that could be applied to an Israeli jet trainer or a Super-Mirage fighter Israel was reported to be trying to develop.

The arms understanding was contained in a memorandum negotiated by Defense Department officials and Samuel Dror, director of the Israeli Purchasing Mission, with headquarters in New York.

Egypt scores U.S. arms aid—Washington's decision to assist Israel in the manufacture of arms was assailed by Egypt Jan. 17. Tahsin Bashir, the government's official spokesman, described the agreement as a "grave turn" in U.S.-Arab relations. He said it was part of an American attempt to assure Israel "weapons supremacy" and to impose a settlement of' the Arab-Israeli conflict.

Another American decision to aid Israel—the resumption of the sale of Phantom jets—had been denounced by President Anwar Sadat Jan. 13. He warned that Washington's support of Israel was endangering U.S. oil interests in the Arab world.

Israel to get U.S. jets. U.S. Administration sources were quoted as saying Feb. 5 that Washington had agreed to sell Israel 42 F-4 Phantom and 90 A-4 Skyhawk jets over the next two–three years.

Although U.S. and Israeli officials had publicly stated that there was no connection between U.S. approval of the plane shipments and Israeli agreement Feb. 2 to an American proposal to negotiate with Egypt, Defense and State Department sources pointed out that the two issues were "not unrelated."

The 132 aircraft were not designed to add to the number of planes in the Israeli air force but to replace many of its more than 150 old French-made jets.

The U.S. agreement to sell Israel more planes was confirmed by Defense Minister Moshe Dayan Feb. 7. "We got the main items we feel we should have got," he said. Dayan issued the confirmation in Washington after concluding high-level talks with Administration officials, including Secretary of

State William P. Rogers and Defense Secretary Melvin R. Laird.

Later in 1972 Dayan met with Secretary of State William P. Rogers and other U.S. officials in Washington Nov. 14. The discussions reviewed the military and political situation in the Middle East.

Dayan said after the meetings that he had brought no "new proposals" and that in his meeting with Rogers he did not discuss his country's continuing military requirements.

U.S. and Israeli officials said in his talks with Deputy Defense Secretary Kenneth Rush Dayan had discussed in general terms Israel's defense needs for the next two-four years.

French-Israeli Mirage agreement. Under an accord signed in Paris Feb. 15, 1972, France agreed to repay Israel for the 50 Mirage jets it had purchased but France had not delivered because of the embargo imposed by President Charles de Gaulle at the time of the 1967 war.

Israel, which had paid $50 million for the aircraft, was to receive $55.1 million, which covered some spare parts also held in France, and $17.1 million in interest. The Mirages were to be turned over to the French air force, alleviating Israel's anxiety that they might have been resold to the Arabs.

U.K. warned on subs to Israel. Egypt protested to Britain March 7 against British construction of two submarines for Israel. The Cairo newspaper Al Ahram reported March 8 that in a meeting with Egyptian Ambassador Kamal Rifaat in London British Foreign Undersecretary Anthony Parsons had confirmed the transaction between the Israeli government and Vickers Shipyard.

Parsons, however, was said to have told Rifaat that the two small subs under construction were to be used in coastal waters and that the deal did not violate Britain's policy of maintaining the military balance of power between Israel and the Arabs.

Atomic & other arms. The Soviet Union claimed Aug. 8, 1972 that Israel was developing a nuclear weapon capability. The newspaper Moskovski Komsomolyets reported that Israel's military establishment "dreams of getting the weapons of mass destruction. With this aim the Weizmann Institute carries out research at the center of nuclear research in the Negev desert." The newspaper noted that "many specialists are convinced that Israel already can produce nuclear warheads."

The article, selected from an East German weekly circulated by the Soviet press agency Novosti, dealt largely with Israeli conventional armaments. Quoting "data of the Israeli Ministry of Finance," the newspaper said "weapons and military materiel worth $3.7 billion were bought abroad since June 1967. In mid-1971, the Israeli army totaled 300,000 soldiers and officers. It had 1,200 tanks, 850 warplanes, 350 motorized guns, 96 rocket units and 52 warships."

The article also said Israel was mass-producing its own supersonic jet planes and had warships equipped with ship-to-ship rockets.

Israel rated strongest in Mideast. U.S. Defense and State Department analysts considered Israel still the strongest power in the Middle East despite the recent Arab decision to back Egypt for renewed pressure on Israel, the New York Times reported Feb. 8, 1973.

In the event that Egypt, Syria Jordan, Iraq and Libya merged their air forces and launched an attack, they would not be expected to defeat Israel even with a 3-1 edge in combat planes, according to the U.S. analysts. Equipped with "longer-range aircraft and better pilots, the Israelis could quickly destroy the neighboring airfields from which such strikes would have to be mounted, and then visit so much punishment, from the air and on the ground, on her tormentors that the game would not be worth the candle," one official was quoted as saying.

Israel to buy more U.S. jets. The U.S. had agreed to sell Israel an additional four squadrons of jet fighter planes and to assist in the production of Israel's own advanced jets, the New York Times reported

March 14, 1973. According to U.S. Defense and State Department officials, the new military commitments had been made by President Nixon in his meeting with Israeli Premier Golda Meir March 1.

The officials said tentative plans called for delivery of about 24 F-4 Phantom fighter-bombers and an equal number of A-4 Skyhawk light attack aircraft over a two-year period, starting in January 1974. These were to be in addition to the 42 F-4s and about 80 A-4s promised by Nixon in December 1971.

According to the Times, the U.S. aid to Israel in building its own aircraft involved production of a Super Mirage, an advanced design based on the French Mirage and powered by the General Electric J-79 engine, also used in the F-4.

Returning to Israel after a 10-day visit to the U.S., Premier Meir had expressed confidence March 11 that Washington would continue to meet Israel's arms requirements. She said her talks with Nixon had provided "no basis or reason for changing our policy" in the Middle East.

U.S. arms sales to Israel. The U.S. had sold nearly $1 billion worth of arms to Israel in a five-year period since the 1967 war, according to declassified Defense Department figures made public May 20. The information was contained in the department's annual report on military and weapons sales from July 1, 1967 through June 30, 1972.

The major portion of the Israeli purchases, $936 million worth, was for F-4 Phantom fighters and A-4 Skyhawk attack planes.

Only two Arab countries in the five-year period had bought a significant amount of American arms: Saudi Arabia $141 million and Jordan $127 million. Lebanon had been sold $3.7 million, and Kuwait, Iraq and Syria had made token purchases.

The Defense Department figures were only for weapons for which a country paid and did not cover military equipment given free under separate aid programs.

Israel lists U.S. arms purchases—Finance Minister Pinhas Sapir said that Israel had purchased $476 million worth of arms from the U.S. in 1972, it was reported Feb. 10. He said the shipments included an undisclosed number of Phantom jets.

Israelis build missile boat fleet. Israel disclosed Feb. 4 that it was building a fleet of missile boats for its navy in a Haifa shipyard.

The commander of the navy, Rear Adm. Benyamin Telem, told a news conference in Tel Aviv that the first vessel would be launched Feb. 19 and that an undisclosed number of others would be delivered to the navy in 1973 and 1974.

The craft weighed 415 tons, was 190.4 feet long and had a speed of about 32 knots. Its armament included two 76-mm. antiaircraft guns, seven missiles, four depth charges and machine guns.

Israel cuts draft service. The Israeli government announced July 15 that starting April 1, 1974 it would reduce the three-year period of compulsory military service for men by three months. The reduction was the first since after the 1967 war when the period of service had been increased from $2\frac{1}{2}$ years to three. A Defense Ministry source said the decision to cut military service was based on a desire to ease the disruption of higher education.

Other Developments

Israel breaks Syrian spy ring. Israeli authorities Dec. 7, 1972 reported smashing a Syrian spy and sabotage ring whose alleged participants included four Israeli Jews. The others were Arabs. The network was said to have been broken before it had "actually managed to do any real harm."

The initial announcement said 21 persons had been arrested as suspects. An additional 20 persons were picked up later, it was reported Dec. 11, but four were released for lack of evidence.

The four Israeli Jewish suspects were identified as Ehud Adiv, 25, David Vered, Yehezkel Cohen, 30, and David Kupfer, 28. They were described as members of Matzpen, a small left-wing Jewish Trotskyite splinter group that supported the cause of the Palestinian Arabs. The four were said to have defected from Matzpen, which they regarded as too moderate, and formed the more radical Revolutionary Communist Union.

A court in Haifa March 25, 1973 convicted three Israeli Arabs and two Israeli Jews on charges of participating in the ring.

In sentences handed down March 26, Daoud Turki, an Arab who reportedly was the initiator of the spy group, and Ehud Adiv, leader of the Jewish faction, received 17 years each. The second Jewish defendant, Dan Vered, was imprisoned for 10 years. Two other Arabs—Subhi Narami and Anais Karawi—received 15-year jail terms. Another Arab, Simon Haddad, was given a two-year sentence.

During the trial, which had started Feb. 11, the defendants had admitted going to Syria where they were trained in weapons and explosives.

Israel marks 25th anniversary. Israel marked its 25th Independence Day May 7, 1973 with a big military parade in Jerusalem. As about 300,000 spectators lined the route of march, thousands of soldiers and hundreds of tanks and other equipment moved through the streets of the city. The highlight was a flyover of scores of Israeli Phantom, Skyhawk and Mirage jets.

The parade was held despite domestic and international protests. Some Israelis had argued that the $6 million spent on the celebration was too extravagant and that the overt display of soldiers and military equipment would damage Israel's image abroad.

During the parade, Arabs in East Jerusalem closed their shops in protest. Most of the four-mile route of the procession ran through the Arab section of Jerusalem.

Jordan filed a protest with the U.N. Security Council May 8. In a letter to Secretary General Kurt Waldheim, Jordanian delegate Abdul Hamid Sharaf charged that "the ugly exhibition of force and militarism on May 7 in the heart of the city of peace and holiness is inseparable from Israel's massive and systematic violations of the spiritual integrity of Jerusalem."

Jerusalem Arabs protest '67 war. Arab merchants in East Jerusalem closed their shops in a brief general strike June 5 to mark the sixth anniversary of the 1967 Arab-Israeli war. Israeli soldiers quickly forced all but a few of the stores to reopen. Ten Arab shopkeepers who refused to reopen were arrested.

There were also scattered Arab protests against the war anniversary in other parts of East Jerusalem and in the West Bank.

New president elected. Ephraim Katchalski, 56, was elected president of Israel April 10. In parliamentary balloting, Katchalski, a candidate of the ruling Labor party, received 66 votes. Ephraim Uhrbach, candidate of the National Religious party, received 41. Katchalski was to succeed Zalman Shazar, who was retiring at the expiration of his five-year term May 25.

A biophysicist, Katchalski had served as head of the biophysics department at the Weitzmann Institute of Science in Israel and as chief scientific adviser to the Defense Ministry.

Katchalski changed his name to Katzir on being elected in accordance with a government policy requiring Hebrew names for state officials.

Oil

Arab Pressure

As Arab-Israeli tensions grew during 1973, the Arab oil-producing countries warned the Western nations and Japan that Arab oil, on which much of the industrialized world depended heavily, might not be available to them very long unless they helped the Arabs against Israel. Some of the industrialized countries indicated quickly that they would not be able to stand up against the Arab "oil weapon."

Saudis link oil flow to U.S. policy. Saudi Arabian Petroleum Minister Sheik Ahmad Zaki Yamani was reported to have warned Secretary of State William P. Rogers and other U.S. officials April 16, 1973 that his country might not increase its oil production for export to the U.S. if Washington did not help in settling the Middle East problem to the satisfaction of the Arab states.

Yamani also was reported to have said that the oil wells were vulnerable to attacks by terrorists and that such activities could only be curbed by a political settlement. Rogers replied that the U.S. opposed terrorism and that its halt was necessary if progress was to be made in achieving a peaceful resolution of the conflict.

Yamani reiterated in a Washington Post interview April 18 that there was a good chance that Saudi Arabia could increase its current production quota of 7.2 million barrels of oil a day to 20 million barrels by 1980 if the U.S. created "the right political atmosphere." The minister said he was specifically referring to U.S. policy toward Israel.

King Faisal of Saudi Arabia warned the U.S. in a statement Aug. 30 that it would be "extremely difficult" for his country to continue supplying oil to the U.S. because of the U.S.' "complete support of Zionism against the Arabs." In another statement made public the same day Faisal, cautioned Arabs against the use of oil as a political weapon.

In response to these apparent conflicting remarks, U.S. Administration oil experts said Saudi Arabia was releasing "contradictory signals" because it still had not worked out a definitive oil policy.

In his first statement, Faisal said in a television interview that his country was "deeply concerned that if the United States does not change its policy in the Middle East and continues to side with Zionism, then, . . . such course of action will affect our relations with our American friends because it will place us in an untenable position in the Arab world."

The Beirut weekly Al Hawadess carried statements Aug. 30 by Faisal and his son Prince Saud al Faisal, undersecretary of the Petroleum Ministry, warning against slogans "which deliberately intend to push the Arabs to gamble with their strongest weapon [oil]." "No one is asking where we would get the money we need if we cut off the oil, not only for supporting our country, but also for providing assistance to our brothers on the front lines" with Israel, the king said.

Saud said the U.S. would not be affected by an immediate halt in Arab oil exports because total U.S. dependence on Arab oil would not occur before the end of the 1970s. Only Western Europe and Japan, with whom the Arabs had no quarrel, would be hurt by an oil cutoff, the prince said.

Another warning by Faisal that he would use his oil in retaliation against U.S. support of Israel appeared in the Sept. 3 issue of Newsweek magazine. Faisal said the U.S. must refrain "from giving unlimited aid to Israel . . . If no American response is forthcoming, one of our conditions for increasing our [oil] production will not have been satisfied."

Yamani warned the U.S. Sept. 18 that Saudi Arabia might cut its oil output if the Arab-Israeli dispute was not resolved.

Yamani made the statement at a panel discussion of the fourth International Industrial Conference in San Francisco. The parley was attended by 650 industrialists from 75 nations, including chief executives from U.S. oil companies. Yamani said "if we cannot solve our economic problems and if we cannot have the right political atmosphere" in the Middle East, Saudi Arabia might have to curtail its oil output. A Middle East settlement must consist of Israeli withdrawal from occupied Arab territories with the active help of the U.S., Yamani said.

A U.S. re-examination of its policies in the Middle East was called for Sept. 18 by Maurice F. Granville, chairman and chief executive officer of Texaco. Speaking to the Independent Natural Gas Association of America in Scottsdale, Ariz., Granville noted that Saudi Arabia had appealed to Americans "to review the actions of their government in regard to the Arab-Israeli dispute and to compare these actions with its stated position of support for peaceful

settlement responsive to the concerns of all the countries involved." Noting the long-standing friendship between the oil companies and Saudi Arabia, Granville said "we must feel concern when those who have been so close to us urge us to review our policies."

Arabs briefly halt oil flow. Libya, Iraq, Kuwait and Algeria temporarily halted the flow of oil to the West May 15 as a symbolic protest against the continued existence of Israel as a state. Although the stoppage was to have lasted only an hour, Libya shut its pumps for 24 hours. The action was taken in response to an appeal issued by a Pan-Arab Trade Union Conference in Cairo earlier in May.

Egyptian President Anwar Sadat had called on Arab states May 14 to use their oil to pressure the U.S. to drop its support of Israel. Speaking to Parliament, Sadat said: "The case is one of protracted struggle and not only on the Suez Canal battle. There is the battle of America's interests, the battle of energy, the battle of Arabs."

Libyan leader Muammar el-Qaddafi had predicted May 13 that oil would be used as "a weapon of Arab self-defense." Speaking at a news conference in Tripoli, Qaddafi charged that an American oil firm operating in Libya, the Oasis Oil Co., employed seven Israeli agents on its staff. Oil industry sources in Libya and an Israeli government official denied the charges May 14.

Libya seizes U.S. oil firm. Libya nationalized a U.S. oil firm June 11 in retaliation for Washington's support of Israel.

The seizure of the Bunker Hunt Oil Co. of Dallas, Tex. was announced in a speech by Qadaffi at a Tripoli rally. Qadaffi describing American oil companies as an extension of the U.S.' "policy of domination" in the Middle East, said the U.S. "deserved a strong slap in the face." He added: "American imperialism has exceeded every limit. The Americans support our Israeli enemy, threaten our security with their aircraft carriers, and from time to time, the Americans threaten our territorial waters." Qaddafi warned "The time might come where there will be a real confrontation with oil companies and the entire American imperialism."

Egyptian President Anwar Sadat and Ugandan president Idi Amin also spoke.

Sadat said June 12 that the nationalization of Bunker Hunt was "the beginning of a battle against American interests in the whole Arab region. America must realize that it cannot protect its interests if it continues defying the Arab nation and supporting Israel without limitations."

The Libyan government had first asked Bunker Hunt in the fall of 1972 for more than 50% control. The company refused and negotiations between the two sides had continued inconclusively since. As a prelude to expropriation, the Libyans had stopped Bunker Hunt from producing oil May 24.

The U.S. State Department disclosed June 12 that Libya had been informed of the U.S. government's reaction to the nationalization of Bunker Hunt. Department spokesman John King said the U.S. "has a right under international law to expect" owners of nationalized property to "receive prompt, adequate and effective compensation from the nationalizing government."

Libya nationalized 51% of the assets of the U.S.-owned Occidental Petroleum Corp., it was reported Aug. 11. Under the negotiated contract, the company received $135 million in cash as initial compensation, with a final amount subject to audit.

Libya gained 51% control of the American-owned Oasis Oil Co. under an agreement announced Aug. 16 by Petroleum Minister Ezzedin Mabrouk. The pact provided for Libyan compensation to Oasis of $135 million in four installments without interest.

Libya announced Sept. 1 the nationalization of 51% of all foreign oil companies operating in the country. The decree was followed by another announcement Sept. 2 that Libya would increase the price of its oil from the current $4.90 a barrel to $6 and would refuse to accept U.S. dollars in payment for the oil.

The nationalization decree affected the Libyan subsidiaries of Exxon, Mobil Oil, Texaco, Standard Oil of California, Atlantic Richfield, W. R. Grace, Royal Dutch Shell and Gelsenberg. The action followed a breakdown in negotiations between the companies and the government, which had set Aug. 25 as the deadline for the takeover.

The Libyan decree gave the firms 30 days to decide on their course of action. Tripoli radio said the government would compensate the companies, with the amount being fixed by a committee of Libyan officials. Each of the companies would be operated by a three-man board comprising two Libyans and one company executive. One of the Libyans would be named president of the board, and majority rule would prevail.

The decision on the price increase was announced Sept. 2 by Premier Abdel Salam Jalloud. He said Libya would "no longer accept payment in U.S. dollars" for its oil because "the dollar has lost its value and we want currency that is convertible into gold."

U.S. oil firm asks support for Arabs. Standard Oil Co. of California urged the U.S. to support the Arab states because their oil resources were vital to the U.S. and the West. The statement, appearing in a company letter mailed July 26 to 40,000 employes and 262,000 stockholders, was made public Aug. 2. It was criticized by supporters of Israel in the U.S.

The letter, signed by Standard Oil Chairman Otto N. Miller, made no reference to Israel in its appeal to the employes and stockholders to foster the "aspirations of the Arab people" and "their efforts toward peace in the Middle East." The statement said, "There is now a feeling in much of the Arab world that the United States has turned its back on the Arab people" at a time when the Arabs' oil was "becoming increasingly important to the future of the Western world."

Miller's remarks drew a rebuke Aug. 3 from the Los Angeles Jewish community and California's two U.S. senators—Allen M. Cranston (D) and John V. Tunney (D). Edward Sanders, president of the Jewish Federation Council of Greater Los Angeles, said Miller's letter "raises serious ethical and moral questions as to the utilization of a vast, profit-making organization to influence American foreign policy."

The Jewish War Veterans (JWV) urged its members and friends Aug. 7 to "institute an immediate boycott of the products" of Standard oil and its subsidiaries. JWV national Commander Norman Tiles said in Hollywood, Fla. that Miller's letter was "an attempt to urge its stockholders to use the tools of Arab blackmail" to subvert U.S. foreign policy in the Middle East.

Miller sought to clarify his remarks in a letter sent Aug. 7 to the Jewish Community Relations Council of San Francisco. He said U.S. efforts at peace in the Middle East should be based on "the legitimate interests of Israel and its people as well as the interests of all other states in the area."

Arab oil ministers meet. Oil ministers of 10 Arab states met in Kuwait Sept. 4 to formulate a common policy on using oil resources as a diplomatic weapon against Israel.

The conferees reportedly had failed to reach agreement on joint action as radical and conservative states posed sharply differing views. It was decided instead to have the matter "left to the heads of state of countries concerned."

Iraq, among the radical states, proposed a cut in oil production for 10 years during which a minimum amount would be exported to the West to finance development plans. Conservative states such as Saudi Arabia and Kuwait cautioned against use of oil as a political weapon. They recommended suspension of any action pending an American response to Saudi King Faisal's warning Aug. 30 to the U.S. regarding its support of Israel.

Other states participating in the conference were Libya, Qatar, Syria, Bahrein, Abu Dhabi, Algeria and Egypt.

Saudis want price increase. Saudi Arabian Petroleum Minister Ahmed Zaki Yamani called Sept. 7 for a revision of the 1971 Teheran Agreement to permit higher prices for the oil-producing countries.

The Teheran accord, aimed at regulating oil prices, expired in 1975. Yamani said the pact was "dead" and proposed that oil producers and major Western companies hold new talks in October to consider an increase in posted prices for oil exports, which determined the governments' revenue. Yamani also demanded an increase in the annual 2.5% price rise allowed to compensate for inflation.

The minister warned that unless the oil companies cooperated in amending the Teheran agreement, "we would have to exercise our rights on our own."

OPEC to ask for higher rates. Following a meeting in Vienna Sept. 15–16, the 11-nation Organization of Petroleum Exporting Countries (OPEC) announced it would demand higher prices from Western oil companies in forthcoming negotiations.

A communique issued after the two-day parley set Oct. 8 as the date for meeting with petroleum representatives in Vienna to revise the Teheran pricing accord.

The OPEC also supported Libya "in any action it takes" to enforce the Sept. 1 nationalization of foreign oil firms.

Nixon for action on oil & Mideast. President Nixon urged legislators to enact seven energy bills before Congress in order to avert a winter heating oil shortage and reduce the U.S.' dependence on Middle East oil producers, who threatened to limit the availability of petroleum supplies to U.S. consumers as political retaliation for U.S. support of Israel.

"If the Congress does not act upon these proposals, it means that we will have an energy crisis. Not perhaps just this winter, but perhaps, certainly, later on as well," Nixon said.

"And if the Congress does not act upon these proposals which, in effect, have as their purpose increasing the domestic capacity of the United States to create its energy, it means that we will be at the mercy of the producers of oil in the Mideast," he added.

Nixon was asked what the Administration was "doing to meet these threats from the Arab countries to use oil as a club to force a change in our Middle East policy?"

"We are having discussions with some of the companies involved," Nixon said. As for the Arab countries involved, the problem was that "it's tied up with the Arab-Israeli dispute." That was why, in talking to Henry A. Kissinger, both before he nominated him as secretary of state and since, "that we have put at the highest priority moving toward making some progress toward the settlement of that dispute."

Another problem was "the radical elements that presently seem to be on the ascendancy in various countries in the Mideast, like Libya. Those elements, of course, we are not in a position to control, although we may be in a position to influence. Influence them for this reason: oil without a market ... doesn't do a country much good. We and Europe are the market. And I think that the responsible Arab leaders will see to it that if they continue to up the price, if they continue to expropriate, if they do expropriate without fair compensation, the inevitable result is that they will lose their markets and other sources will be developed."

Nixon was asked if it was possible "that the threat of limiting the supply of oil would cause a moderation in U.S. support of Israel?"

He said "to suggest that we are going to relate our policy toward Israel, which has to do with the independence of that country to which we are dedicated, to what happens on Arab oil, I think would be highly inappropriate." Both sides were at fault, he said. "Both sides need to start negotiating. That is our position. We're not pro-Israel; and we're not pro-Arab. And we're not any more pro-Arab because they have oil and Israel hasn't. We are pro-peace. And it's the interest of the whole area for us to get those negotiations off dead center. That is why we will use our influence with Israel; and we will use our influence—what influence we have—with the various Arab states."

The

October

1973

War

Conflict on 2 Fronts

Arabs Attack at Suez & on Golan Heights

Six years after their devastating defeat at the hands of Israel in June 1967, Arabs attacked Israelis Oct. 6, 1973. The war erupted on two fronts as Syrian forces pushed back Israeli troops in the Golan Heights and Egyptian tanks crossed the Suez Canal and forced Israeli troops out of their Bar-Lev defense line along the canal. Iraq, Morocco and Jordan sent Arab contingents to fight in this fourth Arab-Israeli war in 25 years.

The war broke out on Yom Kippur, the Jewish Day of Atonement. Premier Golda Meir said in a nationwide address to rally her people that the Israelis were not taken by surprise by the Arab attack even though they were engaged in fasting and prayers in observance of that holy day. She said Israeli intelligence had known for several days that Syrian and Egyptian forces were massing on Israeli lines for a combined attack. Other sources confirmed the Arab buildup, but the outbreak of fighting had not been preceded by mounting tension or diplomatic activity.

Although Israel was aware of the Arab buildup, Defense Minister Moshe Dayan said Oct. 7 that his country had deliberately decided against a preemptive strike in order "to have the political advantage—or whatever you want to call it—of being the side that is attacked."

Both sides blamed each other for starting the hostilities. U.N. truce observers, however, upheld the Israeli claim that the Arabs struck first, saying that Syrian planes attacked in the Golan Heights while the Egyptians simultaneously launched their assault on Israeli forces along the canal.

(The United Nations disclosed Oct. 9 that only three of the 16 U.N. observation posts in the Suez Canal zone area and all but three of the 17 U.N. Golan Heights posts were operating. At the outset of the fighting Oct. 6, Egypt had asked that the U.N. posts on the canal be closed and the observers transferred to Cairo.)

The Soviet Union was reported to have started a major airlift of military equipment to Egypt and Syria to compensate them for their battle losses. The U.S. later began a resupply operation for Israel. But Britain announced an embargo on arms shipments to either side.

The Soviet Union reacted to the outbreak of fighting with bitter denunciations of Israel, while reaffirming support for an overall political settlement.

A government statement issued Oct. 7 blamed Israel for provoking the fighting by refusing to withdraw from all territory

90

occupied in 1967, and also charged that Israel had "unleashed military operations" after concentrating "considerable armed forces on the cease-fire lines" and calling up reservists.

Moscow refrained from calling for a new cease-fire. The New York Times reported Oct. 10 that Soviet officials had said they expected the fighting to place pressure on Israel to make greater concessions in a political settlement. Although the U.S.S.R. had in the past been reported to oppose a new Arab offensive, reports that it had pulled back several thousand advisers and dependents from Arab capitals in recent days suggested to some observers that it had advance knowledge of Syrian and Egyptian plans. Further evidence was the unusually rapid Soviet media coverage of the fighting, without the usual caution in reaction to new situations.

On the diplomatic front, the U.N. Security Council debated the new Middle East war Oct. 8–9 and 11 at the U.S.' request, but failed to take any action to bring the hostilities to an end.

The U.S. also launched independent peace efforts, calling on the Arabs and Israelis to bring the fighting to a halt. Washington appealed directly to the Soviet Union, urging it to refrain from any overt action during the crisis. The U.S. Senate passed a resolution Oct. 8 calling for an end to the war and a return to positions held before the outbreak of hostilities.

Suez-Sinai-Egyptian front. The initial Egyptian communiqué on the outbreak of fighting on the Suez front declared Oct 6 that Cairo's forces that day had crossed to the eastern bank of the canal at five points after repelling an Israeli attempt to land on the Egyptian-held western bank of the waterway. The statement, announced at 2 p.m. Cairo time, a half hour after the outbreak of hostilities, said the attempted Israeli landing was accompanied by air strikes on Ain Sukhna and Zaafarana, 30 and 100 miles south of the city of Suez.

The communiqué said the Egyptian forces had seized almost the entire 100-mile length of the eastern bank of the canal and then enlarged their positions in the continued fighting. Eleven Israeli and 10 Egyptian planes were shot down in dogfights following an Israeli attempt to bomb Egyptian targets, the communique said.

Israel conceded in its communiqué that the Egyptians had crossed the canal at several points by helicopters and small boats and laid down pontoon bridges in two places, enabling them to pour their armor into the Sinai. The communiqué said 10 Egyptian helicopters carrying 30 men each had been downed in the Ras Sudr section, with more than 200 casualties.

Israel claimed its jets Oct. 7 cut nine of 11 bridges across the canal, isolating 400 Egyptian tanks and other forces on the eastern bank. At the same time, the Israelis launched counterattacks, but the Egyptians claimed they were repulsed and that the eastern-bank bridgeheads were being expanded. A Tel Aviv spokesman said Israeli jets struck at Egyptian airfields and other targets as far west as Cairo. Five of the Israeli planes were downed, according to Cairo. In addition, Egyptian planes inflicted heavy losses in men and materiel in attacks on Israeli reserve positions in the central Sinai, Cairo said.

Maj. Gen. Haim Herzog, acting as Israel's military spokesman, acknowledged at a news conference Oct. 8 that all but one or two of the Israeli positions on the Bar-Lev line on the eastern bank of the canal had been overrun by the Egyptians in the previous 24 hours. He declared: "We are involved in a very major war, and so far we are holding our own with minimum forces. We are maintaining supremacy in the air and using the time it provides us to mobilize our forces."

Israel claimed its forces drove the Egyptians back to the canal Oct. 8, that its planes struck surface-to-air missile sites and other targets around Port Said on the northern end of the canal, and that its naval forces hit and damaged an Egyptian minesweeper in the Gulf of Suez south of the canal. Egyptian planes appeared in force and 15 were downed in a series of dogfights in the canal sector, the Israelis reported.

Egypt claimed its troops Oct. 9 raided the Israeli-occupied Egyptian oil fields at Balayim on the Gulf of Suez, setting large fires. The Cairo communiqué conceded the Israeli air strike on Port Said. It also reported the movement of more troops into the Sinai, expanding their penetration to 9 miles, the downing of 24 Israeli Phantom and Skyhawk jets and the repulse of two Israeli armored brigades with the loss of 102 tanks. The Cairo communique claimed the remaining Israeli tanks were "withdrawing eastward in a state of panic" and were being pursued by Egyptian forces. The capture of hundreds of Israeli prisoners, including Col. Assef Yagori, commander of the 190th Armored Brigade, was claimed by the Egyptians.

In naval clashes Oct. 9, Egypt reported it had sunk four Israeli patrol vessels and lost three of its own in a clash in the Mediterranean.

Israel formally acknowledged Oct. 10 that its forces had abandoned the Bar-Lev line on the Suez front. But Maj. Gen. Aharon Yariv, special adviser to the chief of staff, said new defense positions had been established that day "on the Suez front about three to five kilometers, some places six kilometers, facing the Egyptian forces that had crossed the Suez Canal." Yariv said "it is not going to be a short" conflict, that Israel was now engaged in a "war of attrition." He said Israel had done no more than "redress the situation" on the Suez front but had dealt the Syrians a "very severe blow" on the Golan Heights.

A group of Western correspondents confirmed Oct. 10 that Egyptian troops and tanks were continuing to pour into the Sinai and had reached positions 10 miles or more east of the canal in some parts of the sector. The New York Times Oct. 11 quoted British sources as saying that Egypt had more than 30,000 troops in the Sinai and about 450 tanks.

Ground fighting in the Sinai came to a virtual standstill with military activity confined to Israeli artillery shelling and aerial activity. Egypt claimed the downing of six Israeli jets Oct. 10.

Egyptian and Israeli communiqués gave widely divergent descriptions of the fighting Oct. 11. While Cairo was claiming sweeping victories, Israel was reporting a "rather quiet day" along the Suez front.

According to the Egyptian communiqué: Israeli forces suffered heavy losses in lives, tanks and half-tracks in a fierce four-hour fight during an unsuccessful attempt to halt the Egyptian advance.

(Exact location of the battle was not given.) "The enemy then retreated eastward and our forces pursued and encircled part of the retreating enemy forces."

The Egyptians claimed similar successes in the air, shooting down 23 Israeli planes with a loss of six of their own during battles over the Nile Delta, Sinai and Gulf of Suez.

The Israeli communiqué on the day's action was terse, stating only that there had been "local contacts between armor and artillery" with no major advances by either side.

Egypt's Middle East News Agency said Oct. 11 that U.S. Phantom jets from aircraft based in the Mediterranean had joined Israeli jets in attacking Egyptian positions. The U.S. State Department denied the charge as "a mischievous lie."

Golan Heights and Syrian front. Syrian President Hafez al-Assad announced in a broadcast Oct. 6 that his troops and Egyptian forces had launched attacks that day to prevent an Israeli preemptive assault against the two countries. Assad dismissed Israeli charges of a Syrian buildup of troops and armor on its border as a coverup of Israeli intentions to attack Syria first. He said Israel had been massing its forces on the front for a week and Syrian forces "struck to repel this aggression at the right moment."

The first Damascus communiqué on the fighting said Syrian troops occupied a number of Israeli positions, including Mt. Hermon. The Israelis disclaimed the Syrian successes and said they had regained their lost positions, destroying 150 enemy tanks in the first day of fighting on the heights. An Israeli communique said Israeli gunboats sank five Syrian gunboats in a clash in the port of Latakia.

A Syrian tank force pushed 10 miles inside the heights Oct. 7–8, but Israel said its forces had thrown back the Syrians and their soldiers were advancing in the face of strong resistance. The Israelis claimed mastery of the skies almost at the outset of the fighting.

Israeli planes Oct. 8 downed three Soviet-made Sukhoi-20 fighter-bombers over the eastern Galilee in northern Israel. The Syrians were believed trying to bomb the Israeli city of Kiryat Shmona. Syrian jets failed to appear after Israeli planes carried out intensive strikes against five airfields in Syria. Israeli ground forces crushed two Syrian brigades that had spearheaded the assault, destroying "many hundreds" of tanks, according to Lt. Gen. David Elazar, Israeli chief of staff.

Israeli jets Oct. 9 struck deep into Syria, bombing Damascus and Homs. Heavy civilian casualties were reported in the Damascus raid, with six Russians reportedly killed in a bomb strike on the Soviet cultural center. Syrian authorities said three Norwegians, an Indian and a member of the U.N. Truce Supervisory Organization and his wife and daughter also were killed. The principal targets in the raid were said to be the Syrian Defense Ministry, air force headquarters and a radio station. Bombs also fell in the nearby district housing many foreign residences and embassies, where most of the casualties occurred. Unofficial reports said 30 civilians were killed and 70 wounded. Syria claimed four of the six Israeli raiders were downed.

The Israeli strike on Homs set fire to an oil refinery.

Israeli planes Oct. 9 bombed a radar station in Lebanon 18 miles southwest of Beirut, wounding nine Lebanese soldiers. The radar station at El Baruk was capable of picking up Israeli aircraft moving over Lebanon into Syria.

Israeli planes returned to Syria Oct. 10, bombing the Damascus airport, Homs, and the ports of Latakia and Tartus. Syria reported heavy civilian casualties in the latter three cities. Syria said 43 Israeli planes were downed by Syrian and Iraqi planes. Damascus did not list its own losses. Several of the battles were fought in Lebanese airspace. The air strike on Latakia sank a Greek freighter, killing two crewmen and injuring seven.

Israelis retake Golan, cross truce line— Israel's recapture of the Golan Heights and the thrust of Israeli forces beyond the 1967 cease-fire line into Syria was announced Oct. 10 by Israeli military authorities and Premier Golda Meir.

In an address to the nation, Meir said she was "happy and joyful to tell you today that the Golan Heights are in our hands, the settlers are returning to their villages. The Syrian army is past the cease-fire line and we are pushing him still further back." The premier also said Israeli troops were driving the Egyptians back on the Sinai front and "our forces are now close to the canal."

Most of the Israeli settlements on the heights abandoned in the early part of the battle were being reoccupied by Israeli units Oct. 10, while other ground forces were pushing ahead with heavy air and armored support. The Israelis claimed the downing of 17 Syrian jets in dozens of dogfights over the heights, but did not give their own losses. The Syrians were putting up stiff resistance in scattered pockets on the Golan Heights despite powerful Israeli artillery barrages.

Israeli armored forces continued to push out from the 1967 truce line and were reported by a Tel Aviv communiqué Oct. 11 to have broken through enemy lines to a point six miles inside Syria. The advance on the main Quneitra-Damascus highway placed the Israeli army 37 miles from the Syrian capital. Israeli Defense Minister Moshe Dayan said during a visit to the Syrian front that the Israeli attack was aimed at reminding Syria that "the same road that leads to Tel Aviv also leads to Damascus."

The communiqué also said Israeli planes attacked eight airfields in Syria and that the air force knocked down 11 jets on the Syrian and Sinai fronts.

(A Tel Aviv military spokesman said Oct. 11 that Israeli forces had captured several new Soviet T-52 tanks during the heavy fighting on the Golan Heights earlier in the week.)

According to a Damascus communiqué on the Oct. 11 fighting:

Eighty Israeli planes were shot down and 61 Israeli tanks were destroyed when "the enemy mounted a counterattack" on the Golan Heights. Israeli boats attacked the ports of Latakia, Tartus and the oil pipeline terminal at Baniyas. Syrian coastal guns and naval vessels sank eight Israeli boats.

The Israelis claimed sinking two Syrian missile boats in an engagement off Tartus, while suffering no losses of their own.

According to travelers who reached Beirut from Damascus Oct. 11, the Israeli air strike the previous day on Homs had destroyed Syria's major oil refinery plant and a large power plant.

Early Peace Efforts Futile

Kissinger tries to halt war. U.S. Secretary of State Henry A. Kissinger made strong, early diplomatic efforts Oct. 6 to halt the fighting with appeals to Arab and Israeli officials.

U.S. officials evidently were surprised by the Middle East developments. Nixon and Kissinger were alerted at 6 a.m. (EDT) that an outbreak was imminent.

After conferring by telephone with President Nixon, who was in Key Biscayne, Fla., Kissinger telephoned Israeli Foreign Minister Abba Eban and Egyptian Foreign Minister Mohammed H. el-Zayyat, but the plea to "avoid any escalation and continuation of the fighting" proved fruitless.

Kissinger, in New York when the Middle East clash broke out, sent cables Oct. 6 to King Hussein of Jordan and King Faisal of Saudi Arabia, with whom the U.S. maintained close relations. They were asked to "use their good office to urge restraint where they have the influence to do so," State Department spokesman Robert J. McCloskey said. (According to the Middle East News Agency Oct. 7, Faisal had replied to the cable, saying that "unless the U.S. moves at once to contain Israel's aggression, then the situation may explode into a global conflict.")

Kissinger also telephoned Soviet Ambassador Anatoly F. Dobrynin in Washington to urge Soviet restraint during the crisis. Before leaving New York, Kissinger also called U.N. Secretary General Kurt Waldheim and Sir Laurence McIntyre of Australia, president of the Security Council during October, to discuss possible Council action. Follow-up meetings with other Council members were held by John Scali, U.S. ambassador to the U.N.

It was disclosed Oct. 8 that Kissinger had met in Washington Oct. 6 with Huang Chen, head of the Chinese liaison mission to the U.S. China was a strong supporter of the Arab cause.

U.S. military intelligence experts had not indicated that any clash was expected, although the Syrian and Egyptian troop buildups along Israel's frontiers were known in Washington, Administration officials said Oct. 8.

According to the United Press International, the evacuation of Soviet personnel from Syria and indications of heavy Soviet air traffic in and out of Cairo were reported to Washington officials Oct. 5. Dispatches from Tel Aviv also confirmed the reports of a Soviet pullout from Egypt.

If the Soviets had known that any military action was being planned, McCloskey said Oct. 6, they had not informed the U.S. of those facts.

A spokesman for Abba Eban said Oct. 6 that shortly before hostilities broke out, Israel had informed the U.S. and other governments that an attack was likely, that Israel would launch no pre-emptive strike and that it would welcome actions by any "interested parties" to warn Egypt and Syria that Israel was aware of their intentions.

The Administration's efforts at intensive negotiations were highlighted Oct. 8 when it was announced that Nixon had exchanged messages Oct. 7 with Soviet Communist Party General Secretary Leonid I. Brezhnev through regular diplomatic channels. (The emergency hot line between Washington and Moscow was not used, Press Secretary Ronald Ziegler said.) As a consequence of the exchange, U.S. officials said they were hopeful that the detente achieved by Nixon and Brezhnev would avert any confrontation between the U.S. and the Soviet Union in the Middle East.

Nixon, who initiated the exchange of messages with Brezhnev, was said to be acting in accordance with "basic principles" signed May 29, 1972 in which the Soviet Union and the U.S. agreed to "avoid military confrontation and prevent nuclear war" and "to do everything in their power so that conflicts or situations will not arise which would serve to increase international tensions."

Nixon met briefly with reporters Oct. 8 and said the U.S. and Soviet Union shared a desire to limit the Middle East fighting. Kissinger, also present at the meeting, said "our intention is to move forward with the broadest possible support that can be effected."

The U.S. would not attempt a "grandstand play, where the U.S. would go in and unilaterally make a move which then fails," Nixon declared.

U.S. and Soviet leaders remained in "close contact" according to Administration officials. The Soviet Union had given only "minimal" public support to Egypt and Syria, they added.

The Washington Post reported Oct. 9 that Israel's ambassador, Simcha Dinitz, met with Kissinger Oct. 7 shortly after returning from Israel. He informed Kissinger of Israel's principle objectives: to eject the Egyptians and Syrians, and to "deal a devastating blow to the military machine of both Arab states so that it will be impossible for them to launch another aggression for a very long time."

Senate asks cease-fire. The Senate passed a resolution Oct. 8 calling for an immediate cease-fire and a return to positions held before the recent outbreak of war.

The motion, introduced by Senate leaders Mike Mansfield (D, Mont.) and Hugh Scott (R, Pa.), was approved quickly on a voice vote with only a few senators present.

Quick action on the measure, which made no mention of any country as the aggressor, was seen by observers as an Administration effort to forestall any pro-Israel Senate statement during the period when the White House was engaging in broad diplomatic efforts to present a widely accepted proposal before the U.N. Security Council, where anti-Israel sentiment was high. Secretary of State Henry Kissinger had endorsed the Senate action, Scott said.

Sen. Abraham Ribicoff (D, Conn.) and Sen. Henry M. Jackson (R, Wash.) were critical of the resolution. Both had been strong supporters of Israel in the Senate. Jackson said he feared that the U.N. would "turn the resolution into an in-place standstill cease-fire" in which Israel would be forced to relinquish territories occupied since 1967.

U.N. fails to act. The United Nations Security Council held special sessions Oct. 8–9 and 11 to debate the renewed Middle East war but adjourned without passing a resolution.

Members of the Council had expressed reluctance Oct. 10 to meet again as long as military reports showed Arab and Israeli determination to continue fighting. Sir Laurence McIntyre of Australia, Council president for October, said there was "not much point to getting together if it only means another fractious meeting."

The first session was requested Oct. 7 by U.S. Ambassador John A. Scali, on orders from President Nixon relayed by Secretary of State Henry A. Kissinger. A U.S. State Department spokesman, Robert J. McCloskey, said at a news conference Oct. 7 that the U.S. believed Egypt and Syria were responsible for violating the Middle East cease-fire, but it was less interested in passing judgment in the Council than in resolving the crisis.

Scali urged the Council Oct. 8 to act to end the Middle East hostilities and to restore the cease-fire lines existing before the renewed fighting began. He said the U.S. hoped the Council would act in such a way that "the present tragedy can be made a new beginning rather than simply another lost opportunity."

Scali was rebuked by the Chinese representative, Huang Hua, who said it was "preposterous" for the U.S. to ask Egypt and Syria to withdraw to the 1967 cease-fire lines. It was "perfectly just," Huang asserted, for the Arab countries to "rise in resistance to the invading enemies of their own sacred territories."

Soviet Ambassador Yakov A. Malik also expressed support for Egypt and Syria and criticized the Council for meeting at all. The British delegate, Sir Donald Maitland, called for an end to the fighting.

Scali said at the Oct. 8 meeting that reports by U.N. Truce Supervision Organization (UNTSO) representatives in the Middle East indicated Syrian MiG fighters had struck first in the Golan Heights and "the first firing on the Suez front, which took place at the same time as the Syrian attack," came from the Egyptian side of the old cease-fire line.

(UNTSO observation posts along the cease-fire lines reported Egyptian forces were seen crossing the Suez Canal from the western to the eastern banks from five places as the hostilities began, according to the New York Times Oct. 9. Syrian forces crossed the Golan Heights cease-fire line at the same time, the observers reported.)

Egyptian Foreign Minister Mohammed H. el-Zayyat rejected the UNTSO reports, contending the fighting began when Israeli planes attacked Egyptian forces stationed in the areas of Zaafarana and Ain Sukhna on the Gulf of Suez while Israeli naval units were approaching the gulf's western coast.

Israeli Foreign Minister Abba Eban, in reply, requested from Zayyat "some evidence for the odious falsehood about an attack by Israeli naval forces at Sukhna and Zaafarana."

(A similar debate between the two foreign ministers had taken place earlier in the day at a General Assembly session on the conflict called at the request of Syria and Egypt. Eban had said at that time that it was "idiotic" to believe Israel would begin hostilities on Yom Kippur, "a day when there were no communications, no activity, no radio, no ability to summon our reserves, when the majority of our soldiers were in their homes or in their synagogues." Zayyat replied that "the pattern of the first attack is a familiar one for Israel. Israeli aggression is a continuation of its policy of expansionism and consolidation of its occupation in an attempt to break the will of the Arabs.")

The bitter exchanges continued Oct. 9, and Soviet Ambassador Malik walked out of the Council briefly as Israeli Ambassador Yosef Tekoah was expressing his nation's condolences for the "innocent victims" in the Israeli bombing of Damascus that day.

"I am unwilling to hear condolences from murderers and international gangsters," Malik shouted as he left, referring to reports (later disputed) that 30 Soviet citizens were killed in the raid when bombs severely damaged the Soviet cultural center in the Syrian capital.

Tekoah resumed speaking and asserted he was "not surprised that the delegate of the Soviet Union walked out of the room. His country must assume a great share of the responsibility for what has happened. The Soviet Union has identified itself with barbaric hatred and has supplied all kinds of weapons of war to the Arab states," Te-

koah charged. "If it were not for the policies and actions of the Soviet Union, the Middle East might today be in a state of peace instead of in a renewed state of suffering and bloodshed," he said. Malik returned to the room after Tekoah finished speaking.

Syrian Foreign Minister Abdel Halim Khaddam later accused the U.S. of promoting the renewed hostilities and sabotaging the work of the Security Council with what he called "the abusive use of the right of veto."

Other nations stressed the importance of ending the hostilities, with Austria calling for an immediate and unconditional cease-fire.

The majority of the Council—France, Guinea, India, Indonesia, Kenya, Panama, Peru, the Sudan, the Soviet Union and Yugoslavia—reportedly favored a cease-fire only after Israel withdrew from all Arab land occupied after the 1967 war. Britain favored an immediate cease-fire in place; Austria and Australia, like the U.S., sought a return to the old cease-fire lines and an effort for a "genuine reconciliation"; China apparently did not support a cease-fire of any kind.

***Waldheim plea to Security Council*—** Secretary General Kurt Waldheim warned the Security Council Oct. 11 that the Middle East hostilities threatened "the gravest consequences not only for the region itself, but for the world community as a whole."

In a message to Council President McIntyre, Waldheim said he understood the political obstacles to effective Council action to end the fighting. "But after more than five days of this terrible war I feel it is my duty" to urge Council members to overcome these obstacles so "the primary role of the Council can be reasserted in the interests of peace," he said.

Waldheim decried the apparent refusal by all hostile parties "to concede [their] objectives, either military or political. They would appear . . . to be embarked on a war of attrition. Who can possibly benefit from such a development? If the war continues, it will pose an increasing threat to international peace and security in a much wider context."

He said he did not have a concrete proposal, but he urged all the governments concerned to consider alternative courses to war "before it is too late."

Combatants harden positions—Despite Waldheim's warning, positions between the combatants appeared to harden at the U.N. Oct. 11.

Egyptian Foreign Minister Zayyat told the General Assembly that his country respected the U.N. Charter and U.N. resolutions, but refused "to be dictated to, subjected to long occupation, and we refuse to stay occupied."

Zayyat noted Israeli air attacks that had reportedly killed 500 persons and asserted their "result is that our morale is rising, our anger is rising, our determination to put an end to the policy of brigandage and lawlessness is increased. This will be Egypt's contribution this year to the General Assembly."

Zayyat later went before the Security Council to warn that "if these raids on civilian targets and population in our countries continue," Egypt would take appropriate counteraction.

Israeli Foreign Minister Eban said before the Security Council that "Egyptians and Syrians tell us they have the right to attack Israelis. Those who take responsibility for launching a war must take responsibility for the victims."

Eban said Israel's policy was to direct attacks at military targets, but there was "no way of selecting military targets with the assurance that civilians are not going to become casualties." He said many Israeli civilian villages had been struck by Arab ground-to-ground missiles.

Eban said peace would come only through restoration of the cease-fire lines existing before the fighting began. "We are not going to put ourselves in a position of potential suicide," he said. "You cannot overestimate the bitterness that exists in Israel as a result of the surprise attack that took place on the Day of Atonement."

Governments take sides. Reaction from other major capitals ranged from statements of neutrality and calls for a cease-fire, to support for the Arab belligerents from such traditional sympathizers as France and China.

French Foreign Minister Michel Jobert, in an apparent response to critics who wanted his government to condemn the Arabs for reopening the conflict, asked Oct. 8 whether "trying to set foot on one's own territory necessarily constituted an unexpected aggression." Libyan leader Muammar el-Qaddafi had reportedly pressured French President Georges Pompidou to support the Arab side publicly, after Premier Pierre Messmer Oct. 7 implied that Egypt and Syria had fired the first shots.

French leaders were reportedly concerned that Libya might send its French Mirage jets into the war, in violation of the 1969 jet sale contract. The French newspaper Le Monde cited reports that the 70–80 Mirages delivered so far were not equipped with long range fuel tanks, and that few spare parts had been furnished it was reported Oct. 8.

Among French opposition parties, the Socialists condemned the "outbreak of hostilities" and called for "a rapid negotiated solution," while the Communists condemned Israel.

Chinese Foreign Minister Chi Peng-fei met with Syrian, Egyptian and Palestinian envoys in Peking Oct. 9 to express China's "firm support" for the Arabs against Israel's "crimes of flagrantly launching large-scale military aggression." People's Daily said Oct. 8 Israel had acted "to realize its ambition for new territorial expansion." The Peking newspaper also condemned the Soviet Union for supporting Israel by allowing "large numbers of Soviet Jews to emigrate to Israel."

The Yugoslav government called on all "peace-loving forces" to help the Arabs recover territories occupied by Israel. Dahomey and Rwanda became the ninth and tenth black African states to sever relations with Israel Oct. 9, while Ethiopia, Liberia and Nigeria called for an Israeli withdrawal to the pre-1967 cease-fire lines.

Great Britain announced an arms embargo on the opposing sides Oct. 10 but did not indicate whether shipments would be cut off to Saudi Arabia and the Persian Gulf states. They were the only important recipients of British arms in the area but were not directly involved in the fighting. Prime Minister Edward Heath discussed with West German Chancellor Willy Brandt Oct. 7 proposals to develop a joint European Economic Community (EEC) position on restoring the cease-fire. The Italian government called Oct. 9 for urgent discussions among the nine EEC members. Italy's policy of "active equidistance" toward both sides in an attempt to promote a permanent settlement was endorsed Oct. 9 by the Italian Communist party, and reflected the views of Pope Paul VI, who appealed Oct. 10 for international mediation.

Rumania expressed concern Oct. 8 about the renewed fighting but refrained from blaming either side for initiating the action, while charging that continued Israeli occupation of "Arab territories, seized by force" was "a permanent hotbed of tension." Turkey announced a similar stand Oct. 9, proclaiming its neutrality despite a request by the Syrian and Egyptian ambassadors for "more than sympathy for our cause."

Greece announced Oct. 13 it would remain neutral in the war. Foreign Minister Christian Xanthopoulos-Palmas said Greece barred the use of its territory for any war-related action by either side.

West Germany's ruling Social Democratic party called Oct. 14 for big power guarantees for the existence of Israel as a prerequisite for peace in the Middle East.

Pope Paul VI called the war a "catastrophe" Oct. 14 and urged the Arabs and Israelis to seek an immediate peace.

Additional African nations severed diplomatic relations with Israel in a display of solidarity with the Arab countries—Tanzania Oct. 19, Malagasy Republic Oct. 20, Central African Republic Oct. 21, Ethiopia Oct. 23, Nigeria Oct. 25, Ghana and Senegal Oct. 28 and Kenya Nov. 1. Five other African nations had cut their ties with Israel since the outbreak of the war Oct. 6—Rwanda, Cameroon, Dahomey, Upper Volta and Equitorial Guinea. Togo had taken similar action Sept. 21 and Zaire Oct. 4. This brought to 20 the number of African governments that had ended ties with Israel since March 1972.

Aid to the Combatants

Other Arab states pledge action. Iraq and several other Arab states joined Syria

and Egypt in the war against Israel.

The Iraqi military command announced Oct. 10 that its air and ground forces were fighting on the Syrian and Suez fronts. A Beirut report said 18,000 Iraqi troops with 100 tanks had arrived in Syria.

(In reprisal against U S. support of Israel, Iraq Oct. 7 had announced the nationalization of two major American oil firms—Mobil and Exxon. Baghdad said the action was taken because "aggression in the Arab world necessitates directing a blow at American interests in the Arab nation.")

King Hussein placed Jordanian forces on the alert at the outset of the war Oct. 6. The decision was followed by a royal decree Oct. 10 calling up all reservists and mobilizing the country's resources for the "war effort."

Hussein was reported to be under heavy pressure by other Arab governments and his own top army officers to join Syria and Egypt by opening up an eastern front against Israel. At the same time the U.S. and other Western powers were urging Hussein to stay out of the conflict.

Jordanian forces shot down two Israeli planes that had strayed into Jordanian air space, Amman announced Oct. 8.

Financial support of the Egyptian and Syrian armed forces was pledged Oct. 7 by Col. Muammar el-Qaddafi, leader of Libya.

Tunisian President Habib Bourguiba announced Oct. 7 that his country would send troops to the battle zone but expressed doubt of victory "because I know the strength of Israel."

A Moroccan brigade sent to Syria in August reportedly was fighting on the Golan Heights front. Lebanon and South Yemen also pledged support.

Sudanese President Gaafar al-Nimeiry said Oct. 8 that his country's armed units were on their way to the battlefront. He called the conflict a "war of liberation" against Israel and urged other African and nonaligned countries to join.

Saudi Arabia announced a callup Oct. 9 of all members of its armed forces and canceled all army leaves.

Algeria said it had sent jet fighters into action on the Suez front. A small contingent of Kuwait troops stationed on the Suez Canal since 1967 had entered the fighting in the Sinai, the Kuwait government announced Oct. 10.

Soviet Communist Party General Secretary Leonid Brezhnev stressed in an Oct. 8 Moscow speech his hopes that the war would not interfere with the Soviet-U.S. detente, and called for "a just and stable peace" and "guaranteed security for all countries and peoples of the area."

But a message from Brezhnev to Algerian President Houari Boumedienne asked Algerian leaders to use "all means at their disposal and take all the required steps" to support Egypt and Syria, citing an "urgent need for the greatest possible aid and support of the progressive regimes in these countries." The letter, reported Oct. 11, did not detail assistance to be given. Lebanese newspaper An Nahar said Oct. 10 that all Arab governments received similar messages, which included claims that the U.S.S.R. was supplying arms and ammunition "to insure the entire war needs" of the Arabs.

Jordan, Saudis join war—Jordan and Saudi Arabia joined the war against Israel on the northern front, it was announced by both nations Oct. 13 and 14.

It was reported that King Hussein had decided to act after receiving an appeal Oct. 12 from Saudi King Faisal, who contributed heavily to Jordan's budget.

A Jordanian communiqué broadcast by Amman radio Oct. 13 announced that the command had started "moving a detachment of its best military formations" to Syria.

The Jordanian soldiers plus tanks were said to have crossed into Syria near the southern town of Dera. The first clash between Israeli and Jordanian troops was reported by an Amman broadcast Oct. 16. The statement said "the enemy" had been engaged at several points along the front. Meanwhile, the 250-mile Israel-Jordanian cease-fire line remained quiet.

The U.S. Oct. 13 expressed regret at Jordan's decision to enter the conflict, saying it could "serve to prolong and enlarge the war." The U.S. had urged Jordan not to become a belligerent.

The Beirut newspaper Al Nahar reported Oct. 13 that about 1,000 Saudi troops stationed in Jordan had entered Syria Oct. 12 and were engaged in fighting Israel: Saudi Arabia confirmed Oct. 14 that its forces were fighting in Syria.

Jordan's Moslem sheiks Oct. 14 called on Palestinians in the Israeli-occupied West Bank to remain away from their jobs in Israeli-owned factories and farms, saying that "by this boycott you will be contributing to striking the enemy economy."

Tunisia resumed diplomatic relations with Jordan Oct. 14 in response to Amman's entry into the war against Israel. Tunisia had severed ties with Jordan July 15.

Jordan's decision to join the war also prompted Kuwait Oct. 18 to announce resumption of a $46 million annual subsidy to the Amman government's budget. The aid had been suspended in 1970 following the Jordanian army's crushing of the Palestinian commandos in Jordan.

More combatants enter war—U.S. officials reported Oct. 18 that more combatants were entering the war against Israel, including North Korean pilots and North Vietnamese advisers.

According to the report, the North Korean airmen already had clashed with Israeli warplanes, probably south of Cairo, where about 30 of the North

Military Power of Middle East Combatants*

	Population	Army Regulars	Army Reserves	Tanks	Armored Vehicles	Combat Aircraft	Helicopters	Warships
ISRAEL	3,200,000	95,000	180,000	1,700	1,450	488	74	49
EGYPT	35,700,000	260,000	500,000	1,955	2,000	620	190	94
SYRIA	6,700,000	120,000	200,000	1,300	1,000	326	50	25
IRAQ	10,100,000	90,000	250,000	1,065	1,300	224	69	30
JORDAN	2,500,000	68,000	20,000	420	400	52	9	0

*Based on Institute for Strategic Studies, London.

Koreans had been flying defense missions for Egyptian bases for about two months.

The North Vietnamese were said to be with the Syrian forces, advising them in the use of air defenses and artillery.

U.S. and Israeli intelligence confirmed that Iraqi, Algerian and Libyan pilots and planes were now engaged in the fighting.

U.S.S.R. airlift reported. The Soviet Union maintained a press and diplomatic campaign against Isreal throughout the crisis and reportedly began a significant arms airlift to Syria and Egypt while urging noncombatant Arab states to support the war effort. Israeli pickups of U.S. military supplies at bases in the U.S. and Europe were also reported, as U.S. government sources implied that a major effort to resupply Israel was being considered.

An unusually large number of Soviet transport planes had been observed landing at Egyptian and Syrian airports Oct. 9–10. The aircraft, which had apparently taken off in Hungary, included the Antonov 22 transport, capable of carrying fighter planes and tanks. About 30 planes had landed in Syria and an undisclosed number in Egypt. The planes were believed to contain ground-to-air and antitank missiles, ammunition and possibly aircraft.

A Soviet cruiser and two guided-missile destroyers passed through the Dardanelles Oct. 10 in the first reinforcement of the Soviet Mediterranean fleet since the fighting began.

State Department spokesman Robert J. McCloskey said that if reports of a major Soviet resupply effort were true, they "would tend to put a new face on the situation," although he said he was "not in a position to confirm that any of this is taking place."

The Soviet Union replied to U.S. charges of Russian airlifts to the Arabs Oct. 14, by asserting that the U.S. was sending Israel large quantities of weapons in the war against the Arabs and was even providing Israel with American pilots.

President Tito was reported Oct. 14 to have granted the Russians the right to use Yugoslav territory for overflight and refueling in its airlift to Egypt and Syria.

The U.S. protested Belgrade's action Oct. 14.

U.S. officials reported Oct. 17 that it appeared that the Soviets had augmented its airlift with a sea lift transporting tanks and possibly some warplanes to Egypt and Syria.

Sen. Henry M. Jackson (D, Wash.) said Oct. 17 there was a possibility that some of the Soviet ships heading for the war zone were carrying Soviet troops. He said he did not think the Soviet Union would intervene in the fighting as long as it received "clear and unequivocal signals" from the U.S.

Jackson told a rally in Los Angeles Oct. 14 that the U.S. was "withholding from Israel the arms she needs to defend herself" while the Soviet Union's aid to Syria had reached "flood-like proportions." He challenged Secretary of State Henry Kissinger's Oct. 12 assertion that Soviet aid to the Arabs was at "moderate" levels.

Jackson was harsh in his attack on Soviet activities in the Middle East since 1967, which he termed "reckless and irresponsible." He accused the Soviets and Egyptians of violating a cease-fire agreement signed Aug. 7, 1970 on the very day the pact had been arranged.

"My point is very simple," he said. "We have stood by and watched while the Soviet Union has supplied the means by which this bloody war was initiated and is now being fought."

Jackson warned against U.S. support for a cease-fire that would leave Egypt in control of both sides of the Suez Canal, leaving the Soviets free to use the shipping route as a "highway" for the Soviet navy and merchant fleet.

His opposition to an in-place cease-fire settlement also was based on a belief that "Egyptian aggression must not be rewarded by diplomatic maneuvers that will enable Israel's enemies, who decided when the war would start, to decide also when the war will end," Jackson said.

French Foreign Minister Michel Jobert Oct. 18 said the U.S. and Soviet Union were prolonging the war and could bring it to a halt if they wished. Jobert made the statement in reply to opposition deputy charges in the National Assembly that France was taking the side of the Arabs in the conflict.

Soviets vow all-out aid to Arabs—The Soviet Union pledged to provide the Arabs with assistance "in every way" to recover their lands lost to Israel in 1967, according to a communique issued Oct. 15 following talks held in Moscow Oct. 14–15 between Soviet officials and an Algerian mission headed by President Houari Boumedienne.

It was not known whether Boumedienne came to Moscow as a representative of all Arab countries or whether he only represented his own country. The communique stated that the talks had been held in a "frank atmosphere," a Soviet phrase signifying disagreement. The joint statement did not specify what form of all-out assistance the Soviets would take to help the Arabs.

Soviet Premier Alexei Kosygin said later Oct. 15 that his government was interested in "the search for ways of settling the conflict in the Middle East" and in relaxing tensions in Europe. Speaking at a dinner honoring Danish Premier Anker Jorgensen, Kosygin said the Soviet Union "does not seek anything for itself . . . all our actions are aimed at helping the peoples of the Arab countries liberate their lands that were seized by Israel."

The ambassadors of Egypt, Syria, Jordan and Algeria had met with Foreign Minister Andrei A. Gromyko in Moscow Oct. 11. They thanked him for the military assistance his government was providing the Arabs.

U.S. arms sped to Israel. The U.S. announced Oct. 15 it had launched "a massive airlift" of arms to Israel the previous day to redress what it called the military imbalance brought about by an ongoing shipment of Soviet weapons to Egypt and Syria.

A Boeing 707 with Israeli markings was loaded with air-to-air missiles at the Oceana Naval Air Station at Virginia Beach, Va. Oct. 10, according to the Norfolk Ledger-Star.

Pentagon officials reported Oct. 11 that "a minor effort" had been made to speed up delivery on orders of ammunition and air-to-air missiles, but that only a few cargos were involved, all carried by Israeli planes.

Israeli officials were reported Oct. 11 to have met with the Defense Department's Security Assistance Agency. Military sources said they had not asked for immediate replacement of lost equipment, as much as a commitment to take care of future losses.

Egypt urged Saudi Arabia Oct. 9 to stop oil production at U.S.-run wells if the U.S. moved to resupply Israel. The Washington Post reported Oct. 11 that Saudi King Faisal had already warned the U.S. of such a cutoff.

In an apparent reference to the U.S. supply effort for Israel, President Nixon said Oct. 15 that Washington's policy called "for the right of every nation in the Mideast to maintain its independence and security." He said his Administration's current stance was "like the policy we followed in 1958 when Lebanon was involved; it is like the policy we followed in 1970 when Jordan was involved" in fighting the Palestinian commandos. In both cases, Nixon noted, U.S. military action was used or threatened. McCloskey later explained that Nixon did not mean the U.S. was contemplating direct intervention in the current crisis, but was merely expressing a "broad policy objective."

In addition to the competing airlifts, the U.S. and Soviet fleets were reported Oct. 16 to be massing in the Mediterranean and east Atlantic. A U.S. Defense Department spokesman said the Russians had a record 70 ships in the Mediterranean, up from the normal total of 50–60. The attack carrier John F. Kennedy, which had left Scotland Oct. 13, had been ordered to remain in the eastern Atlantic. The U.S. 6th Fleet in the Mediterranean had two attack carriers. A force of 2,000 Marines left the U.S. Oct. 16 to bolster the 6th Fleet as a result of the crisis, the Pentagon said.

In announcing the U.S. airlift decision, State Department spokesman Robert J. McCloskey said Oct. 15 that the equipment was to replace the heavy losses suffered by Israel in the war thus far. McCloskey said the Soviet airlift had begun Oct. 10 and involved about 280 flights that delivered 4,000 tons of military supplies to its two Arab allies. McCloskey said the U.S. had deferred taking action for several days in the hope that diplomatic efforts would end the fighting.

U.S. government sources said the supplies sent to Israel would include 150 M-60 tanks, 25 F-4 Phantom jets and about 50 A-4 Skyhawk light attack bombers. Israel had lost 20–25 F-4s, about 50 or more A-4s, plus some Mirage jets out of its 300-plane force.

Most of the 25 Phantom replacements were said to have arrived in Israel, having been flown by U.S. Air Force pilots across the Atlantic and Mediterranean, with refueling stops at a U.S. Air Force base in the Portuguese Azores. Spain barred the use of its bases for the refueling operations.

The first two days of the airlift was said to have brought into Israel about 500 tons of military equipment in about 30 flights. Other supplies were being sent in by ship. Other equipment reportedly on the way included air-to-air Sidewinder missiles, television-guided Walleye missiles used against ground targets and Shrike missiles, which could be used against Soviet-supplied surface-to-air missiles.

Defense Secretary James Schlesinger said Oct. 18 that the U.S. had "first attempted to tamp down the conflict" when it erupted Oct. 6. But after the U.S. had failed to "persuade the Soviets" to end their military airlift to the Arabs, the U.S. had to respond with its own shipments to Israel, Schlesinger said. This was the first time a U.S. official had publicly acknowledged that Washington had appealed to Moscow for mutual restraint in resupplying the belligerents.

Speaking to newsmen after addressing the AFL-CIO convention in Bal Harbour, Fla., Schlesinger said the U.S. would "absolutely not" send troops to fight in the Middle East. But he noted that Kissinger had said if Soviet forces intervene, the U.S. would have to review its position.

Bahrain Oct. 20 rescinded an agreement granting docking facilities to the U.S. Navy. The government said the accord was canceled after Washington ignored a warning that such action would be taken if it continued its "hostile stand against the Arab nations."

Congressmen back Israeli support—During the second week of fighting in the Middle East, members of Congress signaled the White House that they favored continued U.S. arms aid to Israel.

Four senators—Hubert Humphrey (D, Minn.), Henry Jackson (D, Wash.), Abraham Ribicoff (D, Conn.) and Jacob Javits (R, N.Y.)—introduced a Senate resolution Oct. 18 with the bipartisan support of 63 colleagues. The statement urged the Administration to continue the flow of aircraft and other equipment to Israel "essential to enable Israel to defend itself and deter further aggression."

A similar resolution was introduced in the House the same day by Democratic Leader Thomas P. O'Neill (Mass.) and 220 co-sponsors. House members also called on the Administration to provide shipments sufficient to offset Soviet supplies to the Arabs.

The Senate had passed a related measure on a voice vote Sept. 28. Approval was won for continued arms credit to Israel (without a specific ceiling) until the end of 1975 to permit purchase of 48 F-4 Phantom jets, 36 Skyhawks and other weapons. Sen. Jackson had introduced the measure as an amendment to a military procurement bill.

Despite the widespread Congressional support for arms aid to Israel, the Washington Post reported Oct. 17 that the lawmakers also were adamant in their opposition to committing U.S. troops to the fight. Should any such action be planned by the Administration, however, a wide ranging number of legislators warned President Nixon to seek prior Congressional approval.

Israel raises money in U.S. The Conference of Presidents of Major Jewish Organizations met in Washington Oct. 10 to pledge "solidarity with Israel" and voted to mobilize public support for the war cause.

(Israel's Ambassador Simcha Dinitz told the group that Israel had known of Egypt's and Syria's intentions to attack several days before clashes occurred. Israel chose not to respond, Dinitz said, because "we wanted everyone to be sure this time that Israel has done everything to prevent the war.")

The group also urged the Administration to resupply Israel with military weapons lost during the fighting.

The United Jewish Appeal of Greater New York announced Oct. 8 that $25 million in cash and pledges had been raised since Oct. 6. (The national fund raising goal was $100 million, spokesmen said.) The Israel Bond Organization said it had sold $35 million in bonds during the same three-day period.

U.S. attitudes on fighting examined—A Gallup Poll released Oct. 15 indicated that of 1,500 U.S. adults interviewed, 47% backed Israel in the current Middle East fighting, 6% favored the Arabs and 22% supported neither side. In the survey conducted Oct. 6–10, an unusually large number of persons expressed no opinion when asked, "In this trouble, are your sympathies more with Israel or more with the Arab states?" Nine of 10 persons were aware of the conflict, however.

Britons assail arms embargo. Britain's decision to embargo arms to Israel and other "battlefield" nations was denounced Oct. 15 by British political leaders.

The opposition expressed by several Labor and Conservative members of Parliament was heightened by the Conservative government's acknowledgement that it was training about a dozen Egyptian pilots in Britain to fly helicopters and was sending Scorpion light tanks to Dubai, a Persian Gulf state. A British Foreign Office spokesman said the Egyptians were already qualified pilots and were being trained to fly a new type of helicopter.

One of the critics, Michael Stewart of the Labor party, accused the government of a breach of contract for refusing spare parts for the Centurion tanks sold to Israel.

Nixon asks Congress for $2.2 billion. President Nixon asked Congress Oct. 19 for legislation to provide for $2.2 billion in military aid to Israel, including direct U.S. military grants to that country.

In a special message requesting the emergency aid, Nixon said the bill was needed to give the U.S. "essential flexibility" in its military and diplomatic moves in the Mideast crisis and to prevent a military imbalance "resulting from a large-scale resupply of Syria and Egypt by the Soviet Union."

Nixon implied that some of the funds might not be needed if U.S. efforts "to bring this conflict to a very swift and honorable conclusion" succeeded, but he said "prudent planning" required the U.S. "to prepare for a longer struggle."

U.S. arms deliveries to Israel in recent years of $300 million–$500 million a year had been on a cash or credit basis under the military sales program, but Nixon said "the magnitude of the current conflict coupled with the scale of Soviet supply activities exceed Israel's capacity" to pay. White House Deputy Press Secretary Gerald Warren said most of the $2.2 billion would be in the form of grants, with Israel paying for whatever it could.

Israel had already received shipments costing the U.S. $825 million, including transportation, since the start of hostilities, of which $300 million was in credits previously extended. The $585 million excess would be covered by the new legislation. Nixon said aid so far had included conventional munitions, air-to-air and air-to-ground missiles, artillery, crew-served and individual weapons, fighter plane ordnance, and "replacements" for tanks, aircraft and other materiel destroyed in the fighting.

The request for Israeli aid won immediate support from some congressmen, including Sens. Edmund Muskie (D, Me.), Hubert Humphrey (D, Minn.) and Edward Brooke (R, Mass.), but Rep. George Mahon (D, Tex.) said there was "no need to panic," since Nixon had authority under the 1968 Military Sales Act to sell on credit unlimited amounts of material to a friendly nation for up to 120 days. He said Congress should wait until a "calmer atmosphere" developed, in light of American concern over defense costs and the danger of nuclear war. Sen. Mark Hatfield (R, Ore.) called the message "saber rattling" which will "up the ante in this deadly arms race and lead away from a peaceful resolution."

Aid personnel sent—The State Department announced Oct. 19 that fewer than 50 U.S. Air Force personnel had been sent to Israel during the current supply effort. The men were communications and cargo handling specialists, the announcement said, and no U.S. personnel were "involved in anything remotely resembling any combat assignment." About 50 military personnel had been stationed in Israel before the war, the department said, including embassy attaches and guards.

U.S.' allies bar tie to Israel aid. The New York Times reported Oct. 24 that the U.S. aid shipments had been complicated by the refusal of almost all U.S. European allies to allow their territory or airspace to become involved. The governments of Greece, Turkey, Spain and Italy publicly took that position, and Britain was reported to have privately taken the same stand. Turkey had not publicly protested Soviet overflights of resupply aircraft for Egypt and Syria, the Times reported. The newspaper noted that U.S. military aid to Greece, Turkey and Spain had been granted, and defended in Congress, partly in expectation of cooperation in a Mideast crisis.

The West German Foreign Ministry said Oct. 25 it had told the U.S. to stop all arms shipments to Israel from German territory, to preserve West Germany's "strict neutrality."

U.S. angered at NATO role. The U.S. expressed displeasure over failure by its West European allies to cooperate with Washington at the height of the Middle East crisis. The criticism was particularly directed at the refusal by most North Atlantic Treaty Organization (NATO) members to permit the use of their territory or airspace for U.S. shipment of military supplies to Israel.

Defense Department spokesman Robert J. McCloskey said Oct. 26, "We were struck by a number of our allies going to some lengths to in effect separate publicly from us." He said the supporting of Israel in order to maintain a stable peace in the Middle East was as much in the interest of West Germany and other West European allies as of the U.S. West European behavior in the matter "raises questions as to how that action on their part can be squared with what the Europeans have often referred to as indivisibility on questions of security," McCloskey said.

Defense Secretary James R. Schlesinger said Oct. 26 that several NATO governments, particularly Bonn, were causing the Defense Department to "reflect on" previous concepts of the military alliance.

Secretary of State Henry A. Kissinger Oct. 29 was reported to have expressed "disgust" with NATO's lack of cooperation with the U.S.

McCloskey said Oct. 30 that the criticism he and Schlesinger had leveled at NATO members Oct. 26 was not confined to the U.S. supply lift to Israel. He said Washington also was dissatisfied with the allies' refusal to join the U.S. in obtaining a cease-fire at the U.N. He singled out Britain, which would not support a U.S. request to sponsor a cease-fire resolution in the Security Council in the first week of the war. A department official said Britain had sounded out Egypt that week on the possibility of a truce, but London dropped its efforts after being informed by Cairo that it was not interested.

The U.S. ambassador to NATO, Donald Rumsfeld, was reported to have called on the European allies during the first week of the conflict to curb their trade and political relations with the Soviet Union to pressure Moscow. The NATO members were said to have refused on the ground they had received no information leading them to believe that the U.S. had entered into a confrontation with Moscow.

NATO states rejected American criticism of their stand in the Middle East crisis and also complained about Washington's failure to consult with them on the U.S. military alert. British Foreign Secretary Alec Douglas-Home said Oct. 26 that his government had received "intimation" about the U.S. call-up, but said he did not feel that "consultation" was necessary since the U.S. was not proposing any specific actions to be taken by the other NATO members.

Combatants State Aims

Meir, Sadat, Hussein speak. Egypt and Israel stated their war aims in major addresses delivered by President Anwar Sadat and Premier Golda Meir Oct. 16.

Speaking to the National Assembly and the Central Committee of the Arab Socialist Union, Sadat said Egypt's objective was to recapture the Arab lands won by Israel in 1967 and not to annihilate Israel. In what he called an "Open Letter to President Nixon," the Egyptian leader proposed an immediate cease-fire if Israel accepted the principle of withdrawal from Arab territories under international supervision and an international peace conference at the United Nations, whose participants would include heads of Arab states and Palestinian leaders. He called for restoration of the rights of the Palestinians. Sadat said his country was "ready at this hour" to reopen the Suez Canal for ships of all nations.

Sadat coupled his peace plan with threats to strike at Israeli cities with rockets if Egyptian cities were bombed. He warned that Egypt's Zafir missiles were poised to "hit the very depths of Israel." The missile reportedly had a 235-mile range.

Sadat criticized the U.S. military airlift to Israel but said those shipments "will not terrify us."

(The Syrian Foreign Ministry had said Oct. 15 that Damascus would not accept a cease-fire that did not require Israel to pull its forces back to the 1967 truce line.)

In her address to the Israeli Knesset (Parliament), Premier Meir dismissed Arab peace conditions as "ridiculous." She said Israel thus far had received no proposal for a truce from "any political factor whatsoever." Asserting that the Egyptians and Syrians "have seemingly not yet been beaten enough to evince any desire for a cease-fire," Mrs. Meir said the "cease-fire will come about only when the Arab armies are defeated." She said any truce agreement must include the release of all prisoners.

Mrs. Meir announced in her address that an Israeli task force was fighting the Egyptians on the west bank of the Suez Canal.

The premier praised the U.S. for its support of Israel, but denounced the Soviet Union, Britain and France for their support of the Arabs. She said Moscow's aim was to "derive political benefits from this war." The Israeli leader said "there is reason to believe" that the Soviets were sending Egypt and Syria their experts and technicians in addition to war supplies.

Mrs. Meir called Britain's embargo on arms to both sides a "grave and disgraceful imposition" coming "at a time when we are fighting for our very life." The premier assailed France for its sale of Mirages to Libya, saying the jets were being used by Egypt as proven by the fact that some of them had been shot down by Israeli forces.

Commenting on Jordan's entry into the war, Mrs. Meir indicated that Israeli forces had not yet engaged Amman's troops on the northern front. She said, "We do not want a clash or a war with Jordan and we are still convinced that it is in Jordan's interest not to bring about another war with Israel."

At the conclusion of the debate, the Knesset adopted a resolution supporting the government's conduct of the war and condemning the "one-sided" attitude of France and Britain for their arms embargoes.

Foreign Minister Abba Eban said Oct. 17 that Sadat's proposal was "totally unacceptable." He described it as "a considerable hardening" of Cairo's "already very extreme position." Speaking with correspondents at the U.N., Eban said Israel would offer "a cease-fire for a cease-fire" with no political conditions for a halt to hostilities. He said his country was opposed to a return to the borders that had existed before the 1967 war, but was ready to make substantial concessions in any future negotiations with the Arabs that did not compromise Israel's security.

In his first public appearance since the outbreak of the war, King Hussein of Jordan Oct. 17 called for peace in the Middle East but put forth no specific plan. In a brief address to journalists in Amman, the king assailed Israel for what he termed its "intransigent, arrogant vain policy," and said his country would never be willing to "give up an inch" of its territory. He warned that even if Israel defeated the Arab forces the reverses "will be corrected—if not today or tomorrow, then in the not too distant future."

Nixon, Kissinger hold talks. U.S. efforts to bring a halt to the fighting included a continuing round of diplomatic talks with the Soviet Union, Israel and Arab states.

President Nixon discussed the prospects for peace at the White House Oct. 17 with the foreign ministers of Saudi Arabia (Omar Saqqaf), Morocco (Ahmed Tabibi Benhima), Kuwait (Sheik Saban al-Ahmad al-Jaber) and Algeria (Abdel-aziz Bouteflika).

Saqqaf, spokesman for the group, submitted a peace proposal on behalf of 18 Arab countries, but the plan was not disclosed. Arab sources said the proposal was a compromise between Egyptian President Anwar Sadat's demand for Israeli withdrawal from all Arab territories taken in 1967 and what was believed to be a U.S. suggestion for a cease-fire in place.

After the talks, Nixon said he had told the Arab mission that the U.S. wanted "a fair and just peace and peaceful settlement in the Mideast." Secretary of State Henry A. Kissinger and Assistant Secretary of State Joseph J. Sisco also participated in the discussions.

The meeting between Nixon and the four Arab foreign ministers was said to have been suggested to the President Oct. 12 by King Faisal of Saudi Arabia.

Prior to disclosure of the magnitude of the Soviet military airlift to Egypt and Syria, Secretary Kissinger had said Oct. 12 that although the U.S. did not consider the Soviet shipments "helpful," he did not believe they had reached the point of "irresponsibility" that would threaten the detente between Moscow and Washington. (Kissinger had warned Oct. 8 that Soviet "irresponsibility" in the current crisis would deal a blow to the relaxation of U.S.-Soviet tensions.) Conceding that the Soviet airlift was "substantial," Kissinger said the Soviets were now "less provocative, less incendiary, and less geared to military threats" than they were during the 1967 Middle East crisis.

Kissinger met with Israeli Foreign Minister Abba Eban Oct. 13 and reportedly informed him that the U.S. and the Soviet Union would seek a cease-fire in place on the Syrian and Egyptian fronts. Kissinger reportedly was in close contact with Soviet Ambassador Anatoly F. Dobrynin throughout the crisis.

A difference of opinion within the Nixon Administration on the Middle East crisis was reflected in statements Oct. 16 by Melvin Laird, President Nixon's domestic affairs adviser, and Kissinger's State De-partment spokesman, Robert J. Mc-Closkey. Laird said "a confrontation of sorts" existed between the U.S. and the Soviet Union. "Acts of the Soviet Union are disruptive as far as the opportunities to acquire a cease-fire are concerned," Laird said. He noted that the Administration was "concerned" about Moscow's Oct. 15 pledge that it would do all it could to help the Arabs recover their lands lost to Israel in 1967.

McCloskey stressed the ongoing U.S.-Soviet discussions to achieve a cease-fire. "We are still firmly of the belief that there is an opportunity for the great powers to find the means to end the war and a means to bring about a desirable peace in the area," he said.

Israelis Cross Suez Canal

Egyptian line breached. Israeli forces crossed to the west bank of the canal Oct. 15. The crossing was made by barge and pontoon bridges north of the Great Bitter Lake just south of the canal to cut off a possible Egyptian retreat from the east bank.

As a massive battle between Israeli and Egyptian tanks erupted on both sides of the Suez Canal Oct. 17, the Israelis reported that their bridgehead on the canal's west bank was being expanded and reinforced and that their troops on the west bank were attacking Egypt's Soviet-supplied surface-to-air missiles and other targets. More than 1,000 tanks on each side were committed to the battle, according to foreign military specialists in Cairo.

In previous fighting in the Sinai, Egypt had reported the opening of a major offensive along the entire canal front Oct. 14, claiming that its forces had occupied "large new areas of the desert in violent fighting." The military command said the Egyptians that day had destroyed 150 Israeli tanks and shot down at least 44 Israeli aircraft. Fifteen Israeli planes were said to have been shot down during attempts to bomb airfields in the Nile Delta.

A Tel Aviv communiqué Oct. 14 claimed Israeli forces had repulsed the Egyptian drive, destroyed 220 Egyptian tanks and shot down seven planes. Two of the planes downed were said by the Israelis to be French-built Mirages, apparently sent by Libya to Egypt.

(The Israeli Foreign Ministry protested Oct. 14 to the French charge d'affaires that Libyan Mirages had participated "in attacks by the Egyptian air force on Israeli targets." The French government responded to the Israeli charge by calling on Libya to provide Paris with "every clarification" of the incidents.)

The last Israeli stronghold on the Bar-Lev defense line along the canal surrendered to Egyptian forces Oct. 13. Thirty-seven Israeli defenders who had been holding out since Oct. 6 were taken prisoner under Red Cross supervision. In other developments Oct. 13, the Egyptians claimed inflicting heavy losses on Israeli armor and shooting down 16 Israeli planes and helicopters.

In reporting the crossing of the canal to the west bank Oct. 15, an Israeli military spokesman said Oct. 16 that the task force was "fairly large." In addition to the canal crossing, the Israelis launched a counteroffensive in the middle of the Egyptian lines on the Sinai.

A Tel Aviv report Oct. 18 said Israeli forces were locked in battle with the Egyptians on both sides of the canal and that since Oct. 15 the western bank spearhead had been reinforced by troops, tanks, halftracks and artillery. An Egyptian counterattack against those troops Oct. 18 had been "broken," an Israeli spokesman said. Israeli forces destroyed 110 Egyptian tanks on both sides of the waterway, and 19 Egyptian planes were downed—16 around the canal and three over the Mediterranean, according to Israeli accounts. The Israelis also claimed the shooting down of six Egyptian helicopters, some of which were carrying troops into the Sinai.

Israel had claimed the destruction of 90–100 Egyptian tanks during the first day of the battle Oct. 17. Israeli aircraft flying close support missions along the canal during the day also bombed SAM sites on the west bank and military targets near Port Said.

An Egyptian communique Oct. 18 said the fighting was "ferocious." It said the Israeli infiltration force on the west bank was under siege and was being attacked.

The Egyptians had said the previous day that the Israeli force was gone, that of the seven tanks that had crossed the canal, three were destroyed and four withdrew. The command said 15 Israeli jets and three helicopters were downed in the Oct. 18 fighting.

Israel said Oct. 19 that its forces had pushed 15 miles into Egypt, destroying artillery and missile batteries. The Tel Aviv communique also said the Israeli force on the west bank now totaled 10,000 men and 200 tanks. An Israeli spokesman said 10 Egyptian surface-to-air missiles were knocked out in the central region of the canal south of Ismailia during the fighting Oct. 19, that at least 70 Egyptian tanks were destroyed and 25 planes downed.

Israeli forces Oct. 20 pushed out in three directions from the west bank bridgehead, "enlarging and deepening" their salient, according to a Tel Aviv spokesman. Maj. Gen. Uzi Narkiss placed the Israeli penetration about 20 miles and said the road leading from Ismailia south to Suez city had been cut. Ten Egyptian planes and 60–70 Egyptian tanks were destroyed, he said. Egypt claimed 85 Israeli tanks and 56 halftracks were destroyed in the day's fighting on the western and eastern banks.

Egypt acknowledged for the first time Oct. 21 the seriousness of the Israeli west bank bridgehead but expressed confidence in the outcome. A military spokesman conceded that the Israelis had established two positions on the west bank, at Deversoir and Serapeum, north of the Great Bitter Lake.

Egyptian sources charged Oct. 21 that the U.S. was flying replacement jets for Israel into Egyptian territory at El Arish, an air base in the Sinai, about 80 miles east of the canal.

656 Israelis die in 8 days. The Israeli forces reported Oct. 14 that 656 Israelis had been killed in eight days of fighting on the Syrian and Sinai fronts. The dead included Maj. Gen. Avraham Mendler, commander of an armored division, who had been killed in the Sinai Oct. 13 when his halftrack was struck by an Egyptian shell. The Israelis did not give the number of their wounded.

(In a briefing Oct. 22, Israeli Maj. Gen. Shlomo Gazit had said that since the outbreak of fighting Oct. 6, Israeli forces had destroyed 240 Egyptian planes and more than 1,000 tanks. He placed Syrian, Iraqi and Jordanian losses on the northern front at 212 planes and 1,000 tanks.

(The U.S. Defense Department Oct. 23 estimated that total Arab casualties at 15,000 killed and wounded, with Israeli losses slightly less than 5,000. The department estimated that Arab equipment losses totaled about 450 planes and 1,900 tanks and Israeli losses at 120 planes and more than 800 tanks and armored vehicles.)

Syrian front. Israeli forces on the Syrian front Oct. 11–12 neared Sassa, about 20 miles from Damascus. Israeli troops pushed into the town Oct. 15, but the Syrians claimed they were driven out Oct. 17. The fighting during the seven-day period was marked by sharp air and armored clashes and Israeli naval attacks against Syrian ports used for the landing of Soviet supplies.

It was believed the Israelis were deliberately halting any further advance into Syria in order to concentrate their major efforts in the Sinai.

Syria claimed the downing of 35 Israeli planes Oct. 12 that attacked military bases around Damascus and other targets. The official announcement said Israeli missile boats attacking the ports of Latakia and Tartus sank three freighters belonging to the Soviet Union, Japan and Greece. Eight Israeli missile boats were sunk in the operation, according to Damascus.

(At a meeting of the U.N. Security Council Oct. 12, Soviet delegate Yakov A. Malik called the sinking of the Russian merchant ship in Tartus and other Israeli strikes on Syrian ports "barbarous" attacks. Israeli delegate Yosef Tekoah expressed regret for the sinking of civilian ships, but noted that Syria and Egypt were patrolling wide areas along their coasts, and their vessels were being engaged by the Israelis.)

In the ground fighting Oct. 12 Syria claimed the destruction of more than 40 Israeli tanks and 20 armored vehicles. Israeli troops were said to have broken through Syrian defense lines west of the Quneitra-Damascus highway, but their advance was blocked by a Syrian counterattack.

Israeli forces reported encountering Iraqi troops for the first time Oct. 12 and claimed Oct. 13 to have destroyed most of an Iraqi division in a major tank and artillery duel 12 miles inside Syria. At least 70 Iraqi tanks were said to have been destroyed. The Baghdad units involved in the day's fighting were part of a 12,000-man force committed to the fighting earlier in the week.

Israel reported that a helicopter-borne commando unit landed behind Syrian lines about 60 miles northeast of Damascus, blowing up a bridge and attacking a convoy of Iraqi forces. Israeli military spokesman Haim Herzog said Oct. 13 that half the Syrian air force had been knocked out and most of Syria's military airfields and radar defenses had been put out of action.

The Syrian command reported holding Israeli troops to a standoff in air and artillery battles on the Golan Heights Oct. 13–14. It was the first mention of clashes continuing on the heights despite an Israeli advance far beyond that sector. Israel lost 50 tanks, three artillery batteries, and five planes in the day's action. The Syrian command also reported that two Israeli ships were sunk by Syrian navy and coastal guns off Latakia.

Israeli artillery shelled Syrian positions within four miles of Damascus, a Tel Aviv spokesman reported Oct. 14. Israeli military sources said the Syrians were forming two large strong-points on the approaches to Damascus for the defense of the capital.

The destruction of the remnants of Iraqi forces was claimed by the Israeli command Oct. 15. The mop-up battle was said to have taken place on the southeast flank of the push toward Damascus. Israel claimed five Syrian jets were downed. A Syrian communique reported the downing of five Israeli aircraft.

Syrian President Hafez al-Assad conceded in a speech Oct. 15 that Israeli forces had achieved a "limited breakthrough" in his country's defenses the previous week. He said Syrian troops were now counterattacking "from new places."

Western sources in Damascus claimed that intense Syrian artillery fire Oct. 16–17 forced the Israelis to abandon Sassa, which they had occupied Oct. 15. The advance Israeli units were said to be operating in a salient around the village of Soukhatlyah, about 3–5 miles in front of the general Israeli line, now about 15 miles northeast of the 1967 truce line.

A Syrian military communiqué said Syrian and Iraqi tanks had pushed Israeli forces back from their advanced positions near Sassa Oct. 16. Another communiqué said at least 40 Israeli tanks and 30 other vehicles were destroyed by Syrian tanks and artillery on all sectors Oct. 17.

Sharp air, tank and artillery battles were fought along the Golan front Oct. 18–19, according to Damascus reports. Jordanian King Hussein visited his troops at the front Oct. 18. He said that in fighting alongside the Syrians they had "liberated new positions."

Syria announced its planes bombed an oil refinery at Haifa Oct. 20, but Israeli sources denied the attack. Syrian Deputy Premier for Economic Affairs Mohammed Naidar said the Haifa installation was bombed in retaliation for Israeli strikes on Syrian economic targets, which he said had caused more than $300 million in damage and 100 civilian casualties.

A large buildup of Syrian, Iraqi and Jordanian tanks and armored vehicles was reported Oct. 21 on the central and southern sectors.

Commandos shell Israel—Palestinian commandos were reported Oct. 13 to have been shelling Israeli towns and settlements along the Lebanese border, but causing only light casualties and little damage. The attacks, also involving ground forays, had been ordered by commando leader Yasir Arafat at the outbreak of the war in a coordinated action with Syrian forces on the northern front.

One of the principal targets of the commando assaults was the Israeli town of Kiryat Shmona, which had been struck by about 30 rockets.

More than 1,000 guerrillas were said to have responded to Arafat's call to attack Israel.

Arabs Unleash 'Oil Weapon'

Making good on a frequently reiterated warning, the Arab oil-producing countries came to the aid of the Arab combatants by first curtailing oil production and shipments and then completely embargoing oil shipments to Israel's supporters.

Arabs cut oil output. Ministers of 11 nations of the Organization of Arab Petroleum Exporting Countrties agreed in Kuwait Oct. 17 on a coordinated program of oil production and export cuts in an attempt to force a change in the Middle East policy of the U.S.

The largest producer, Saudi Arabia, announced Oct. 18 it was immediately slashing oil production by 10% and would cut off all shipments to the U.S. if it continued to supply arms to Israel and refused to "modify" its pro-Israel policy. The reduction would continue until Nov. 30, after which further reductions would be announced.

It was reported later that Saudi Arabia had actually ordered an embargo on oil shipments to the U.S., and the other Arab oil countries soon did likewise.

The Persian Gulf state of Abu Dhabi announced Oct. 18 it was stopping all oil shipments to the U.S. and would do the same to any other country that supported Israel.

The Kuwait meeting had announced that each country would reduce production by 5% each month over the previous month until Israel withdrew from the territories occupied during the 1967 war and agreed to respect the rights of Palestinian refugees, which were not defined.

The ministers' statement said the cutback was not intended to "harm the Arabs' friends," although they acknowledged some hardships would result in Europe, which they hoped would bring pressures on the U.S. to change its pro-Israel policy.

Officials in France, which had given the Arabs diplomatic support, were reported Oct. 17 to have received assurances that deliveries to France would not be affected.

The different interpretations of the decision reached in Kuwait were prompted by a reported division at the Kuwait conference, with Kuwait, Saudi Arabia and Egypt opting for a more moderate policy and Libya, Algeria and Iraq urging radical measures. Each country was apparently interpreting the conference recommendation in its own way. The other nations at the conference were Abu Dhabi, Bahrain, Dubai, Qatar and Syria.

The nations at the conference had been producing about 19.6 million barrels daily, about 40% of production in non-Communist countries. Only one million barrels of crude oil had been sold directly to the U.S., where it constituted about 6% of current daily consumption of 17.4 million barrels. But the U.S. also consumed nearly another million barrels of oil products processed in third countries from Middle Eastern crude, which would be affected if the production cut were across the board.

Saudi Arabia had been exporting over 500,000 barrels of crude a day to the U.S. A 10% cut, combined with the cessation of Abu Dhabi's daily U.S. shipments of 180,000 barrels, would cause an immediate loss to the U.S. of over 230,000 barrels, about 1.3% of consumption. Coupled with predictions that the U.S. would need increasingly large Middle East shipments to meet growing needs, the cuts were expected to have an immediate impact on the tight U.S. fuel supply situation.

The cutbacks were expected to have a far more serious effect in Europe, which filled well over half its oil needs from Arab sources, and Japan, which received 45% of its oil from Arab countries.

The New York Times reported Oct. 17 that Japanese government officials and oil company executives expressed private bitterness at the Arab moves, in light of the long-standing compliance by most Japanese firms with the economic boycott against Israel. M.A.H. Luns, Secretary General of the North Atlantic Treaty Organization (NATO) said Oct. 14 that a halt in Arab shipments of oil would "come very close to a hostile act."

Oil prices increased. The six largest Persian Gulf oil-producing countries announced in Kuwait Oct. 17 a 17% increase

in the price of their crude oil, and a 70% increase in taxes to be paid by oil companies on oil produced and sold by the companies.

Talks begun Oct. 8 between the producers and the companies in Vienna had broken down Oct. 12 after the companies refused demands for substantial revision of the 1971 Teheran agreement, which had called for limited annual price increases through 1975.

The six nations—Iran, Saudi Arabia, Iraq, Abu Dhabi, Kuwait and Qatar—accounted for over one half of non-Communist countries' oil exports. They said the "action was unrelated to the Middle East war." Iran, a neutral in the conflict, was not a participant in the curb on exports to the U.S.

The countries set a market price on their own oil of $3.65 per barrel for light crude, up from $3.12.

Arabs impose total ban against U.S. Arab oil-producing states carried out their threat to embargo all petroleum exports to the U.S. for its support of Israel.

Libya Oct. 19 ordered a complete halt in shipments of crude oil and petroleum products to the U.S. At the same time Tripoli raised the price of its oil for other importers from $4.90 to $8.25 a barrel. Libyan exports to the U.S. had totaled about 142,000 barrels a day of crude oil and indirectly 100,000 barrels of petroleum products, or about 1.4% of total U.S. consumption.

Riyadh radio announced Oct. 20 that Saudi Arabia had decided to halt all oil exports to the U.S. in view of Washington's aid to Israel.

Algeria had announced it would reduce by 10% its annual oil production, it was reported Oct. 20.

The Arab boycott of U.S. markets became total when Kuwait, Bahrain, Qatar and Dubai announced a cutoff of their supplies Oct. 21.

Action against others. Iraq retaliated Oct. 21 against the Netherlands' support of Israel by nationalizing the Dutch share of the Basra Oil Co. At the same time, Iraq denounced the Oct. 17 decision by the Organization of Arab Petroleum Exporting Countries to cut oil production. The Baghdad statement said the cutback would only harm Western Europe and Japan, which it said were friendly to the Arab cause.

Libya announced Oct. 30 it was suspending oil deliveries to the Netherlands. It was the seventh Arab country to do so.

Ahmed Abdel Meguid, Egyptian ambassador to the United Nations, warned Oct. 31 that all Arab oil for Canada (25% of Canada's oil imports) would be cut off if Canada did not take "positive steps" to change its Middle Eastern policies. These, Meguid said, were "less than neutral" and favored Israel.

Arabs widen production cuts. The Organization of Arab Petroleum Exporting Countries (OAPEC) announced Nov. 5, following a two-day meeting in Kuwait, that each of its 11 members would reduce their oil production in November to 75% of the September output, with an additional drop of 5% in December.

The 25% cutoff would include the complete embargoes already imposed on shipments to the U.S. and the Netherlands for their pro-Israel policy. The conference statement said the cutbacks would be arranged so that countries friendly to the Arab cause would not be deprived of their normal flow of oil.

The conference decided to send Saudi Petroleum Minister Sheik Ahmed Zaki al-Yamani and Algerian Industry and Power Minister Belaid Abdesselam on a tour of Western Europe to explain the organization's views and the decisions taken at the conference.

Yamani had said Nov. 4 that Saudi Arabia was "tracking down every last barrel of oil that reached the United States." He said his country had computer records on the destination of all Saudi oil shipments, including refineries in Trinidad, Puerto Rico and Canada, that shipped products to the U.S.

The 11 OAPEC nations were Abu Dhabi, Algeria, Bahrain, Dubai, Egypt, Iraq, Kuwait, Libya, Qatar, Saudi Arabia and Syria.

The Middle East Economic Survey, a Beirut publication, said Nov. 3 that Saudi Arabia had divided countries into three categories for the purpose of oil supplies: embargoed, exempt or most favored, and not exempt but not embargoed either. Among the most favored nations listed were France, Spain, Jordan, Lebanon, Malaysia, Pakistan, Tunisia and Egypt.

Arabs threaten U.S. business. The International Confederation of Arab Trade Unions called on all Arab nations Nov. 4 after a four-day meeting in Tripoli, Libya to impose a partial boycott on business dealings with the U.S., the Netherlands and other countries supporting Israel.

The delegations recommended boycotts of air and sea transportation of U.S. and Dutch firms as well as companies of other unspecified nations backing Israel, and of goods manufactured in the U.S., the Netherlands and other countries. The conference also suggested that all Arab nations sever diplomatic relations with the U.S. and the Netherlands.

Halting the Fighting

U.N. Orders Cease-Fire

The U.N. Security Council called on the belligerents Oct. 22, 1973 "to cease all firing and terminate all military activity," but two more resolutions were needed Oct. 22 and 25 to even make a start toward halting the hostilities.

First cease-fire call. The U.N. Security Council adopted the first cease-fire proposal Oct. 22. The resolution was sponsored by the U.S. and the Soviet Union and had been formulated on the basis of talks held in Moscow Oct. 20–21 between Secretary of State Henry A. Kissinger and Soviet Communist party leader Leonid Brezhnev. President Nixon had dispatched Kissinger to Moscow at the request of Brezhnev.

Meeting at the request of the U.S. and the Soviet Union, the Council went into session the night of Oct. 21 and adopted its joint resolution early Oct. 22 by a 14–0 vote, with China not participating. A three-point draft called for (1) a cease-fire in place to go into effect "no later than 12 hours" after adoption of the resolution, (2) implementation of the Council's Resolution 242, adopted at the end of the Israeli-Arab war of 1967, and (3) a start to Arab-Israeli negotiations with the objective of "establishing a just and durable peace in the Middle East."

Chinese delegate Huang Hua, charging that the U.S. and the Soviet Union sought to impose their own views on the Council, said the only resolution his country would support would be one that condemned Israel.

Israeli delegate Yosef Tekoah agreed to the truce but said his country's acceptance was conditioned on participation by all states taking part in the fighting, including the Palestinian commandos. He also demanded an exchange of all prisoners and said Southern Yemen must lift its blockade of Israeli ships in Bab al Mandeb, the strait linking the Red Sea and the Gulf of Aden.

Egyptian delegate Mohammed el-Zayyat denounced Tekoah's conditions and said they were "null and void" unless adopted by the U.S. and the Soviet Union.

The Council met again Oct. 23 at the request of Egypt, which charged that Israel had violated the cease-fire. By a 14–0 vote (China again not voting), the Council confirmed its previous call for an end to hostilities and urged both sides to return to the positions they had held when the first cease-fire went into effect. The resolution also called for U.N. observers to supervise the truce.

Tekoah denied Egyptian charges of Israeli truce violations. He accused the Egyptians instead of cease-fire breaches, citing 13 specific attacks on Israeli positions in the Sinai.

At the close of the session, Secretary General Kurt Waldheim announced that Syria would obey the cease-fire resolution adopted Oct. 22. The Syrians said their acceptance was conditional on Israeli withdrawal from the territories occupied in 1967 and on the protection "of the legitimate rights of the Palestinians."

Jordan had announced acceptance of the cease-fire Oct. 22. But an Amman communiqué said the Jordanian force fighting on the Syrian-Israeli front remained under Syrian orders and would not disband. Iraq and the Palestinian commandos Oct. 22 rejected the U.N. call for a cease-fire. A commando spokesman in Damascus, Abu Nidal, said "there is nothing to be gained by talking with Israel."

Reaction to truce proposals—Egypt announced Oct. 22 that it accepted the cease-fire resolution approved by the U.N. Security Council that day, but only on condition that Israel also adhered to it. Cairo, however, interpreted the resolution to mean that Israeli forces must withdraw immediately from the current cease-fire lines as well as from the Arab areas it had been occupying since the 1967 war.

The Egyptian statement said President Anwar Sadat had decided to obey the U.N. truce call after receiving assurances Oct. 21 from Soviet Communist party leader Leonid Brezhnev. Sadat did not say what the assurances were.

Israeli Premier Golda Meir explained her government's acceptance of the cease-fire at a special session of the Knesset (parliament) Oct. 23. She gave three reasons why her government agreed to comply: Israel "by its nature, has no wish for war, does not desire loss of life"; "the cease-fire proposal has come when our position is firm on both fronts, . . ."; "we responded to the call by the United States and its President out of appreciation and esteem for its positive policy in the Middle East at this time." Mrs. Meir warned that if Egypt "persisted in belligerent activity, we shall deem ourselves free to take any action and move called for by the situation."

Mrs. Meir reported on her meeting with U.S. Secretary of State Henry A. Kissinger, who had stopped off briefly in Israel Oct. 22 to report on the discussions he had just concluded with Soviet officials in Moscow. She said her talks with him convinced her that the U.S. did not oppose the two basic points Israel regarded as necessary for a Middle East peace. These were that peace must be achieved through direct negotiations between Israel and the Arabs and that borders must be negotiated by the parties concerned.

The Soviet Union accused Israel Oct. 23 of renewing hostilities in violation of the U.N. cease-fire resolution by attacking Egyptian military positions and "peaceful populated localities." The statement warned Israel of the "gravest consequences" if the fighting did not stop.

Israeli Foreign Minister Abba Eban said Oct. 24 his government would continue to seek "an early beginning" of peace negotiations with the Arabs. He saw no breakdown in the truce and emphasized that the current cease-fire lines were "not boundaries—the boundaries will be negotiated later."

Eban said priority in any negotiations with the Arabs would be the immediate and unconditional return of war prisoners. He said as of Oct. 24 Israel held 1,300 captives—988 Egyptians, 295 Syrians, 12 Iraqis and five Moroccans. About 360 Israelis were believed missing and presumed captured.

China charged Oct. 24 that the joint U.S.-Soviet cease-fire resolution was an attempt to "put out the blazing fire of this just war." The statement asserted that "in order to continue their scramble for hegemony in the Middle East, the two superpowers are nakedly pursuing big-power politics and imposing a new 'no war, no peace' situation on the people of the Arab countries."

The Soviet Union Oct. 24 denied Chinese accusations and said Peking was seeking to undermine Moscow's relations with the Arab nations. The statement was in the form of a commentary by an analyst for the Soviet news agency Tass, Yuri Kornilov. He said China's refusal to support the U.S.-Soviet resolution at the U.N. showed that Peking was "not interested in the settlement of the Middle East conflict." The statement scorned China for not giving the Arabs "any real aid" since the outbreak of the war.

Peace force approved. The U.N. Security Council approved a resolution Oct. 25 establishing a U.N. peace-keeping force to insure implementation of the cease-fire in the Middle East.

The vote on the latest resolution was 14–0, with China not voting. The force was to exclude troops of the five permanent Council members and was initially to be composed of soldiers of Austria, Finland and Sweden.

Adoption of the draft followed a request to the Council by Egypt Oct. 24 that it send U.S. and Soviet troops to the Middle East to compel Israel to withdraw its forces to the Sinai positions it had occupied Oct. 22 when the first truce went into effect. The appeal, also sent by President Anwar Sadat to President Nixon and Soviet Communist party chairman Leonid Brezhnev, was rejected outright by the U.S.

Soviet delegate Yakov A. Malik declared at the Oct. 24 session that Cairo's request for troops from the two superpowers was justified, but he refused to commit his government.

An original proposal submitted earlier Oct. 25 by eight non-permanent Council members had called for a U.N. peace-keeping team that did not exclude the five permanent members—the U.S., Soviet Union, China, France and Britain. U.S. objections to this aspect of the resolution forced a revision.

The resolution also empowered Secretary General Kurt Waldheim to increase the number of U.N. military observers on both sides in the Middle East. They currently totaled 259. Waldheim also announced that he was transferring to Egypt 900 troops from Austria, Finland and Sweden with the U.N. peace-keeping force in Cyprus. He appointed Maj. Gen. Ensio P. H. Siilasvuo of Finland as interim commander.

The Council's Oct. 24–25 meeting was held at Egypt's request to take up its renewed charges of Israeli truce violations. Soviet delegate Malik called on the U.S. Oct. 24 "to bring Israel to order" and urged U.N. member nations to sever diplomatic relations with Israel.

Israeli delegate Yosef Tekoah denied the charges of Israeli truce violations, saying that Egyptian forces had opened fire earlier Oct. 24 but that fighting now

---

U.N. Resolutions on Cease-Fire, Emergency Force

Oct. 22 resolution

The Security Council,

1. Calls upon all parties to the present fighting to cease all firing and terminate all military activity immediately, no later than 12 hours after the moment of the adoption of this decision in the positions they now occupy;

2. Calls upon the parties concerned to start immediately after the cease-fire the implementation of Security Council Resolution 242 in all of its parts;

3. Decides that immediately and concurrently with the cease-fire, negotiations start between the parties concerned under appropriate auspices aimed at establishing a just and durable peace in the Middle East.

Oct. 23 resolution

The Security Council, referring to its resolution 338 (1973) of 22 October 1973,

1. Confirms its decision on an immediate cessation of all kinds of firing and of all military action, and urges that the forces be returned to the positions they occupied at the moment the cease-fire became effective.

2. Requests the Secretary General to take measures for immediate dispatch of United Nations observers to supervise the observance of the cease-fire between the forces of Israel and the Arab Republic of Egypt, using for this purpose the personnel of the United Nations now in the Middle East and first of all the personnel now in Cairo.

Oct. 25 resolution

The Security Council,

Recalling its Resolutions 338 (1973) of 22 October, 1973, and 339 (1973) of 23 October, 1973,

Noting with regret the reported repeated violations of the cease-fire in noncompliance with Resolutions 338 (1973) and 339 (1973),

Noting with concern from the Secretary General's report that the United Nations military observers have not yet been enabled to place themselves on both sides of the cease-fire line,

1. Demands that immediate and complete cease-fire be observed and that the parties return to the positions occupied by them at 16:50 hours G.M.T. on 22 October, 1973;

2. Requests the Secretary General, as an immediate step, to increase the number of United Nations military observers on both sides;

3. Decides to set up immediately under its authority a United Nations emergency force to be composed of personnel drawn from states members of the United Nations except permanent members of the Security Council, and requests the Secretary General to report within 24 hours on the steps taken to this effect;

4. Requests the Secretary General to report to the Council on an urgent and continuing basis on the state of implementation of this resolution as well as Resolutions 338 (1973) and 339 (1973);

5. Requests all member states to extend their full cooperation to the United Nations in the implementation of this resolution as well as Resolutions 338 (1973) and 339 (1973).

had subsided for the first time since war broke out Oct. 6.

Syria accepts cease-fire. Syrian President Hafez al-Assad announced Oct. 29 that he had accepted the cease-fire Oct. 24 on the basis of Soviet "guarantees" that Israel would withdraw from all occupied Arab territories and recognize the rights of the Palestinian people. Assad warned that if these conditions were not attained through "the new political stage of the battle," Syria would "resume the armed struggle."

(A Baghdad government press report Oct. 29 said Iraq had decided to withdraw its troops from the Egyptian and Syrian fronts. The statement said the decision had been made in view of the acceptance by Syria and Egypt of the U.N. Security Council cease-fire, which Iraq had rejected.)

U.S. Forces on Alert

Soviet action countered. American military forces were placed on a "precautionary alert" Oct. 25 at key bases in the U.S. and abroad. The action was taken in response to a reported alert of Soviet airborne troops and possible Soviet plans to unilaterally send troops into the Middle East war zone under the guise of a peace-keeping force.

Secretary of State Henry A. Kissinger explained the U.S. emergency move in a news conference in Washington.

The alert order was issued from the Defense Department's National Military Command Center and signed by Adm. Thomas H. Moorer, chairman of the Joint Chiefs of Staff, acting under instructions of Defense Secretary James R. Schlesinger. The decision was made by the National Security Council, whose members included President Nixon, Kissinger and Schlesinger.

U.S. suspicions of Moscow's intentions in the Middle East crisis were said to have been aroused by a report, according to American intelligence sources, that 40,-000 Soviet airborne troops had been transferred to staging areas in the southern part of the Soviet Union in the past week for possible airlift to Egypt.

Information also was said to have been received that an unusually large number of Soviet AN-22 transport planes were landing at Egyptian airports. It was not certain whether they were carrying Soviet troops or military supplies. U.S. officials said the Administration also was concerned about the presence of about 6,000 Soviet "naval infantrymen" on ships in the Mediterranean. Some of those vessels were already in Syrian ports, it was believed.

U.S. officials stressed that the precautionary alert did not put the country on a war footing. It provided for cancellation of leaves, the return of men to their units and preparation to move out if necessary. Among the actions taken: 50–60 B-52 heavy bombers were ordered to return from their base at Guam to the U.S. and a third U.S. attack carrier, the John F. Kennedy, was ordered into the Mediterranean from its post in the eastern Atlantic.

Kissinger explains U.S. action—Secretary of State Henry A. Kissinger told an Oct. 25 news conference in Washington that the U.S. had called the military alert as a "precautionary step" in response to evidence that the Soviet Union may have intended to intervene unilaterally in the Middle East.

Kissinger said the "ambiguity" of certain Soviet "actions and communications and certain readiness measures that were observed" led the President to decide to "make clear our attitude toward unilateral steps." He said the evidence that led to the decision would be made available "from the conclusion of the present diplomatic efforts." A questioner cited a report by Sen. Henry Jackson (D, Wash.) that the Soviet Union had delivered a "brutal, tough" note to the U.S. warning of unilateral action. Kissinger said Jackson "does not participate in our deliberations," and he refused to discuss the content of diplomatic communications. But he said the Administration had been "puzzled by the behavior of some Soviet representatives in the discussions that took place," possibly referring to a meeting with Soviet Ambassador Anatoly Dobrynin Oct. 24.

Kissinger said the U.S. did "not now consider" itself "in a confrontation with the Soviet Union" and was "not aware of any Soviet forces that may have been introduced into Egypt." He reiterated his view that the nuclear superpowers had a special "responsibility" to keep confrontations "within bounds that do not threaten civilized life." He said the latest U.S. move derived from this view and from a resolve to "resist any attempt to exploit a policy of detente to weaken our alliances." He said the introduction of great power forces would either "transplant the great power rivalry into the Middle East" or "impose a military condominium."

Kissinger summarized Soviet-American developments throughout the latest crisis. He said the U.S. had tried "to bring about a moderation in the level of outside supplies that was introduced into the area" in the first week of the fighting and had "attempted to work with the Soviet Union on a cease-fire resolution." He said the U.S. still aimed to use the present situation to work out a settlement, since "the chances for peace in the Middle East are quite promising."

The secretary of state implied that the U.S. would be willing to pressure Israel to make major concessions in any negotiations that might occur. He said "the conditions that produced this war were clearly intolerable to the Arab nations " and that the U.S. was prepared "to lend its diplomatic weight" both "bilaterally" and "unilaterally" to seek a solution "just to all sides." He said Israel, in the Security Council resolution 338, had "been given an opportunity for the negotiations it has sought for all of its existence, and it must be ready for the just and durable peace."

(Time magazine reported in its Nov. 5 issue that the note described by Jackson, sent by Soviet Communist leader Leonid I. Brezhnev, had threatened Soviet "destruction of the state of Israel" if Israel did not stop its advance. But the New York Times cited a U.S. State Department spokesman as denying Oct. 28 that the Brezhnev letter had made any specific reference to Israel.)

Kissinger said a question, asking whether the military alert had been de-signed with domestic political considerations in mind, was "a symptom of what is happening to our country" and denied the charge. He implied that "crises of authority" in the U.S. "for a period of months" may have influenced the Soviet Union to gamble on a unilateral Mideast intervention. He insisted that the alert decision had been made unanimously by the National Security Council.

Soviets dispute U.S. on action. Communist party General Secretary Leonid I. Brezhnev accused the U.S. Oct. 26 of the "artificial drumming up" of a crisis to justify its worldwide military alert.

In an address to the World Peace Congress in Moscow, Brezhnev assailed "fantastic rumors" of Soviet plans for unilateral military intervention in the crisis. The Soviet leader, however, did not deny outright that his country had taken precautionary action of its own. He said "events of the last few days forced us to be vigilant. Urgent and decisive measures are necessary to guarantee the fulfillment of the [U.N. Security Council] cease-fire resolution and the withdrawal" of Israeli troops on the Suez front from previously held positions.

Brezhnev disclosed that the U.S.S.R. had sent "representatives" to the Middle East to observe the cease-fire and expressed hope that the U.S. would do the same.

Brezhnev said Israel had defied the Security Council's resolution to withdraw to the Oct. 22 positions when the Council issued its first truce call. He implied that U.S. arms shipment and support was responsible for the Israeli action.

Brezhnev repeated Moscow's desire for a just and stable peace in the Middle East. He said his government was prepared to offer guarantees for the final borders and the security of all states in the area, including Israel.

Despite his criticism of the U.S. role in the latest Middle East crisis, Brezhnev reaffirmed the Soviety policy of maintaining a detente with Washington.

President Nixon's explanation of the U.S. alert at a news conference Oct. 26 was dismissed four hours later by the Soviet government as "absurd." The Soviet statement, published by the news agency

Tass October 27, said: The U.S. alert, "which by no means promoted the relaxation of international tensions, was obviously taken in an attempt to intimidate the Soviet Union." "It is appropriate to tell the initiators of this step that they picked the wrong address."

Nixon explains. President Nixon, at a televised news conference, explained his administration's actions.

Nixon said his personal relationship with Soviet leader Leonid I. Brezhnev was instrumental in defusing the Middle East crisis and asserted that "the outlook for a permanent peace is the best that it has been in 20 years."

Nixon said that the cease-fire was "holding" and that the U.S. would send "observers" to the scene if the U.N. secretary general requested.

He spoke of the "very significant and potentially explosive crisis" that had developed three days before. The U.S. had obtained information, Nixon said, "which led us to believe that the Soviet Union was planning to send a very substantial" military force to the Mideast. He then had ordered the precautionary world-wide military alert for U.S. forces "to indicate to the Soviet Union that we could not accept any unilateral move on their part to move military forces into the Mideast." He had sent an "urgent message" to Brezhnev, Nixon said, not to take that course but to help support the U.N. resolution to exclude major powers from participating in a peace-keeping force.

Nixon's optimism about a lasting peace was based on the agreement by the Soviet Union and the U.S. to participate "in trying to expedite the talks between the parties involved." This did not mean that the two major powers "will impose a settlement," he said, but "that we will use our influence with the nations in the area to expedite a settlement."

The week's developments, Nixon believed, pointed up that the Soviet Union and the U.S. were in agreement that it was "not in their interest to have a confrontation" in the Middle East despite their "admittedly" different objectives in the area.

The President said there were "enormous incentives" for the major powers to find a solution, "to get the ne-

gotiating track moving again" but this time "to a conclusion—not simply a temporary truce but a permanent peace."

During the question period, Nixon described the tenor of the recent exchange of messages with Brezhnev as "very firm" and leaving "very little to the imagination" on both sides. "And it's because he and I know each other," he added, "and it's because we have had this personal contact that notes exchanged in that way result in a settlement rather than a confrontation."

He said the upcoming negotiating would be "very, very tough" but "all parties are going to approach this problem of trying to reach a settlement with a more sober and a more determined attitude than ever before." None of the Mideast countries involved could "afford another war" and both the Soviet Union and the U.S., Nixon said, "now realize that we cannot allow our differences in the Mideast to jeopardize even greater interests that we have, for example, in continuing a detente in Europe. . . ." Nixon suggested "that with all of the criticism of detente," without it, "we might have had a major conflict in the Middle East."

The President said the potential of an oil cutoff gave urgency to his settlement effort. He referred to a previous U.S. statement "that raised a little difficulty in Europe to the effect that our European friends hadn't been as cooperative as they might've been in attempting to help us work out" the settlement. "I can only say on that score," he continued, "that Europe, which gets 80% of its oil from the Mideast, would have frozen to death this winter unless there'd been a settlement. And Japan, of course, is in the same position."

U.S. ends military alert. The U.S. ended its worldwide military alert Oct. 31. The Defense Department announced that the nearly 2.2 million troops of the U.S. European command and the sailors of the Atlantic Fleet had returned to "normal status." The 30,000 men of the Mediterranean 6th Fleet, however, remained on heightened alert because of the continuing tensions in the Middle East.

Defense Department spokesman Jerry W. Friedheim said it appeared that the 50,-000 Soviet troops alerted in the Soviet

Union and Eastern Europe had returned to normal duties.

The U.S. had moved a naval task force into the Indian Ocean Oct. 30. Its destination was the Persian Gulf. In reporting the decision Oct. 29, the Defense Department at first had said it was in response to a Soviet naval buildup in the Mediterranean and the alert of U.S. troops. Several hours later the department said there was no connection, that the action was taken only "to demonstrate we can operate" in the Indian Ocean.

Alert questioned in U.S. Several major American newspapers and news magazines reported public suspicion that the U.S. military alert had been influenced by the political "fire storm" of reaction resulting from the widening Watergate scandal.

This view was rejected by Congressional leaders Oct. 25, immediately after the alert was ordered, although many were reported to have expressed reservations privately.

Newsweek, in its Nov. 5 issue, suggested that the President's "flourish of crisis diplomacy" was a device to divert attention from his domestic political troubles. According to Newsweek, an unnamed Administration aide said that "we had a problem and we decided to make the most of it."

Time's Nov. 5 issue questioned "whether the alert scare [was] necessary." After citing the doubts of "some military experts" that Soviet actions toward the Middle East warranted the military response ordered by the President, Time concluded that "perhaps some less dramatic action might have ended the crisis."

The Washington Post reported Oct. 26 that there was bipartisan support for the President's warning to the Soviets "despite" privately expressed reservations and an "undercurrent of suspicion that the President might have escalated the crisis. . . . to . . . take people's minds off his domestic problems."

Battlefield Developments

Egyptians encircled at Suez. Israeli forces on the west bank of the Suez Canal, reinforced, by Oct. 23 were reported to have cut off Egypt's 20,000-man III Corps on the southern end of the east bank of the waterway. The Israelis' thrust placed them about 20–25 miles inside Egypt and about 30 miles from Cairo. In addition to the isolated Egyptian salient, another Egyptian force, estimated at about 60,000 men, was on the east bank to the north and was cut off from the III Corps.

Israel announced Oct. 25 that it planned to supply plasma to the trapped Egyptian troops through the Red Cross and said the men were in no immediate danger of dying of thirst or hunger. Israel had cut the water pipelines to the eastern bank.

A foreign policy adviser to President Anwar Sadat, Ashraf Ghorbal, accused Israel Oct. 25 of continued violation of the cease-fire and of cutting the vital road from Cairo to Suez city at the southern end of the canal. He asserted that "Israel is cheating on the cease-fire and it is a shame that the United States is helping it to cheat."

In the fighting, the trapped Egyptian force attempted to battle its way out of the encirclement Oct. 24 but was beaten back by the Israelis and lost 15 MiGs, according to Israeli accounts.

The clash was one of several sporadic outbreaks that had occurred since the first cease-fire officially went into effect at 6.52 p.m. Oct. 22, 12 hours after the U.N. Security Council approved a resolution calling an end to hostilities.

An Egyptian communiqué said Oct. 24 that an Israeli attempt to storm the city of Suez on the east bank was thrown back with a loss of 13 tanks. The communiqué conceded that Israel controlled a 4.3-mile "gap" north of the Great Bitter Lake area. The statement alleged that the Israelis had "taken advantage" of the Oct. 22 and 24 cease-fires to "spread southwards under cover of darkness from the bridgehead areas north of the Great Bitter Lake." The communiqué discounted Israeli claims that it held "475 square miles of Egyptian territory on the west bank." Egypt contended that it held 1,158 square miles on the east bank, extending 120 miles from north to south, with the penetration varying from 7–10 miles.

The Israelis claimed the capture Oct. 24 of Adabiya, 10 miles south of Suez. This placed their salient about 30 miles inside Egypt, controlling territory from the outskirts of Ismailia in the north to Adabiya to the south—about half the length of the Suez Canal.

Syrian front fighting abates. Unlike the Suez front, fighting on the northern sector in Syria virtually came to a halt following Damascus' acceptance of the U.N. cease-fire resolution Oct. 24. Sporadic clashes had continued after the first truce Oct. 22, but by Oct. 25 military activity had practically stopped, except for occasional artillery exchanges.

Prior to the Syrian agreement to the truce, a Damascus military communiqué earlier Oct. 24 said 11 Israeli jets had been downed Oct. 23 and that 60 other planes were driven off following an attempt to bomb an air base and civilian targets near the capital.

Fighting on Mt. Hermon abated Oct. 23 after Israeli forces dislodged Palestinian and Syrian troops from two observation posts seized by the Syrians in the early days of the war. The Israelis then pushed further northward on the slope, beyond the 1967 cease-fire line.

In fighting prior to the U,N. truce calls, Israeli and Syrian planes clashed between Mt. Hermon and Damascus Oct. 21, with the Syrians claiming destruction of 11 Israeli jets. The dogfights were coupled with heavy ground fighting in the Mt. Hermon sector. The communique said Syrian artillery Oct. 20–21 destroyed or silenced nine Israeli artillery batteries, a rocket base and three observation posts.

Truce Progress

Expanded U.N. truce force approved. The United Nations Security Council Oct. 27 approved, by a 14-0 vote, the establishment of a 7,000-man U.N. peacekeeping force to be stationed as a buffer between Israeli and Egyptian troops in the Sinai. The first contingent of 900 U.N. officers and men already had arrived in Egypt on the basis of an earlier Council resolution approved Oct. 25.

The 7,000-man force had been proposed by Secretary General Kurt Waldheim at an emergency session of the Council Oct. 26. The meeting had been requested by Egypt to protest what it called continued Israeli violations of the cease-fire. Egyptian delegate Mohammed H. el-Zayyat said the 20,000 men of the Egyptian III Corps trapped on the east bank of the Suez Canal were being pressured by Israeli forces "into surrender or death of thirst or hunger." Israeli delegate Yosef Tekoah replied that "it is natural for an encircled army to try to break out. However, it surely cannot expect the Israeli forces not to return fire."

The U.N. force was to operate for an initial period of six months at a cost of $30 million to be shared by all U.N. members. China did not participate in the vote approving the truce unit and served notice it would not pay for its upkeep.

Chief delegates John A. Scali of the U.S. and Yakov A. Malik of the Soviet Union had engaged in a sharp exchange on interpretation of the authority of the peace force prior to the balloting. Malik insisted that the Council, in which his country had a veto, must control both the secretary general's peace-keeping activities and the broad operations of the U.N. observers. He also wanted the force to include members of the Warsaw Pact nations. Scali demanded greater autonomy for the observer force and opposed inclusion of Soviet bloc troops.

A spokesman for the Soviet delegation, Nikolai N. Loginov, said Oct. 29 that his government would share the cost of the U.N. peace-keeping force as long as it considered the observers to be acting in a lawful and legitimate manner. He emphasized, however, that Moscow would continue to regard the force as legitimate only if its operations were carried out under Council authority.

Meanwhile, the cease-fire on the Suez front was generally holding except for two Egyptian violations reported by the Israelis. A Tel Aviv communique said III Corps soldiers attempted Oct. 26 to bridge the canal and cross to the west bank but were repulsed after several hours of fighting. Both sides exchanged heavy artillery fire, and Israeli jets struck at Egyptian positions.

In another action Oct. 26, a Liberian-flag tanker sailing from the Israeli port of Elath was damaged by an Egyptian mine in the Gulf of Suez. Two crewmen, reportedly Israelis, were wounded.

In the second engagement, Israeli forces claimed they had downed three Egyptian helicopters on the east bank of the canal in the III Corps vicinity Oct. 28. The aircraft were shot down over Israeli positions in the Ras Masala sector—two by Israeli planes and the third by ground fire, according to a Tel Aviv communiqué.

More nations join UNEF. The United Nations Emergency Force (UNEF) created to prevent a renewal of hostilities between Israel and the Arabs was further expanded with the inclusion of seven nations to join the four already represented in the force—Austria, Finland, Ireland and Sweden.

Canada Oct. 28 accepted a request from Secretary General Kurt Waldheim to provide logistic support for UNEF.

The U.S. Nov. 2 endorsed a Security Council compromise to include Poland in a similar logistic role. The agreement also authorized five other nations to provide geographic balance on the peacekeeping contingent. They were Ghana, Indonesia, Nepal, Panama and Peru. Fourteen of the 15 Council members accepted the accord. China dissociated itself from the agreement, charging that UNEF was a U.S.-Soviet plot to promote their influence in the region.

The acceptance of Canada and Poland was the result of a compromise arranged by Yugoslavia, India and six smaller nations on the Council. The U.S. and the Soviet Union had been in sharp dispute the previous five days over the geographical distribution of the members of the force. Soviet delegate Yakov A. Malik at first had accepted Canada's membership, agreeing to Waldheim's suggestion that Ottawa's forces be limited to the less politically sensitive task of logistics, rather than taking an active part by patrolling or observing. Malik later made his acceptance of Canada conditional on the inclusion of a Warsaw Pact nation in UNEF to counterbalance the presence of a North Atlantic Treaty Organization (NATO) member on the force. U.S. chief delegate John A. Scali had opposed the idea of a

Warsaw Pact state in UNEF but later dropped his objections following consultations in Washington between U.S. officials and Soviet Ambassador Anatoly F. Dobrynin. Scali also withdrew his support of Israel's position that it would oppose the inclusion of any nation in UNEF that did not have diplomatic relations with Jerusalem.

Waldheim was reported Nov. 6 to have agreed to accept a U.S.-Soviet offer to provide 36 men each for the U.N. Truce Supervision Organization (UNTSO) to observe the cease-fire in the Middle East. Waldheim was authorized under a Security Council resolution of Oct. 25 to expand UNTSO. The U.S. had eight men on the force, which had been created to report truce violations on the Arab-Israeli borders. UNTSO men were to serve alongside UNEF troops.

A U.N. liaison officer with the Egyptian government in Cairo, Col. Ake Bendrik of Sweden, was relieved of his post at Waldheim's request because of statements he had made that angered Egypt and Israel, it was reported Nov. 1. Bendrik had aroused Cairo's indignation when he told a news briefing Oct. 29 that UNEF did not have the means of determining where Egyptian and Israeli positions were Oct. 22 when the truce went into effect. Egypt had been demanding that Israel withdraw to the Oct. 22 lines, which would reduce Israel's salient on the west bank of the Suez Canal and relieve the plight of the trapped Egyptian III Corps on the east bank. Bendrik later admitted that the U.N. force was under a mandate to determine the Oct. 22 lines.

Bendrik reportedly antagonized the Israelis by telling a news briefing that their forces were not in Suez city on the west bank. This statement was regarded as a diplomatic effort to avoid taking sides between Israel's claims that its forces were in the city, and Egypt's contentions that its forces were in complete control of Suez city.

Trapped Egyptian forces supplied. The Egyptian III Corps trapped on the east bank of the Suez Canal began receiving relief supplies Oct. 29 with Israeli permission. The first 30 of 125 trucks carrying food, water and medical supplies were driven by U.N. personnel from Cairo to Suez city, and from there the cargo was transshipped across the waterway on Egyptian boats and barges.

Meanwhile, Israel and Egypt became embroiled in a dispute over the exchange of war prisoners. Egypt conditioned the return of the captives on the pullback of Israeli forces to the canal's west bank cease-fire lines of Oct. 22, while Israel linked the resupply of the trapped III Corps to the freeing of Israeli POWs.

The relief of the Egyptian force had been worked out in direct negotiations Oct. 28 between Israeli and Egyptian military officers under U.N. auspices, the first such meeting between the two sides in 17 years. The discussions, also dealing with the general aspects of the cease-fire, were conducted in Israeli-occupied territory on the west bank. Two meetings were held—one between Israeli Gen. Aharon Yariv and an unidentified Egyptian general; a second meeting was held later between Lt. Gen. Haim Bar-Lev, former Israeli chief of staff, and Brig. Gen. Bashir Sherif.

The plan to relieve the III Corps had been advanced by U.S. Secretary of State Henry A. Kissinger. American officials said he had made direct contacts Oct. 26 "with the governments involved, including Israel, Egypt and the Soviet Union."

Israeli officials said they were reluctant to alleviate the plight of the III Corps but agreed only after heavy diplomatic pressure by the U.S. American authorities were said to have transmitted a warning to the Israelis Oct. 26 that unless the Egyptian soldiers were given relief, the Soviet Union might intervene militarily to rescue the force.

Defense Minister Moshe Dayan told the Israeli Parliament Oct. 30 that his government's agreement to permit food and water to be sent to the Egyptian soldiers "was not a humanitarian gesture." He said Israel had yielded under a threat of losing vital U.S. arms supplies.

Dayan was replying to opposition criticism for permitting the Egyptians to be resupplied without insisting that Cairo agree first to an exchange of prisoners.

Wounded POWs to be exchanged. Israel and Egypt agreed Oct. 30 on the exchange of wounded prisoners "as soon as feasible." The arrangement, worked out in

meetings on the west bank of the Suez Canal between Maj. Gen. Aharon Yariv and senior Egyptian officers, also provided for Egyptian submission to the International Committee of the Red Cross (ICRC) of a list of Israeli POWs they held. Israel already had given the ICRC a list of Arab prisoners it said it held—6,000 Egyptians, 300 Syrians, 15 Iraqis and a number of Moroccans. The Israeli-Egyptian accord also provided for the release of about 10 Israelis captured by the Egyptians in the 1967 war.

The Israeli diplomatic mission in Geneva received from the ICRC Oct. 31 an Egyptian list of 39 Israeli POWs. A previous Egyptian list handed the Israelis Oct. 16 contained 46 names. Israel had estimated that about 450 Israelis were in Arab captivity—350 in Egypt and 100 in Syria.

In related developments: The Egyptian government had offered Oct. 30 to release all Israeli prisoners "only when Israeli forces returned to the Oct. 22 cease-fire line." This was regarded as a softening of Cairo's position, since previously it had insisted that no POWs would be returned until a final peace settlement was negotiated.

Israeli officials had said Oct. 29 that continuation of the cease-fire was contingent on the early identification and release of Israeli prisoners. The Israelis said they had been in contact with "the highest levels" of the U.S. government to get American help to secure the release of the captives.

The Soviet Union Oct. 29 prevented the 15-member U.N. Security Council from asking Egypt, Syria and Israel to cooperate with the Red Cross on prisoners. Fourteen Council members agreed to issue the appeal to the parties in the dispute in the name of Secretary General Kurt Waldheim and Sir Laurance McIntrye, Council president for October. The matter was dropped after Soviet delegate Yakov Malik reportedly had objected on the grounds that the prisoner issue must be linked to the withdrawal of Israeli forces to the Oct. 22 lines.

In a related development, Israel announced Nov. 5 it had agreed with Egypt on the exchange of 44 wounded Israeli prisoners for more than 400 wounded Egyptians. The communiqué said, however, that the Egyptians "continue to delay the implementation of the agreement." It said only one wounded Israeli had been returned.

Syria, which had thus far refused to discuss the prisoner issue with Israel, accused Israel Oct. 31 of violating the 1949 Geneva Convention on the protection of war victims. Damascus said unless Israel complied with the agreement it would not submit lists of Israeli captives. Syrian Deputy Foreign Minister Raphael Abdul Ghani said Israel must return Syrians expelled from villages occupied during the recent fighting and must return the bodies of Syrians killed.

Israel charges POW atrocities. The Israeli army radio announced Nov. 4 that Syrian troops had killed 12 Israeli prisoners of war on the northern Golan Heights front. The broadcast said the bodies of the men had been found tied hand and foot on the battlefield in a bunker in the Khushniya area of the heights.

Israel gave the International Red Cross documents and photographs relating to the alleged atrocities.

Israel's chief U.N. delegate, Yosef Tekoah, told a rally in New York Nov. 5 that "our forces found in two places on the Syrian front Israeli soldiers killed, their hands tied and their eyes covered by their captors." Tekoah said he also had received reports of Israeli soldiers shot after capture and of others displayed on television and "forced to be photographed in humiliating positions."

Sinai, Syria truce violations. Violations of the cease-fire on the Sinai and Syrian fronts were reported by the Israelis and Arabs.

Israel claimed Egyptian forces attacked Israeli positions along the east bank of the Suez Canal Oct. 31–Nov. 1. Six soldiers of the trapped Egyptian III Corps were killed in two separate attacks on Israeli positions Oct. 31. The Egyptians threatened Nov. 1 to break through Israeli lines and move deeper into the Sinai but were driven back by Israeli troops, artillery and tanks, Tel Aviv reported.

An attempt by the III Corps Nov. 3 to bridge the canal for a crossing to the west bank between Suez city and the Bitter Lakes was stopped by Israeli counterat-

tacks. The attempted thrust precipitated a three hour exchange of artillery, mortar and small-arms fire. Another Israeli communiqué said the Egyptians also had tried unsuccessfully to establish a new forward line in the Gidi Pass region of the Sinai.

Three exchanges of fire erupted Nov. 4 on the western bank of the canal south of Ismailia, at a point northwest of the Ismailia-Cairo highway and at the southernmost end of the III Corps lines on the east bank near Ayur, according to the Israelis.

On the northern front, Syria charged that the Israelis had violated the truce Nov. 6–7. In the first outbreak of fighting since the cease-fire, Israeli planes fired missiles at Syrian positions Nov. 6 in the southern and central sector of the Golan Heights, according to Damascus. The communique said Syrian planes and artillery blunted the Israeli strike. Israel said it had no information on the incident.

An Israeli ground force attempting to advance Nov. 7 on forward Syrian positions was intercepted and stopped by Syrian troops, a Damascus communiqué said.

An official of the U.N. Emergency Force (UNEF), Rudolf Stajduhar of Yugoslavia, said in Cairo Nov. 3 that UNEF was becoming effective in easing Israeli-Egyptian troop tensions. He said a Finnish contingent earlier in the week had intervened in a dispute between both sides in Suez city, preventing what appeared to be an imminent clash. A compromise enabled civilians in the area to pass back and forth through Israeli lines, Stajduhar said.

Stajduhar disclosed that Maj. Gen. Ensio Siilasvuo, interim UNEF commander, Oct. 30 had relayed to Israeli Defense Minister Moshe Dayan a Security Council call to have his forces withdraw to the Oct. 22 truce lines. Dayan said no action could be taken on the request until Premier Golda Meir returned from her visit to Washington.

Sadat threatens to renew war. Egyptian President Anwar Sadat threatened Oct. 31 to resume the war unless Israel withdrew its forces to the Oct. 22 truce line by the time U.S. Secretary of State Henry A. Kissinger visited Cairo Nov. 6–7.

Sadat told a news conference that his troops were capable of wiping out the Israeli forces on the west bank of the Suez Canal but said, "We don't want to violate the cease-fire" and cause more bloodshed. He said the exchange of Israeli prisoners would take place only when Israeli troops withdrew to the Oct. 22 cease-fire lines, which would considerably reduce their salient on the west bank and lift the siege of Egypt's III Corps.

Sadat said he had received an Israeli message "four or five days ago" from British Prime Minister Edward Heath, relayed by Soviet Communist party General Secretary Leonid I. Brezhnev. Sadat said the note suggested that if Egypt lifted the anti-Israeli naval blockade of the Strait of Bab el Mandeb at the entrance to the Red Sea, Israel would free the trapped III Corps. Sadat said the blockade would be discussed later in the context of "disengagement," apparently referring to Israeli withdrawal from the Sinai.

The Egyptian leader said he had accepted the cease-fire because of U.S. "intervention" on behalf of Israel. "I would not fight the United States," he said. U.S. and Soviet assurances that they would guarantee the truce lines and implementation of the U.N. Security Council resolutions also prompted Egypt to accept the truce, Sadat said.

Fahmy, Meir in Washington talks. President Nixon and Secretary of State Henry A. Kissinger met in Washington with top-ranking Egyptian and Israeli officials in an attempt to bring the two sides closer to direct negotiations for a permanent settlement of the Middle East conflict.

Kissinger met Oct. 29–30 with Egypt's acting foreign minister, Ismail Fahmy, and the two met Oct. 31 with Nixon. (Fahmy was named foreign minister Oct. 31. He replaced Mohammed H. el-Zayyat, who was appointed special adviser to President Anwar Sadat.)

Nixon and Kissinger held talks Nov. 1 with Israeli Premier Golda Meir, who flew to Washington amid reports the U.S. was applying pressure to Israel to make concessions to the Egyptians on several key issues.

The Soviet Union simultaneously continued its talks with Egypt and the U.S. Moscow was reported Oct. 31 to have sent an experienced diplomat, Vasily Kuznetsov, to Cairo to confer with Sadat.

Soviet Ambassador Anatoly Dobrynin met with Nixon and Kissinger at Camp David, Md. Oct. 31.

Fahmy, named Egypt's foreign minister Oct. 31, met with Kissinger for nearly four hours Oct. 30 and with Kissinger and Nixon for less than an hour Oct. 31. All three expressed satisfaction with the talks. Fahmy reportedly stressed to the U.S. leaders that peace talks could not be held unless Israel withdrew to the Oct. 22 cease-fire lines, and insisted that a final settlement of the Middle East conflict would be incomplete without Israeli withdrawal to its boundaries prior to the 1967 Arab-Israeli war.

(Sadat said Oct. 31 he preferred a U.N.-sponsored peace conference, rather than direct peace talks with Israel. State Department officials, on the other hand, were reported to have said Nov. 1 that the U.S. had worked out an agreement with the Soviet Union for direct Arab-Israeli talks.)

Mrs. Meir arrived in Washington Oct. 31 amid reports the U.S. was pressuring Israel to observe the Oct. 22 cease-fire lines, open a supply corridor under U.N. supervision to the trapped Egyptian III Corps, and make concessions on terms for an overall settlement of the Middle East conflict.

Mrs. Meir met Kissinger for breakfast Nov. 1 and later conferred for more than an hour with Nixon. She said at a press conference after the meetings that she had been reassured of U.S. support for Israel's "security and well-being" and denied repeatedly that the U.S. was pressuring Israel to make unilateral concessions to the Arabs.

(The U.S. confirmed that Nixon and Kissinger had not asked Israel to pull back to the Oct. 22 lines. Press sources said, however, that the U.S. tended to accept the Egyptian contention that Israel had violated the cease-fire by completing the encirclement of Egypt's III Corps after Oct. 22.)

Mrs. Meir asserted "not one living person" could say with accuracy where the Oct. 22 lines actually were, and only direct negotiations could resolve this dispute. She added that Israel was prepared to negotiate with Egypt and Syria "tomorrow," anywhere in the world.

The Israeli premier declined to say what Arab territory Israel would refuse to give up in such negotiations, apart from insisting it would never return East Jerusalem to Jordan.

Mrs. Meir said her talk with Nixon had made it clear Israel and the U.S. shared "a common goal"—the preservation of the cease-fire—and sought "a true and lasting peace" in the Middle East.

Pompidou asks EEC meeting on Mideast. French President Georges Pompidou sent letters to the heads of government of European Economic Community (EEC) nations Oct. 31 proposing a meeting at the highest level before the end of 1973 to "compare and harmonize" their policies on the Middle East and other issues.

Apparently angry over what he saw as Soviet-U.S. disregard of Europe during the renewed Arab-Israeli war, he told a French Cabinet meeting Oct. 31 that the Middle East cease-fire, "planned and put into effect without the participation of Europe in any form," was a "dangerous" course of action. He said that private understandings between the U.S. and the Soviet Union worked against Europe's direct historical, geographic and economic links to the Middle East.

EEC urges troop pullback. In an attempt to avert an Arab oil boycott threatened against nations adopting a pro-Israeli policy, the foreign ministers of the European Economic Community (EEC) adopted a joint statement Nov. 6 calling on Israel and Egypt to return to the cease-fire lines of Oct. 22—before Israeli troops completed their encirclement of the Egyptian III Corps.

The statement, approved at the end of a two-day meeting in Brussels, called on Israel to "end the territorial occupation which it has maintained since the conflict of 1967" and declared that peace in the Middle East was incompatible with "the acquisition of territory by force." It also stated that any peace settlement must take account of "the legitimate rights" of the Palestinian refugees and supported international guarantees negotiated through the U.N.

The ministers did not act on a Netherlands request for a pooling of oil resources by EEC members if the Netherlands began to run out of oil because of the Arab oil boycott against it.

France and Britain had been the most vigorous opponents of a joint EEC oil pool because they feared such a policy might jeopardize their privileged position with the Arabs on assured petroleum supplies.

Israel places death toll at 1,854. Israel announced Nov. 6 that 1,854 of its soldiers had been killed in the October War. The total number of wounded was not given, but the army said about 1,800 wounded soldiers remained hospitalized.

The casualty figures were for the period starting Oct. 6, when the hostilities erupted, and ending at the truce of Oct. 24. There had been other Israeli battle losses since then.

6-Point Egyptian-Israel truce accord. Israel and Egypt accepted a six-point U.S.-sponsored agreement aimed at strengthening the cease-fire and dealing with other matters relating to the recent hostilities. The agreement had been drawn up by U.S. Secretary of State Henry A. Kissinger in talks he had held in Cairo Nov. 7 with Egyptian President Anwar Sadat. They also negotiated re-establishment of diplomatic relations between the U.S. and Egypt, broken in 1967.

The U.S. announced the accord Nov. 9. It was immediately accepted by Egypt. Israel delayed its endorsement until Nov. 10.

The text of the six-point plan:

■ Egypt and Israel agree to observe scrupulously the cease-fire called for by the United Nations Security Council.

■ Both sides agree that discussions between them will begin immediately to settle the question of the return to the Oct. 22 positions in the framework of agreement on the disengagement and separation of forces under the auspices of the United Nations.

■ The town of Suez will receive daily supplies of food, water and medicine. All wounded civilians in the town of Suez will be evacuated.

■ There shall be no impediment to the movement of nonmilitary supplies to the east bank [occupied by the encircled Egyptian III Corps].

■ The Israeli checkpoints on the Cairo-Suez road will be replaced by United Nations checkpoints. At the Suez end of the road, Israeli officers can participate with the United Nations to supervise the non-military nature of the cargo at the bank of the canal.

■ As soon as the United Nations checkpoints are established on the Cairo-Suez road, there will be an exchange of all prisoners of war, including wounded.

The peace plan had been conveyed to Israel by U.S. Assistant Secretary of State Joseph J. Sisco at a meeting in Tel Aviv Nov. 7 with Prime Minister Golda Meir, Defense Minister Moshe Dayan and Deputy Premier Yigal Allon.

The peace proposal had been scheduled to be signed Nov. 10, but the ceremony was delayed because of Israeli efforts to seek clarification of some of the points it regarded as too vague. Israel wanted assurances that Egypt would lift the naval blockade of the Straits of Bab el Mandeb at the entrance to the Red Sea that blocked Israeli shipping. Premier Meir discussed this point Nov. 9 with U.S. Ambassador Kenneth B. Keating. Egypt had never acknowledged the blockade and was therefore not publicly asked to disavow it in the agreement with Kissinger.

U.S. Defense Department officials had said there had been no actual blockade of the strait, that Egyptian and South Yemeni vessels had patrolled the area but had not actually stopped any shipping. Israel refuted this view, saying that the Egyptians had turned back all Israel-bound shipping.

Israel also had expressed concern about other issues of the agreement, including the sequence in which the six points would go into effect and as it applied to the release of prisoners.

An Israeli government statement Nov. 10 finally approving the accord said Israel's "positive decision in principle concerning the signature of a cease-fire agreement with Egypt remains in force."

Kissinger's talks in Cairo were part of a Middle East mission he had undertaken in an effort to strengthen the tenuous Middle East cease-fire. He had left Washington Nov. 5 and conferred with King Hassan II in Morocco and with President Habib Bourguiba in Tunisia Nov. 6. After departing from Cairo Nov. 8, Kissinger and his party stopped in Amman and conferred for five hours with Jordanian King Hussein. Kissinger flew to Riyadh later Nov. 8 where he met with Saudi Arabia King Faisal.

Kissinger's tour of the five Middle East nations had been preceded by a week of intense diplomatic talks in Washington with Arab and Israeli leaders. He conferred Nov. 2 with Syrian Deputy Foreign Minister Mohammed F. Ismail and held further discussions with Egyptian Foreign Minister Ismail Fahmy, with whom he had met Oct. 29-30. Kissinger's meeting with Ismail was Syria's first significant diplomatic contact with the U.S. in a year.

The secretary of state met again Nov. 3 with Fahmy and Premier Golda Meir, who had delayed her departure scheduled for Nov. 3.

Egyptian officials reported that President Sadat conducted a one-day mission Nov. 1, holding strategy talks in Damascus with Syrian President Hafez al-Assad and with other Arab officials in Kuwait and Saudi Arabia. Soon after Sadat's return to Cairo, he conferred with visiting Algerian President Houari Boumedienne.

Col. Muammar el-Qaddafi, Libyan leader, left Damascus Nov. 5 after official visits to Syria and Iraq. Meanwhile Libyan officials denounced the cease-fire and said the Arab "battle against Israel must continue because if it is halted it will be difficult to resume." The Libyan authorities also denounced Soviet support of the truce and assailed Moscow for permitting the continued emigration of Soviet Jews to Israel.

Assad conferred with Boumedienne in Damascus Nov. 2.

The Soviet Union was reported Oct. 31 to have sent a note to the Palestine Liberation Organization (PLO) asking whether it was interested in participating in a Middle East peace conference and in the creation of a Palestinian state. Although the PLO had promised to study the proposal, the Palestinian resistance movement in general was said to be favorable to the idea of taking part in an international conference.

Israeli Foreign Ministry sources said Nov. 1 that Israel would continue to oppose inclusion of the Palestine guerrilla movement in any international parley in line with its policy of holding talks only with representatives of Arab countries.

U.S., Egypt resume ties—The resumption of U.S.-Egyptian ties had been agreed to by Kissinger and Sadat at their first meeting Nov. 7. A statement by State Department spokesman Robert J. McCloskey, who accompanied Kissinger, said both nations had "agreed in principle to resume diplomatic relations at an early date."

Egypt had severed diplomatic relations with Washington at the start of the 1967 war after charging that U.S. planes were assisting Israeli forces in the conflict.

Israel to resupply III Corps—The trapped III Corps Nov. 6 received the last of the 125 supply trucks Israel had agreed to permit to be driven through its lines to provide the surrounded Egyptians with food and water. The Israelis immediately agreed to allow another 50 truckloads of supplies to be brought to the Egyptians. Israeli government sources said the decision was taken to avoid a breakdown in negotiations between Egyptian officials and U.S. Secretary of State Henry A. Kissinger.

A senior Israeli officer in the area, Maj. Gen. Ariel Sharon, asserted Nov. 7 that the III Corps had its own natural water supplies and access to food in Suez city and was in no immediate danger of being forced to surrender through hunger or thirst. Sharon said there were several springs, wells and water holes within the III Corps' defense perimeter.

Kissinger quoted on peace prospects—Al Ahram editor Mohammed Hassanien Heykal quoted U.S. Secretary of State Henry A. Kissinger as telling him Nov. 7 that "Peace is not just around the corner," that it might take "some six months or even a year before we see **anything concrete emerge**" from a scheduled Arab-Israeli peace conference.

Heykal said Kissinger made the statement in Cairo following his meeting with President Sadat.

Although the U.S. was pledged to protect Israel's security, Kissinger had told Heykal that "We do not believe" those relations "are irreconcilable with the ties which we wish to maintain and strengthen" with Egypt.

Kissinger said the U.S. had asked for a cease-fire one day after the outbreak of the war, not to protect Israel, but for the benefit of the Arabs. "All our experts believed that if you restarted the war, you would be exposing yourself to a decisive attack by the Israeli forces," Kissinger said. He told Heykal that a resumption of the war held other dangers, that it would either provoke Soviet military intervention or lead to the sending of Soviet forces into Egypt, "never to leave."

As for American arms aid to Israel, Kissinger said the U.S. "could not—either today or tomorrow—allow Soviet arms to win a big victory, even if it was not decisive, against United States arms. This has nothing to do with Israel or you."

Kissinger completes Mideast visit— On the final leg of his Middle East tour, Kissinger stopped over in Riyadh Nov. 8–9 to confer with Saudi Arabian officials. Saudi authorities disclosed Nov. 9 that Kissinger had been told in his talks with King Faisal and other government officials that Saudi Arabia would not lift its oil embargo against the U.S. until Israel withdrew from all Arab territories it had occupied since 1967. The change in the current cease-fire lines in the Sinai would not in itself prompt Saudi Arabia to relax its oil cutoff, according to U.S. and Saudi officials.

Foreign Minister Omar Saqqaf said Kissinger had impressed King Faisal "as a sincere man" prepared "to do his best to bring about a peaceful settlement."

Egypt & Israel begin POW exchange. Israel and Egypt began exchanging prisoners of war Nov. 15 after resolving a dispute over their cease-fire lines that had threatened to collapse the U.S.-sponsored six-point plan aimed at strengthening the truce. Both nations had signed the agreement Nov. 11.

The first group of prisoners to be returned under sponsorship of the International Committee of the Red Cross were wounded. An ICRC planeload of 26 injured Israelis flew from Cairo to Tel Aviv, while 44 wounded Egyptians were airlifted from Tel Aviv to Cairo. A total of 238 Israeli and some 8,400 Egyptian POWs were to be repatriated under the agreement in about a week's time.

Defense Minister Moshe Dayan, who greeted the Israeli prisoners at Lod airport, said he was encouraged by the prisoner accord with Egypt because "it is the result of talks at a table, not of meeting them with tanks and guns on the battlefield."

The agreement aimed at implementing the truce had been signed Nov. 11 in a tent set up at Kilometer 101, 63 miles from Cairo, an Israeli military checkpoint on the road from Cairo to Suez city. The accord was signed by Israeli Maj. Gen. Aharon Yariv, Premier Golda Meir's principal military adviser, and Egyptian Maj. Gen. Mohammed Abdel Ghany el-Gamasy. The discussions were held under the auspices of the United Nations, with the U.N. Emergency Force (UNEF) commander, Gen. Ensio Siilasvuo, and two civilian aides sitting at the head of the table. (Siilasvuo had recently been promoted from interim commander to commander.)

UNEF takes over ckeckpoints—Following the agreement on POWs, the two sides immediately became embroiled in a dispute that centered on control of checkpoints on the Cairo-Suez highway. This was vital for supplying the trapped Egyptian III Corps on the east bank of the Suez Canal. Israel said it was prepared to turn over the checkpoints to UNEF as the agreement provided but was opposed to Egyptian demands that it pull its forces away from positions along the sides of the highway.

Finnish troops of UNEF engaged in fist-fights with Israeli soldiers Nov. 12 after the Finns established two checkpoints, at Kilometer 101 and Kilometer 119, just outside Suez. The Finns took over the two points after another meeting between Israelis and Egyptians broke up in disagreement. The Finnish commander said the Israeli force invaded Kilometer 119 checkpoint and threatened to open fire if the UNEF force did not pull out. It was then that the fistfights erupted. The Finns called in 50-60 UNEF reinforcements and the tension abated. The Israelis, however, posted their forces just outside the checkpoints.

Despite UNEF control of the two checkpoints, Israeli troops Nov. 13 continued to maintain control of the highway leading to Suez.

In addition to release of the prisoners and the return of Cairo-Suez checkpoints to UNEF, the Israelis and Egyptians agreed Nov. 14 on the supply of food, water and medicine for Suez and evacuation of wounded from the city, and the shipment of nonmilitary supplies to the III Corps. The other two points of the six-point agreement were the strict observance of the cease-fire, which was largely being fulfilled, and the return of troops to the Oct. 22 truce line, which remained to be negotiated.

An Israeli spokesman in Jerusalem said Nov. 15 that Israeli troops would remain in control of the area along the Cairo-Suez highway, that Israeli liaison officers would accompany every vehicle that moved on the highway and that Israeli officers would have the right to inspect all supply convoys bound for the III Corps. Israeli troops also were to be stationed at the western entrance to Suez, where all supplies destined for the city were to be inspected.

U.S. ends airlift to Israel. The U.S. virtually ended its airlift of military supplies to Israel Nov. 14.

Defense Department spokesman Jerry W. Friedheim said "the emergency that called for the airlift supplies is essentially over," that six planeloads of equipment were being flown to Israel Nov. 14. He said additional military equipment was being sent by ship, but he did not rule out all future flights to Israel.

The U.S. Air Force had reported that since the start of the American airlift Oct. 14 about 570 flights of transport planes had brought 22,600 tons of materiel to Israel to replace losses suffered in the fighting.

Friedheim disclosed that the Soviet airlift to Syria and Egypt was continuing but on a lesser scale than during the war. He said four or five Soviet planes had landed in the two countries Nov. 13, compared with the average of more than 80 a day when the airlift was at its peak. The Arab states were beginning to receive the bulk of their equipment from the Soviet Union by ship. According to the Defense Department, 28 Soviet ships carrying arms were at sea or unloading at Arab ports on a given day recently.

Friedheim estimated that the Russians had sent Egypt and Syria about 100,000 tons of supplies.

Deputy Secretary of State Kenneth Rush told the House Appropriation Committee's Subcommittee on Foreign Operations Nov. 14 that the U.S. was determined to replace Israeli arms losses and to send it additional equipment to maintain the military balance in the Middle East. Rush noted that despite the cease-fire, Egypt and Syria were re-equip-ping their forces with "large infusions of Soviet military equipment."

U.S. ends 6th Fleet alert. The U.S. Defense Department announced Nov. 19 it had canceled the six-week old military alert for the 60 ships of the American 6th Fleet in the Mediterranean.

Department spokesman Jerry W. Friedheim said now that Middle East tensions had eased the ships would stop at Mediterranean ports while some others would return to ports in the U.S.

Friedheim said the Soviet Union had reduced its Mediterranean fleet from 95 ships to more than 70.

Aftermath

Problems & Disputes

The cease-fire, by officially halting the October 1973 war, helped bring to greater prominence a number of war-related problems involving the combatants, their supporters and even innocent third parties.

Israeli Controversy
Over War Leadership

Israelis debate policy. Widespread debate within Israel on matters relating to the war resulted in the resignation of a Cabinet minister, repeated public demonstrations and a demand by the opposition for a delay in a peace settlement until after national elections.

Justice Minister Yaacov S. Shapiro announced Oct. 30 that he was resigning from the Cabinet. He had called Oct. 24 for the resignation of Defense Minister Moshe Dayan because of allegedly inadequate preparations for the war and failure to interpret correctly evidence of Egyptian and Syrian war preparations. Dyan Oct. 25 offered to resign, but Premier Golda Meir expressed full confidence in him.

The conservative Likud opposition coalition demanded Oct. 31 that the government make no decisions on the terms of any permanent peace settlement until after the parliamentary elections, set for Dec. 31. The elections had been postponed Oct. 24. Likud had denounced the Cabinet's "serious failure" in not launching a preemptive strike, when it resumed criticism of the government Oct. 22, saying "the concept of national unity died the moment the government accepted the cease-fire without even informing us."

Demonstrations in Tel Aviv entered their third consecutive day Oct. 31, with protesters, including relatives of prisoners held by the Arabs, demanding a strong government position on prisoner return and opposing the resupply of the encircled Egyptian III Corps on the east bank of the Suez Canal.

Other critics complained of inadequacies in military tactics and command experience, while massive opposition reportedly developed against return of any of the lands gained in the 1967 war, in order to provide Israel with "strategic depth" in case of a renewed Arab attack. According to Newsweek Magazine Oct. 29, public opinion polls before the war had shown only about 30% of the population in favor of indefinite retention of the lands. On the other hand, Deputy Prime Minister Yigal Allon said the war had ended Israel's "exaggerated confidence in ourselves and our attitude of condescending scorn for the Arabs "

Maj. Gen. Ariel Sharon, who had led his forces to the west bank of the Suez Canal, asserted in an interview published

130

in foreign newspapers Nov. 9 that the Israeli high commanders had moved too slowly and cautiously from the outbreak of hostilities and had "failed to understand the element of time, which was critical." Sharon said Israel had enough forces at the outset to prevent what he called "the disaster that befell us for 24–48 hours."

Sharon said the Israeli commanders did not fully exploit his crossing of the canal. He said higher headquarters had delayed for 36–40 hours the moving of reinforcements across to the bridgehead. The delay meant that the Egyptian III Corps on the east bank south of the bridgehead had not been encircled or reduced as a military force by the time the first cease-fire was called Oct. 22.

Sharon also blamed top Israeli officers for preventing his own force from racing north to encircle the Egyptian II Corps on the east bank in the north even after the west bank bridgehead was reinforced by a second Israeli armored division.

Sharon said Israel "could have taken more risks" since alleged Soviet intentions to intervene militarily in the Middle East and U.S. pressure on Israel "were not serious." As a result, Israel "lost, at least temporarily, our power of deterrence over the Arabs," Sharon said.

Sharon was tacitly rebuked Nov. 10 by Lt. Gen. David Elazar, chief of staff, who said he deplored "biased and one-sided descriptions and interviews . . . which serve no constructive purpose but only personal enhancement, even if this entails casting unfair aspersions on comrades in arms."

Defense Minister Moshe Dayan Nov. 10 ordered Elazar to take action against Sharon "in accordance with the guidelines of the attorney general."

Sharon's views were disputed Nov. 11 by Lt. Gen. Haim Bar-Lev, who had been assigned to the southern front and was one of Sharon's superiors. Bar-Lev said the plan to cross the canal was not an individual decision. He said it had been in the making since the end of the 1967 war, that "the bridge prepared at the crossing point . . . was in accordance with the operational doctrine" of the Israeli armed forces. "The command decided on the time, the place and the target, and this was recorded in written operational orders and in the orders to the commanders, which were heard by 30–40 officers," Bar-Lev said.

Bar-Lev conceded there had been shortcomings in the conduct of the war. One matter that called for investigation, he said, was why soldiers at the front had not been on alert when the war broke out Oct. 6.

The Israeli government Nov. 11 ordered a two-level investigation of the conduct of the war. One probe would deal with political decision-making, the other would concentrate on the military aspects.

The government's war policies were further assailed in the Knesset (Parliament) Nov. 13 after Premier Golda Meir delivered an address expressing confidence that Israel and Egypt would settle their differences and carry out the cease-fire agreement. She reviewed the events of the past two weeks and emphasized the need for Israel to retain some of the Arab lands won in the 1967 war. She said Israel had learned from the war the "value in depth and defensible borders. We have not learned that we must return to the lines of June 4, 1967, which tempt our neighbors to aggression."

After Mrs. Meir's speech, opposition Gahal leader Menahem Begin accused the premier and her Cabinet of "criminal negligence" during the war and asked them to resign. Pointing to Mrs. Meir and her ministers, Begin said, "You knew well in advance of the massive Egyptian and Syrian preparations for an imminent attack and yet you did not even admit this to your own government and you overruled your own chief of staff when he wanted to stage a preemptive attack." Begin had attacked the government Oct. 24 for accepting the cease-fire, which he said "awarded Egypt and Syria a prize for their aggression."

U. S., Israeli intelligence failure cited. The New York Times reported Oct. 31 that U.S. intelligence officials had begun an evaluation of the failure by U.S. and Israeli intelligence agencies to predict the Arab attack.

According to the Times, evidence of a buildup in both Syria and Egypt had been accumulated by Israeli sources in the weeks before the attack but had been discounted as fall maneuvers. Israel had detected bridge-building equipment on the west bank of the Suez as long as one and a half years ago, but both Israel and the U.S. believed Egypt incapable of a major canal crossing.

Three days before the Oct. 6 attack, U.S. intelligence learned that the U.S.S.R. had diverted commercial Soviet aircraft to Syria and Egypt to evacuate Soviet dependents, but the U.S. believed the Soviets might have been responding to information that Israel was planning an attack.

Israel sets judicial probe of war. The Israeli Cabinet Nov. 18 ordered a judicial inquiry into the country's alleged failures and shortcomings in the war. The probe would parallel a military investigation of the conflict ordered by the government Nov. 11.

Supreme Court Chief Justice Shimon Agranat was directed to appoint a five-member commission that would be headed by a judge with power of subpoena. It would be instructed to investigate "the information available before the Yom Kippur war concerning the enemy movements and intentions to open war as well as assessment of the information by the competent military and civilian bodies." The commission also would attempt to clarify "the Israel defense forces' deployment in general, its preparedness before the Yom Kippur war and its actions until the enemy was contained."

Mrs. Meir wins confidence vote. Israel's ruling Labor party gave Premier Golda Meir a vote of confidence Dec. 6 after she had accepted full responsibility for the setbacks suffered by Israel at the start of the October war.

The party's Central Committee voted 291–33 to continue Mrs. Meir and her top aides in office, thus rejecting an attempt by younger party members to oust the leadership for its failure to mobilize the country until a few hours before the Arab attack Oct. 6.

In requesting the confidence vote, the premier said "I am responsible for anything that may have happened." She conceded that "there was a fatal mistake of

evaluation" of the intelligence reports of an Arab build-up. "The information was in our hands, including mine, and I have tortured myself not a little since then."

On the question of retaining Arab territories, Mrs. Meir said "I don't believe we can give back everything." She warned that "the voices heard inside Israel calling for returning everything can damage our interests at the peace negotiations and encourage the Arabs to harden their line."

The confidence vote followed adoption by the Labor party Dec. 5 of a revised compromise plank on peace terms with the Arabs. The draft, drawn up at a Central Committee meeting Nov. 28, averted an open break between the party's moderates and hard-liners on what position Israel should take at the forthcoming peace conference with the Arabs.

The party's secretary general, Aharon Yadlin, announcing details of the plank Nov. 28, said Israel would seek to attain the following:

"An end to all hostilities, blockade and boycott."

"Defensible borders that will assure Israel's capacity to protect herself effectively against military attack or attempted blockade and will be based on territorial compromise. The peace borders will replace cease-fire lines, Israel shall not return to the lines of June 4, 1967, which had invited aggression."

This aspect of the plank was a reaffirmation of the principle of secure and defensible borders but specifically broached for the first time the possibility of territorial compromises.

The plank also firmly rejected the formation of a Palestinian state on the West Bank of the Jordan River. It was vague on the establishment of Israeli settlements in the occupied territories, merely saying that "steps will be taken to continue and to consolidate settlements in accordance with decisions to be taken by the Israeli government from time to time, with priority given to security considerations."

The party debate Dec. 5 was marked by direct and indirect criticism of Defense Minister Moshe Dayan's continuance in the party's top leadership. He replied that he accepted blame for the "failures" of the defense establishment in the October war.

International Tensions

U.S. seeks to end allied rift. The U.S. was reported Nov. 2 to have contacted its three principal allies in West Europe in an effort to settle their dispute over American policies and actions during the recent Middle East crisis.

An Administration official said a letter from President Nixon had been delivered Nov. 1 to Chancellor Willy Brandt in reply to the West German leader's message of Oct. 28. Brandt was said to have complained about U.S. failure to inform its allies of its actions during the crisis and of the continued American shipment of military supplies to Israel after the Oct. 22 cease-fire. President Nixon was said to have reassured Brandt of fuller consultations in the future. The President reportedly had made similar pledges to Britain and Italy.

U.S. Secretary of State Henry A. Kissinger called in the ambassadors of the North Atlantic Treaty Organization (NATO) Nov. 2 to brief them on his forthcoming trip to the Middle East.

U.S. Defense Secretary James R. Schlesinger disclosed Nov. 9 that at a meeting of NATO defense ministers in The Hague he had worked out an accord with the Bonn government for possible future shipment to Israel of U.S. arms in West Germany. Under the U.S.-Bonn arrangement, such supplies destined for Israel could be stocked in West Germany but were not to be carried in Israeli ships. West Germany had protested Oct. 25 the loading of American supplies aboard an Israeli freighter in Bremerhaven.

The dispute had prompted Schlesinger to warn that the U.S. might have to withdraw some of its equipment, and possibly some of its troops, from West Germany. On returning from the NATO meeting Nov. 8, Schlesinger said such action was no longer being considered because of the "common understanding" he had reached with West German Defense Minister Georg Leber.

French Foreign Minister Michel Jobert Nov. 12 assailed the U.S. as well as the Soviet Union for their role in the October crisis. He said the understanding reached between the two superpowers had not prevented war, that Western Europe was being "treated like a nonperson, humiliated all along the line," while the U.S. and the Soviet Union were delivering arms to their allies in the Middle East and conducting secret talks toward a cease-fire. Jobert warned the U.S. that Europe was in the very center of the "second battle" of the Middle East war—the battle for Arab oil upon which Europe was heavily dependent.

Meir seeks Socialist support. Israeli Premier Golda Meir met with world Socialist leaders in London Nov. 11 in an effort to muster support for her government.

The closed-door meeting of the Socialist International representing 20 countries was called at Mrs. Meir's initiative. She opened the session with a denunciation of a Nov. 6 declaration of the foreign ministers of the European Economic Community (EEC) regarded as pro-Arab because it supported Egypt's position in the dispute over the cease-fire lines on the Sinai front. The Israeli premier was particularly critical of the statement urging Israel "to end the territorial occupation which it has maintained since the conflict of 1967."

Two European leaders at the meeting—West German Chancellor Willy Brandt and Netherlands Premier Joop den Uyl—were said to have replied that the EEC statement went no further than the U.N. Security Council resolution on territories adopted after the 1967 war.

British Labor party leader Harold Wilson, reporting later on the meeting, said at least two representatives did not support Mrs. Meir's views. They were Prime Ministers Dom Mintoff of Malta and Seewoosagur Ramgoolan of Mauritius.

Mrs. Meir met with British Prime Minister Edward Heath Nov. 12 and urged his help in obtaining the release of Israeli prisoners, especially those held by Syria. The Israeli leader had told a news conference earlier that "many of those taken prisoner by Syria are not alive any more." She repeated her government's claim that some of the captives had been executed.

The EEC statement on Israel had been denounced Nov. 9 by Israeli Foreign Minister Abba Eban. He asserted that the nine European governments that had endorsed the declaration were more concerned about their oil supplies than peace in the Middle East.

In a message sent to the West German Parliament Nov. 9, Chancellor Brandt said his government was committed to the survival of Israel despite its dependence on Arab oil. Referring to the Arabs' use of an oil embargo to exert political pressure, Brandt said, "Friendship cannot be made by black-mail and threats."

U.S. considers pact with Israel. Secretary of State Henry A. Kissinger said Nov. 12 that the U.S. was considering a mutual security treaty with Israel as one possible way of guaranteeing Israel's boundaries after it withdrew from all or part of the occupied Arab areas.

Kissinger made the statement during a television interview in Peking, following his peace mission to five Middle East capitals.

Kissinger acknowledged that it would be "a very serious problem" for Israel's security for it to yield Arab territory occupied since the 1967 war as a result of a peace agreement. After such an accord was signed, "the question of guarantees will arise and we have to then ask ... what sort of guarantees—unilateral, several countries and so forth" can be offered Israel, Kissinger said.

Kissinger was questioned about a suggestion recently made by U.S. Senate Foreign Relations Committee Chairman J. W. Fulbright (D, Ark.) that the U.S. induce Israel to accept a peace agreement in exchange for a treaty that would oblige the U.S. to come to its defense in the event of war. The secretary replied that all U.S. Administrations had supported Israel. "This has been our policy in the absence of any formal arrangement and it has never been challenged no matter which Administration was in office."

The U.S. was not prepared to drop its support of Israel because of the Arab oil embargo, Kissinger said. "While we are highly respectful of the views of the Arab world," he said, "it is not possible for us to be swayed in the major orientation of our policy by the monopoly position or the temporary monopoly position enjoyed by a few nations."

Questioned about possible pressure on Israel to make concessions to the Arabs during peace talks, Kissinger replied: "Israel has always agreed that final borders will not be the cease-fire lines either in 1967 or 1973 and we have every hope that through the process of negotiations a mutually acceptable settlement will be achieved."

Oil Pressure

Singapore cuts U.S. military fuel. Singapore stopped all fuel supplies to U.S. military forces in the Pacific in response to an Arab threat to cut off oil exports to Singapore, industrial sources in the country reported Nov. 14. The U.S. embassy in Singapore confirmed the same day that "Certain companies in Singapore are no longer able to supply petroleum to the United States Department of Defense under their current contracts."

Prime Minister Lee Kuan Yew was reported to have ordered refineries in Singapore Nov. 12 to stop supplying the American market. His action followed a statement by a Saudi Arabian diplomat to Singapore newsmen that "Our policy is clear—no supplies of our oil are to go to any United States military buyers."

Canada bars U.S. oil cutoff. Prime Minister Pierre Elliot Trudeau said Nov. 13 that Canada would not cut off petroleum exports to the U.S., even if a cutoff were requested by Arab nations.

In a diplomatic note to the U.S. that day, Canada said it would continue to export oil and refined products to the U.S. if they were not required in Canada. Energy Minister Donald Macdonald had said Nov. 5 that Canada might bar some refined product exports if requested by the Arabs. Most of Canada's exports were of crude oil.

Japan under pressure. Japan faced a serious threat to its economy because of the Arab oil cutbacks, a government official warned Nov. 12, 1973.

Eimei Yamashita, vice minister of the Ministry of International Trade and Industry, made the statement after submitting an emergency action plan to Prime Minister Kakuei Tanaka to cope with the energy crisis. He said the fuel shortage might reduce Japan's economic growth rate for the current fiscal year ending March 1974 from 10% to 5%. About 83% of Japan's oil imports came from the Middle East—45% from the Arab countries and 38% from Iran.

The Japanese Foreign Ministry had said Nov. 8 that Tokyo had rejected a request by Arab nations to sever diplomatic relations with Israel, impose an official embargo on trade with Israel and provide military assistance to the Arab states. Ministry spokesman Mizuo Kuroda said the Arab states, which he did not identify, had informed Japan that compliance with their request would place Japan in the "friendly" nation category, assuring it of uninterrupted oil supplies.

U.S. Secretary of State Henry A. Kissinger conferred with Tanaka and other Japanese officials in Tokyo Nov. 15-16. The discussions dealt almost exclusively with the effects of the oit cutoff on Japan's economy.

Japan urges Israeli withdrawal—Yielding to Arab oil pressure, Japan called on Israel Nov. 22 to pull its forces out of occupied Arab territories and implied that Tokyo might break diplomatic relations with Jerusalem if it did not do so.

A Cabinet statement said Japan "will continue to observe the situation in the Middle East with grave concern, and depending on future developments, may have to reconsider its policy toward Israel." The statement cited the 1967 U.N. Security Council Resolution 242 as the basis for urging Israeli withdrawal from Arab areas taken in the Six-Day War.

Foreign Minister Masayoshi Ohira called in 10 Arab ambassadors and Israeli Ambassador Eytan Ronn to inform them of Japan's new pro-Arab policy on the Middle East. Tokyo's shift followed Arab demands that it sever ties and trade with Israel and supply Arabs with arms if it wanted to be exempt from Arab oil cutbacks.

The U.S. State Department Nov. 23 said it regretted that Japan had "found it necessary to make a statement" favoring the Arab position on the Middle East.

The Israeli Foreign Ministry Nov. 26 denounced Tokyo's stand, saying "It is distressing to find a power like Japan yielding to pressure of our enemies and to their threats against the industry and economy of Japan and the sovereignty of free nations." The ministry noted that Japan had previously supported Israel's view of Resolution 242, that it interpreted it to mean that Israel would withdraw to borders to be determined by both parties in negotiations.

Iraq ignores Arab oil cutback. Oil industry sources in Beirut reported Nov. 13 that Iraq was not abiding by the Nov. 5 decision by Arab oil producers to cut production 25%.

Iraq was reportedly continuing to ship oil through Mediterranean and Persian Gulf terminals. A total of 700,000 barrels a day was coming through the Kirukuk pipeline for ship loadings at Banias, Syria. A similar daily amount had been sent through the pipeline branch to Tripoli, Lebanon in the past 10 days, the report said.

An Iraqi government statement warned against creation of a general "shortfall in supplies" to all industrial users. "This approach would provide grounds for the advocates of an aggressive policy in the United States to launch new military adventures in the Arab region," it said.

Arabs ease Europe oil curb. The Organization of Arab Petroleum Exporting Countries (OAPEC) announced at a meeting in Vienna Nov. 18 that its member states would cancel the scheduled December 5% reduction in exports for most countries of the European Economic Community (EEC). The total embargo against the Netherlands and the U.S., however, would continue.

An OAPEC communiqué made public after the meeting said that "in appreciation of the political stand taken by the Common Market countries in their [Nov. 6] communiqué regarding the Middle East crisis," the organization had decided "not to implement the 5% reduction for the month of December" for the EEC member nations.

Belgium calls for Israeli pullback—
Belgian Foreign Minister Renaat van Els-
lande called on Israel Nov. 27 to
withdraw from Arab lands occupied in the
1967 war. Speaking to the Belgian
Parliament, he also called for a "solution
to the Palestinian problem" and
recognition of Israel's sovereignty in con-
formity with Resolution 242. Van Els-
lande said his government's position on
the Middle East was consistent and that
his call for Israeli withdrawal was not the
result of Arab pressure.

Israel cuts fuel consumption—Israeli
Communications Minister Shimon Peres
announced Nov. 12 that his country had
decided to reduce consumption of fuel
as a gesture of solidarity with countries
affected by the Arab oil cutoff.

Peres said Israel's supply situation
was satisfactory, but many of its citizens
"would like to identify with a country
like Holland," which had introduced radical conservation measures because of the
petroleum shortage.

The Ministerial Council of the Organization of African Unity called Nov. 21 for
a total oil embargo by all oil-producing
countries, Arab and non-Arab, against Israel, Portugal, Rhodesia and South
Africa.

U.S. warns Arabs on oil embargo. Secretary of State Henry. A. Kissinger
warned Nov. 21 that the U.S. might have
to consider retaliatory action if the Arab
oil embargo continued "unreasonably and
indefinitely."

Speaking at a Washington news
conference, Kissinger said the U.S. "has
full understanding for actions . . . taken
[by Arab oil producers] when the war was
going on, by which the parties and their
friends attempted to demonstrate how
seriously they took the situation." But he
said "those countries who are engaging in
economic pressure against the United
States should consider" whether their
continued embargo was now appropriate
while peace efforts were in progress.
Asserting that the U.S. commitment to a
peaceful Middle East settlement would
not be influenced by the oil cutoff, the secretary stated, "We will not be pushed be-

yond this point by any pressure." Any
U.S. reprisals would be taken "with
enormous reluctance and we are still
hopeful that matters will not reach this
point," Kissinger declared. He did not
specify what form such countermeasures
would take or whether a deadline had been
set.

Among other aspects of the Middle
East crisis discussed by Kissinger:

The secretary said "it was obvious" that
Israel would have to relinquish Arab lands
it had occupied since the 1967 war in any
peace agreement. He did not specify,
however, what Israel's permanent
boundaries should be, saying that a final
accord negotiated by Israel and the Arabs
"will have to have an element of security
arrangements" and "may have to have an
element of outside guarantees," a
reference to a possible U.S. security
treaty with Israel. The other facets of a
peace pact should include a solution of the
Palestinian problem and a settlement of
the status of Jerusalem, he said.

U.S. officials had said Nov. 19 that the
U.S. had no plans then to retaliate for the
Arab oil embargo.

State Department spokesman George S.
Vest was asked whether the U.S. was still
willing to sell Saudi Arabia military
equipment in view of that country's suspension of oil exports to the U.S. He
replied that there was "no basic change
in policy" on that deal but that the matter would remain under review.

Secretary of Agriculture Earl L. Butz
told a news conference that proposals
had been received from "many quarters"
for a halt to U.S. grain shipments to
Arab nations in reprisal for the oil ban.
Butz said that such action "would simply
irritate the situation, make negotiations
more difficult and would not put any pressure on the Arab countries."

Butz said American grain exports to
the Arab states were "not high enough
to be significant, and in view of the fact
that the Russian nation has a much easier
grain situation than a year ago they
could very easily make up the deficit of
anything we cut off."

Saudis warn U.S. against reprisals—
Saudi Arabian Oil Minister Ahmed Zaki
Yamani warned Nov. 22 that his country

would cut its oil production by 80% if the U.S., Western Europe or Japan took any action to counter the Arab oil embargo.

Responding directly to Kissinger's remarks about possible, unspecified American reprisals, Yamani said if the U.S. attempted to use military means, Saudi Arabia would blow up its oil fields. He cautioned Western Europe and Japan against joining the U.S. in any move, saying "your whole economy will definitely collapse all of a sudden."

Yamani made his statement in a television interview in Copenhagen.

Shah Mohammed Riza Pahlevi of Iran called on the Arabs to end their oil boycott in a Beirut weekly newspaper interview published Nov. 22. "Since you have accepted the cease-fire and moves toward a peaceful settlement, why are you continuing to shut off oil supplies and reducing production?" the shah asked.

Suez Talks Founder

Israel, Egypt impasse on truce line. Israeli and Egyptian military negotiators held another meeting at Kilometer 101 Nov. 19 but remained deadlocked over the withdrawal of forces along the Suez Canal.

The Israeli-Egyptian disagreement centered over conflicting interpretations of one point of the six-point cease-fire accord—the pullback of Israeli forces on the west bank of the canal to the truce line of Oct. 22. Israel contended that this line was impossible to define, that an Israeli pullback would amount to a unilateral withdrawal and would prejudice prospects for future mutual disengagement. The Israelis further believed that if their troops returned to the Oct. 22 line, they would face entrapment on the west bank of the canal. An Israeli official observed Nov. 19 that "instead of having the Egyptian III Corps in a pocket, we would put our own forces in an Egyptian pocket."

Egypt rejected a proposal made by Israeli Premier Golda Meir Nov. 16 that both sides withdraw to either side of the canal and that the United Nations Emergency Force establish a buffer zone between the two armies.

Disengagement talks broken off. Israeli and Egyptian military negotiators broke off their talks at Kilometer 101 Nov. 29 after reaching an impasse on disengagement of their forces along the Suez Canal. No date was set for a new meeting.

According to sources close to the negotiations, Israeli Maj. Gen. Aharon Yariv had repeated his government's proposal that Israeli forces eventually withdraw to the Mitla Pass in the Sinai, 20 miles east of the canal, in exchange for an agreement by Egypt to thin out its forces along the eastern bank of the waterway. Yariv said no further progress could be expected on the withdrawal problem before the projected Geneva peace conference.

Israeli sources said the talks had broken down over Egyptian demands that Israeli troops return to the Oct. 22 positions on the west bank of the canal and pull back 20-23 miles from the eastern side of the territory they had held in the Sinai since 1967.

An Egyptian spokesman blamed Israel for the deadlock, charging that its delegation was "stalling and even backtracking" on some of Yariv's earlier statements.

Previous meetings between Yariv and his Egyptian counterpart, Maj. Gen. Mohammed Abdel Ghany el-Gamasy, had been held Nov. 22–26.

Charge Israel builds canal causeway— Egypt charged Nov. 17 that Israeli forces were building a causeway across the Suez Canal in violation of the truce and said this action was creating "a great change in the canal's structure as an international waterway." According to Cairo's complaint, the Israelis were bulldozing thousands of tons of dirt into the canal on both banks in the area of Deversoir, north of the Great Bitter Lake.

A U.N. patrol investigating the allegation confirmed the report, saying it appeared the causeway "consisted of large concrete pipes, permitting the flow of water, and hard surface." The U.N. statement would not judge whether the change was minor or major in the canal's use as a waterway.

The Israeli command said Nov. 17 that it had only three pontoon bridges spanning the canal in the Deversoir area, which had been first set up by the Israelis in crossing to the west bank in October.

Israelis, Egyptians exchange fire— Israeli and Egyptian forces exchanged heavy machine-gun and mortar fire Nov. 29 less than two miles from Kilometer 101 as the negotiations began. A provisional report issued by the United Nations Emergency Force (UNEF) said the Egyptians had started the shooting and that the Israelis returned the fire.

An Egyptian spokesman disputed the UNEF report, saying Cairo's forces had returned the fire after coming under attack by three Israeli armored cars. The spokesman said the Israelis had fired at Egyptians in two other areas.

An Israeli spokesman said one of two Israelis hit by Egyptian sniper fire died Nov. 28.

U.N. seeks renewal of truce talks. The commander of the United Nations Emergency Force (UNEF), Maj. Gen. Ensio Siilasvuo, held separate meetings with Egyptian and Israeli officials in an effort to get both sides to resume the truce talks that had broken down Nov. 29.

Siilasvuo first conferred in Cairo Nov. 30 with Egyptian War Minister Ahmed Ismail and then flew to Jerusalem, where he met Dec. 2 with Israeli Defense Minister Moshe Dayan and Maj. Gen. Aharon Yariv, Israel's chief negotiator at the truce talks.

Egyptian Foreign Minister Ismail Fahmy had called on the U.S. and the Soviet Union Nov. 30 to break the truce deadlock by pressuring Israel to withdraw its forces to the Oct. 22 cease-fire lines. Fahmy's request was delivered in separate meetings held with U.S. Ambassador Hermann F. Eilts and Soviet Ambassador Vladimir M. Vinogradov.

President Anwar Sadat conferred with the two envoys Dec. 1, reportedly calling on them to persuade Israel to return to the Oct. 22 lines.

Israeli Premier Golda Meir expressed optimism Dec. 1 that the Israeli-Egyptian truce talks would be resumed. She disclosed that Israel had offered proposals to Egypt that "went beyond what they could have expected to demand to achieve

complete disengagement." She said Egypt had turned down the unspecified proposal and had demanded an Israeli withdrawal that "went beyond the purpose of preserving the cease-fire."

Premier Meir was dubious about U.S. security guarantees for Israel. She asked: "Are the Americans now, after Vietnam, in a position to guarantee our security? How? By sending troops?"

Israel indicated Dec. 1 that the Egyptians had lifted the blockade of the Bab el Mandeb Strait at the entrance to the Red Sea. The blockade had been imposed at the start of the October war. Maj. Gen. Aharon Yariv, Israel's negotiator at the Kilometer 101 truce talks, said in an interview that the cease-fire "now prevails at sea as well as on land."

U.S. to pay UNEF cost. The U.S. became the first of the big five powers to agree Nov. 21 to pay its portion of the cost of operating the United Nations Emergency Force (UNEF).

UNEF's total upkeep for the first six months of operation was estimated at $30 million. The U.S. was to pay $8,668,000, the largest share. Britain was to pay $1,-841,000, the Soviet Union $4,497,000 and France $2,032,000. China had announced it would not pay its $1,907,000 share because it was opposed to UNEF.

The Indonesian Defense Ministry announced Nov. 22 that it had indefinitely postponed the dispatch of its contingent to UNEF. A ministry spokesman attributed the delay to technical reasons.

Arab Views & Actions

Arab summit: 'practical solidarity.' The heads of 15 Arab states and Palestinian leaders held a summit conference in Staoueli, Algeria Nov. 26–28 to review the October war with Israel and to plan future Arab strategy.

A communique issued at the conclusion of the parley Nov. 28 endorsed "political efforts" toward a Middle East peace agreement, but only on condition that Israel withdraw from all the occupied Arab territories, "notably Jerusalem," that is, the former Jordanian sector of the city. The conference gave implicit approval to Egypt's decision to enter into peace negotiations with Israel, scheduled to start in Geneva Dec. 18.

In a declaration issued at the conclusion of the conference, the Arab heads of state stated that Egyptian and Syrian armed forces had "inflicted severe blows on the Israeli aggressors. The Arab peoples and their governments gained in this fight a sharp awareness of their responsibilities and their material and human means. This awareness resulted in practical solidarity which showed its efficiency and which forms a new dimension in the process of Arab liberation."

The declaration pointed out that the "cease-fire is not yet peace," and cited two "paramount and unchangeable" conditions to achieve that end: "evacuation by Israel of the occupied Arab territories, and first of all Jerusalem; and re-establishment of the full national rights for the Palestinian people."

A separate resolution on oil adopted by the conferees called for its continued use "as an economic weapon" to force Israeli withdrawal from occupied Arab areas and to grant the Palestinians their "national rights." It asked that the oil embargo against nations supporting Israel be maintained, that there be a continued reduction of oil output until revenues of the oil producing states did not exceed one quarter of their oil revenues in 1972 and that there be a ban on the "re-exporting of oil from one state to a hostile state."

Egyptian President Anwar Sadat had called for the prolonged use of the "oil weapon" in a speech to the delegates earlier Nov. 28. He said the Arabs should "pursue this long and bitter struggle" with Israel "through all means, political, economic and military."

The conference Nov. 27 also officially recognized the Palestine Liberation Organization (PLO), headed by Yasir Arafat who was in attendance, as the sole legitimate representative of the Palestinian people. The decision was regarded as a blow to Jordanian King Hussein, who had repeatedly insisted on being the principal spokesman for the Palestinians.

Hussein did not attend the conference but was represented at the meeting by Bahjat Talhouni, head of the king's Cabinet. Hussein's absence was said to have been based on his opposition to a reported conference plan to support creation of a Palestinian state in the Israeli-occupied West Bank and Gaza Strip. The final summit communique did not specifically mention this plan.

Hussein had said Nov. 26 that his country would not attend the Geneva conference if the Arab summit meeting designated the PLO as the exclusive, representative of the Palestinians.

The summit talks were boycotted by Libyan leader Col. Muammar el-Qaddafi and Iraqi President Ahmed Hassan al-Bakr because of their opposition to Arab policies. A Baghdad announcement had said Nov. 19 that Iraq "does not regard that the convening of the Arab summit conference will achieve the Arab masses' aims of liberation and continuation of the struggle against" Israel.

Qaddafi had said he would not attend because Libya in effect "would be asked to recognize Israel."

Libya scores Egypt-Israel talks. Col. Muammar el-Qaddafi, Libyan leader, denounced the U.S. and the Soviet Union for stopping the Arab-Israeli war and assailed Egypt for entering into negotiations with Israel.

In an interview published in a Beirut magazine Nov. 12, Qaddafi said, "The war should have gone on, for years if need be, until the Arab or Israeli side finished the other off completely." The conflict was "one of survival between two deadly opposed nations, religions and civilizations" and the Middle East "has no room for both antagonists," he said.

The Libyan leader criticized U.S.-Soviet peace moves: "Their presence and intervention in the Middle East is unacceptable, . . . because each is serving its own interests rather than that of the Arabs or the Israelis."

In another statement, Qaddafi said he was "extremely furious" at the cease-fire negotiations currently being conducted by Israel and Egypt. Qaddafi's remarks were contained in a cablegram sent to Egyptian President Anwar Sadat and made public Nov. 15 by the Libyan press agency. He also criticized Sadat for launching the war against Israel and then agreeing to the

U.N. cease-fire without consulting Libya. Acceptance of the truce, Qaddafi complained, "gave the enemy [Israel] an opportunity to make up for his losses in arms and men. We recognized Israel in principle and accepted direct negotiations, which naturally lead to peace with her."

While visiting Paris Nov. 25, Qaddafi told a news conference that the only way to resolve the Middle East crisis was for all Jews who emigrated to Israel after 1948 to return to the land of their origin and for the Palestinians to regain their homes in Israel. Qaddafi asserted that Libya would welcome back Jews who had left and give them full citizenship. He said European countries must bar all further emigration to Israel.

Libya closed its embassy in Cairo Dec. 1. The move was in apparent protest against Egypt's conduct of the war against Israel, its acceptance of a cease-fire and the decision of the Arab summit meeting endorsing a peace conference with Israel.

Arabs to withdraw U.S. bank funds. A withdrawal of Arab funds from U.S. banks to finance development projects in Arab countries had been agreed by a meeting of the Arab League in Cairo, it was reported Dec. 6.

League spokesmen said there would be a "gradual withdrawal of deposits" and that "special committees will meet to discuss what percentages would be withdrawn and how the money would be invested." Egypt and Syria were to get top priority for the development programs, it was reported.

The Arabs were believed to have about $10 billion on deposit in Western banks in both official and private funds.

Arab Weapons

Syria gets Soviet arms. The Soviet Union was shipping large quantities of arms to Syria, while the Syrians were at the same time seeking to purchase military equipment from the West, the New York Times reported in a dispatch from Damascus Nov. 18.

The report said the newly-shipped Soviet matériel already had been put into service by the Syrians and that convoys carrying new Russian tanks had been seen in recent days moving on the highway from the port of Homs to Damascus.

The Times report said the equipment Syria sought to buy from the West included electronic devices and other air-defense gear to counteract jamming by Israeli planes of Syria's radar system. The Syrians were believed offering cash in convertible Western currencies, which reportedly was being provided by Saudi Arabia and Kuwait.

U.S. suspects Soviet A-arms in Egypt. U.S. defense officials said Nov. 21 that the Soviet Union might have sent atomic warheads to Egypt during the height of the fighting in October and that some of the weapons might still be there under Soviet control. The report was followed by an Egyptian appeal to other Arab states Nov. 23 to acquire or manufacture atomic bombs as a counter-deterrent to Israel's nuclear capability.

According to American intelligence cited by the U.S. officials, the Soviet atomic warheads were for Soviet-built Scud missiles, also shipped to Egypt before or during the fighting. The missiles, had an estimated range of 160–180 miles, within reach of Israeli cities if fired from northeast Egypt.

U.S. intelligence had confirmed Nov. 2 that the Scuds had been brought into Egypt but at the time said there was "no confirmatory evidence" that they were armed with nuclear warheads.

Secretary of State Henry A. Kissinger told reporters at a news conference Nov. 21 that "we have no confirmed evidence that the Soviet Union has introduced nuclear weapons in Egypt. There are Soviet public statements rejecting this allegation." Kissinger added: "If the Soviet Union were known to introduce nuclear weapons into local conflict this would be a fundamental shift in traditional practices and one hard to reconcile with an effort to bring about a responsible solution." These views were similar to those believed transmitted by Kissinger to Soviet Ambassador Anatoly F. Dobrynin Oct. 24 just prior to the ordering of U.S. military alert in response to reports of possible Soviet military intervention in the Middle East.

The shipment of Soviet atomic weapons into Egypt also was questioned by two members of the U.S. Senate Armed Services Committee Nov. 21. Sen. Stuart S. Symington (D, Mo.) said he had investigated the reports and was "convinced" they were not true. Sen. John C. Stennis (D, Miss.), committee chairman, said he was "not impressed" with the reports.

Arabs urged to seek atomic weapons—
The suggestion that the Arabs arm themselves with atomic weapons was made Nov. 23 by Mohammed Hassanien Heykal, editor of the semiofficial Egyptian newspaper Al Ahram.

Heykal wrote that acquisition of nuclear weapons was necessary because he was convinced that Israel was in possession of atomic weapons and might use them to "blackmail" the Arabs. He said a high-level American visitor had told him recently that the U.S. had feared during the fighting in October that the Israelis "might lose their nerve and use the three [atom] bombs they had in order to repel the Arab offensive."

Heykal said the Arabs "have the means of making an atom bomb" and urged that Arab scientists pool their efforts to accomplish this.

Heykal disclosed that the late President Gamal Abdel Nasser had attempted to start an atom bomb development project. He said Col. Muammar el-Qaddafi, Libyan leader, had tried to buy an atomic bomb in 1970 but "soon realized that atomic bombs were not for sale."

Heykal implied that Egypt had an understanding with the Soviet Union and China for nuclear weapons assistance if Israel posed an atomic threat before the Arabs could get their own nuclear arms.

Prisoners & Peace Talks

POW exchanges & atrocities. The exchange of Israeli and Egyptian prisoners of war was completed Nov. 22. Since the start of the repatriation of the POWs Nov. 15, an airlift supervised by the

International Committee of the Red Cross (ICRC) had returned 241 Israelis and 8,031 Egyptians, an ICRC official said.

Defense Minister Moshe Dayan who greeted the last of the returning Israeli prisoners at Lod airport near Tel Aviv, said Nov. 22 that the Egyptians may have murdered some captured Israelis. Dayan said some Israelis taken by the Egyptians during the war "are no longer living and were not returned. Apparently they were murdered or died in some other way."

Israel had filed a complaint with the ICRC in Geneva Nov. 10, charging that Syria had murdered 28 Israeli prisoners of war. The ICRC replied to the Israelis that it could not investigate the allegations, but it transmitted the Israeli statement to Syrian authorities, the Israeli state radio announced Nov. 11. Israel had filed a similar complaint about the alleged incident with U.N. Secretary General Kurt Waldheim Nov. 8.

The alleged Syrian atrocities were cited Nov. 26 by U.S. Rep. Bella Abzug (D, N.Y.), who had returned from a recent Congressional mission to Israel. She displayed photographs at a New York news conference, which she said showed the bodies of Israeli soldiers found at several places on the Golan Heights after the territory was retaken from Syrian forces. Israeli sources had informed her that the men had been blindfolded and murdered, Abzug said. She said the photographs were given her by Premier Golda Meir. A total of about 30 Israeli prisoners had been found under similar circumstances elsewhere on the Golan Heights, Abzug said.

Israeli Foreign Minister Abba Eban had said Nov. 22 that Damascus must free Israeli prisoners before Israel "can sit with Syria at a peace conference." Eban said he had discussed details of the proposed parley in Washington Nov. 21 with Secretary of State Henry A. Kissinger.

Eban had met with U.N. Secretary General Kurt Waldheim at U.N. headquarters Nov. 10 to discuss the return of Israeli prisoners from Syria. The minister urged "vigorous international action" to gain their release.

Syria announced Nov. 23 that it would not exchange prisoners with Israel for the present. It said the exchange "will be carried out only within the framework of a total Israeli withdrawal from occupied Arab lands."

Israel filed a complaint with Waldheim charging that at least 42 Israeli soldiers taken prisoner on the Syrian front in the October war were murdered, it was reported Dec. 9.

The document claimed that the captives had been slain by Syrian, Moroccan and Iraqi soldiers. It said the prisoners had been beaten and knifed, while others were bound and executed.

The document included a copy of a complaint to the International Committee of the Red Cross (ICRC), requesting that it investigate the Israeli accusations of "murder, brutality and other grave breaches of the Geneva Conventions." The Israelis also charged that before the outbreak of the war Oct. 6, Syrian soldiers had been ordered to remove the identity tags from dead Israelis to make identification difficult and that some of these disks were later discovered in possession of captured Syrians.

Syria's chief delegate to the U.N., Haissam Kelani, said Dec. 9 that he knew nothing about the Israeli charges but that Israel's first allegation of Syrian atrocities made Nov. 10 was "completely false." Kelani in turn accused Israel of violating the Geneva Conventions by expelling 24,000 Syrians from their villages in the battle zone.

Another Israeli complaint submitted to the U.N. Dec. 10 for the first time accused Egypt of murdering at least 28 Israeli POWs. The memorandum also said that in the early days of their imprisonment the captives had been denied sufficient food and water, sanitary facilities or medical care. Israel had sent the ICRC a report on this alleged incident Dec. 9.

Egyptian authorities Dec. 10 denied the Israeli atrocity charges. Maj. Gen. Ezzedin Mokhtar, spokesman for the high command, accused Israel instead of violating the Geneva Conventions by torturing military and civilian prisoners captured on the west bank of the Suez Canal. Mokhtar said Israel "had stopped food and drink for prisoners so that they were about to perish."

Israel accepts peace conference bid. The Israeli Cabinet announced Nov. 25 that it had accepted in principle a U.S. proposal to attend a peace conference on the Middle East, scheduled to start in Geneva Dec. 18. Jordan also had agreed in principle to be present.

An Israeli source said acceptance had been qualified because Israel had not yet received a formal request. "Upon receipt of an official invitation, it will be discussed by the Cabinet and a formal decision will be taken," it was stated.

The semi-official Egyptian newspaper Al Ahram reported Nov. 24 that President Anwar Sadat had informed Palestinian commando leader Yasir Arafat that Cairo would not attend the peace parley until Israeli forces withdrew to the Oct. 22 cease-fire lines on the Sinai front.

Dayan for retaining Arab areas—Defense Minister Moshe Dayan asserted Nov. 23 that in the forthcoming peace conference Israel must insist on retaining former Arab territories for its security. "Woe betide us if we are not strong," he said. "The Americans will not support us and the Arabs will not pity us."

Dayan alluded to Secretary of State Henry A. Kissinger's Nov. 12 suggestion that Israel withdraw from the Arab territories in exchange for security guarantees. Such international guarantees, the defense minister said, could supplement defensible borders, but were no substitute for them. Therefore, Dayan said, Israel must retain the Golan Heights, the Jordan Valley and the radar installations in the hills of Nablus in the West Bank, the Gidi and Mitla passes in the Sinai, and Sharm el Sheik, which controlled the passage between the Red Sea and the Gulf of Aqaba.

Egypt accepts Geneva conference bid. Egypt formally announced Dec. 8 that it would participate in the Geneva peace conference.

Deputy Premier Abdel Kader Hatem told Parliament, however, that Cairo would not permit the parley to be used by Israel to return to the prewar stalemate. He said: "We have accepted the cease-fire because we are keen to preserve peace. The real threat to peace is Israeli refusal to implement the United Nations resolutions." Hatem warned that although Egypt had accepted an invitation to attend the conference, it was also "prepared to liberate the occupied Arab territories, whatever the sacrifices."

President Anwar Sadat met with Syrian President Hafez al-Assad in Cairo Dec. 11 to plan diplomatic strategy for the conference. Assad had arrived in the Egyptian capital Dec. 10 from Libya, where he and Sadat had conferred by telephone with Libyan leader Muammar el-Qaddafi.

Syrian Deputy Foreign Minister Zakharia Ismail had said Dec. 6 that his country would not attend the Geneva conference unless Israel agreed beforehand to withdraw its forces to the truce lines of Oct. 22 on the Syrian and Egyptian fronts. Ismail noted that Israel did not contest that the U.N. Security Council Resolution 339 (the resolution of Oct. 23) implied a pullback to the Oct. 22 lines on the Syrian front but had wrongly linked the application of the resolution with the matter of prisoners of war. Since the resolution "does not mention the Geneva Conventions," the POWs and withdrawal were therefore "two completely different problems," Ismail said.

Israel lists conditions—Defense Minister Moshe Dayan told the Israeli Knesset Dec. 10 that according to a Cabinet decision, the Israeli delegation to the Geneva conference would not "sit with the Syrians" if they failed to supply a list of Israeli prisoners they held. However, he said Israel would not boycott the talks if Syria did not provide the figures.

A government source said later that the Israeli delegation would attend even if the Syrians were there but would have no dealings with them if Damascus did not produce the list.

Dayan gave a different interpretation of the Cabinet decision Dec. 11, saying it meant that "if Syria doesn't provide [prisoner] lists and they are participants at the conference, we shall not come to the conference."

Kissinger tours Mideast. U.S. Secretary of State Henry A. Kissinger visited Algiers, Cairo, Riyadh, Damascus, Amman, Beirut and Jerusalem Dec. 13–17 to discuss last-minute procedural and substantive problems involved in the Geneva conference.

Kissinger's first stop was in Algiers, where he conferred for two hours Dec. 13 with Algerian President Houari Boumedienne. Foreign Minister Abdel Aziz Bouteflika said later that as a result of the talks, relations between Algeria and the U.S. were now at "a turning point" and that a "dialogue" was in progress. Diplomatic ties between the two countries had been severed in 1967.

Kissinger flew to Cairo and met Dec. 13–14 with Egyptian President Anwar Sadat. At the end of their discussions Kissinger said he and Sadat had "agreed that disengagement of forces—separation of forces—should be the principal subject of the first phase" of the Geneva peace conference, permitting United Nations troops to act as a buffer between the Israeli and Egyptian armies.

Sadat expressed satisfaction with "the long fruitful discussions" with Kissinger. He said Egyptian representatives would "gather in the same room" with the Israeli delegation in Geneva but would hold no "direct negotiations" with them.

At his meeting in Riyadh Dec. 14 with King Faisal, Kissinger and the Saudi Arabian monarch discussed the diplomatic details preparatory to the Geneva parley and the Arab oil embargo.

Kissinger's six-hour meeting in Damascus Dec. 15 with President Hafez al-Assad was the first high-level discussions between Syrian and U.S. officials since 1967 and the first visit to Damascus by a U.S. secretary of state since 1953. An American official said afterward that U.S.-Syrian contacts, broken off in 1967, could be expected to be resumed soon.

Kissinger flew to Amman and met with Jordanian King Hussein and Prime Minister Zaid al-Rifai Dec. 15–16. The secretary said he had achieved a "complete identity" of views with the Jordanians.

The secretary went to Lebanon later Dec. 16 and conferred with government officials, including President Suleiman

Franjieh and Premier Takieddin Solh. Kissinger's flight was diverted from Beirut to Riyaq, about 30 miles to the east, for security reasons. Lebanese officials feared the presence of a large number of anti-American protesters at the Beirut airfield and the possible appearance of armed Palestinians, who lived at a nearby refugee camp. The talks were held at a military airbase at Riyaq.

The last leg of Kissinger's Middle East tour was Jerusalem, where he held talks Dec. 17 with Israeli government leaders, including Premier Golda Meir, Defense Minister Moshe Dayan and Foreign Minister Abba Eban. Israeli officials said later that their government's reaffirmation to attend the Geneva conference had been given in exchange for Kissinger's pledge of American support for Israel at the talks.

A statement issued by Premier Meir's office later Dec. 17 reiterated that Israel would not confer with the Syrians at Geneva unless they provided a list of Israeli prisoners they held and permitted Red Cross officials to visit them.

Geneva peace conference postponed. The Middle East peace conference scheduled to start in Geneva Dec. 18 was postponed until Dec. 21. The delay was said to have been caused by disagreement on procedural questions, particularly the role of the United Nations Security Council at the meeting.

Israel had insisted the conference be held under the aegis of the U.S. and the Soviet Union. It opposed the Arabs' demands that the U.N. have a major part at the parley on the ground that the U.N. was biased against Israel.

Syria announced Dec. 18 that it would not join Egypt and Jordan at the conference. A Damascus statement said the decision to boycott was taken because the U.S. and Israel would turn the conference "into a meeting to discuss partial issues leading to endless discussions with the aim of weakening the basic cause"—getting Israel to withdraw from Arab lands and safeguarding the rights of the Palestinians.

Egypt Dec. 18 reaffirmed its decision to attend the Geneva talks despite Syria's refusal to participate.

The start of the talks was formally announced by the U.S. and the Soviet Union Dec. 18. A joint announcement was released in Madrid by aides to U.S. Secretary of State Henry A. Kissinger, who had arrived in the Spanish capital following a tour of Middle East capitals to set the stage for the parley.

Kissinger and Soviet Foreign Minister Andrei A. Gromyko were to be co-chairmen at the meetings. The text of identical letters delivered to Secretary General Kurt Waldheim by the U.S. and the Soviet Union relegated the U.N. to a minor role even though it said the conference would be held under its auspices. The statement said: "The parties have agreed that the conference should be under the co-chairmanship of the Soviet Union and the United States." It said both sides also had "agreed that the question of other participants from the Middle East area will be discussed during the first stage of the conference."

The U.S. and the Soviet Union called on Waldheim to participate in the opening, ceremonial meetings and to send a representative to keep him informed of the progress.

Waldheim's "full and effective role" at the Geneva conference had been affirmed in a resolution adopted at a closed meeting of the U.N. Security Council Dec. 15. The resolution, also stating that the conclave would be held under U.N. auspices, was approved by 10 affirmative votes of the non-permanent members. The U.S., Britain, France, and the Soviet Union abstained. China dissociated itself from the vote. U.S. acting chief delegate W. Tapley Bennett said he abstained "because I did not have the authorization to support" the resolution. "We would have preferred a consensus approach," rather than a formal resolution, he said.

Truce Breaches

Israeli-Syrian clashes. Israeli and Syrian forces engaged in tank and artillery duels on the Golan Heights front Dec. 2–3.

Damascus claimed that in a three-hour exchange of fire Dec. 2 in the Hurfah and Mizrat Beit Jinan areas Syrian forces destroyed an Israeli engineering unit, three tanks, a bulldozer and an ammunition dump. An Israeli spokesman said his side suffered casualties.

A Damascus communique claimed 15 Israelis were killed or wounded Dec. 3 in heavy exchanges of artillery and tank fire in the central sector of the 50-mile northern front. One Syrian soldier was killed and four others wounded, the report said. Israel said four of its soldiers were wounded.

Israel also exchanged sporadic fire with Egyptian forces on the Suez front Dec. 2. Egypt claimed it had downed an Israeli Phantom jet Dec. 5 east of Ismailia. Israel denied the claim, but acknowledged that two of its soldiers were killed and one wounded that day when their jeep struck a mine on the west bank. Four other Israeli soldiers were wounded near Ismailia by Egyptian small arms fire, the spokesman said.

Israeli and Egyptian planes clashed over the Gulf of Suez Dec. 6. Israel claimed it had downed an Egyptian MiG-21 just south of the Suez Canal and that all its own planes had returned safely. Cairo said an Israeli Phantom was shot down and that no Egyptian planes were lost. Both sides contended that the dogfight resulted from violation of each other's airspace.

Israel reported clashes on the Suez front Dec. 8, saying 10 Israeli soldiers were wounded in artillery exchanges near Nafisha, southwest of Ismailia.

A United Nations spokesman in Cairo reported Dec. 10 that Egyptian forces Dec. 8 had committed 22 truce violations and the Israelis five. Eight other incidents were reported.

Israeli death toll at 2,412—New figures released by the Israeli armed forces Dec. 8 placed its death toll in the October war and its aftermath at 2,412. This was 558 more than the last official count Nov. 6.

The new figure included 293 soldiers missing in action and certified as dead. The total number of missing was placed at 508—406 on the Egyptian front and 102 on the Syrian front. The new death toll included 57 men who were killed or died of their wounds after the cease-fire went into effect Oct. 25.

Egyptians down Israeli plane. Egypt claimed an Israeli "spy plane" was shot down Dec. 13 in the southern sector of the Suez Canal front. An Israeli army spokesman acknowledged that an unmanned Israeli robot plane on a patrol flight was diverted from its course and crashed into Egyptian territory Dec. 13.

Egypt protested to the U.S. Dec. 13 against what it called a violation of its airspace by a U.S. "spy plane" Dec. 10.

Suez truce violations. The cease-fire along the Suez Canal front was broken continually by sporadic clashes between Israeli and Egyptian forces Dec. 19-31. The United Nations Emergency Force (UNEF) attributed hundreds of violations to both sides during that period.

Most of the fighting consisted of small-arms shooting, but there were some artillery and tank-gun duels. The clashes were centered largely south of the canal in the area of the Israeli bridgehead on the western bank and were marked by small ground advances by Egyptian troops.

Among the major incidents:

Clashes Dec. 19 endangered Finnish troops of UNEF. UNEF commander, Lt. Gen. Ensio Sillasvuo, protested to the Egyptians and Israelis. He urged both sides to practice "restraint, observation of the cease-fire and insure the safety" of UNEF personnel.

A Finnish soldier was wounded Dec. 22 in an exchange of gunfire between the Israelis and Egyptians on the outskirts of the city of Suez.

Israel reported Dec. 27 that the Egyptians were building two causeways across the canal in the northern sector where both shores of the waterway were controlled by the Egyptian II Corps.

Israeli and Egyptian forces fought a five-hour battle Dec. 27 about nine miles northwest of Kilometer 101 on the Cairo-Suez road on the west bank. The clash was among 40 breaches of the truce that also included an artillery duel west of Ismailia and a tank-gun battle in the Sinai.

Egypt claimed its air defenses shot down an Israeli plane that intruded over Egyptian lines Dec. 28 near Suez city.

The Egyptians reported their ground guns shot down another Israeli plane Dec. 29 east of Lake Timsah in the southern sector. Israel acknowledged loss of the aircraft but said it was an unmanned observation plane that was hit over Israeli-held territory.

Egypt's semi-official newspaper Al Ahram reported Dec. 31 that a military supply route had been clandestinely opened to the trapped III Corps on the eastern bank. Under the cease-fire agreement, the isolated Egyptian troops were permitted to receive only food, water and medicine. The military equipment was believed reaching the III Corps across the northern end of the Gulf of Suez. Al Ahram claimed that two parts of the III Corps had established contact, thus "trapping the Israeli forces west of the canal in a pincer."

Oil Developments

U.S. urges Arabs end oil ban. Secretary of State Henry A. Kissinger said Dec. 6 that the U.S. again had called on the Arabs to end their oil embargo.

Speaking at a Washington news conference, Kissinger said since the U.S. was actively engaged in efforts to achieve peace in the Middle East, "We continue to believe that discriminatory measures against the United States and pressures are no longer appropriate."

"What the United States might do if other countries treat us unreasonably . . .; we will leave until that situation arises," he said. Kissinger stressed the need for cooperation rather than confrontation between the Arabs and the U.S. as "we are approaching the negotiations" at the Geneva peace conference.

Kissinger conceded that the Soviet Union had played "a constructive role" in setting up the Geneva conference. He cautioned, however, that Soviet attempts "to push extremist solutions" at the parley "would make a settlement extremely difficult."

He expressed doubt about the establishment of a joint U.S.-Soviet peace-keeping force to guarantee a settlement, but he did not rule it out. The U.S., he said, would "consider the question of guarantees in its broadest sense" as proposed by any of the parties.

The Soviet Union denied speculation in the West European press that Moscow

was involved in the Arab oil embargo. The newspaper Sovestskaya Rossiya Dec. 4 singled out the London Times and the Frankfurter Allgemine of West Germany for "starting an anti-Soviet ballyhoo resorting to concoctions and lies" and placing the blame "at the wrong door." The newspaper added: "Everyone knows who is to blame for the present energy crisis in Western Europe. They are the imperialist and Zionist circles stubbornly resisting a just Middle East settlement."

Kissinger meets Saudi on oil ban— Saudi Arabian Petroleum Minister Sheik Ahmed Zaki al-Yamani conferred in Washington Dec. 5 with Secretary of State Kissinger and other American officials on the Arab oil embargo against the U.S. Yamani told newsmen after his meetings that his country was prepared to lift its total ban as soon as the Israelis "start withdrawing" their forces from occupied Arab lands. "I think that when the Israelis decide to withdraw, and there is a timetable for that, there will be a timetable to increase production step by step in a manner which corresponds with the timetable of the withdrawal," Yamani said.

On the question of Arab recognition of Israel, Yamani said, "So many Arab leaders have announced they are prepared to sign a peace treaty with Israel that the question of the existence of Israel is not an issue. . . . It is not tied to the oil issue in any case."

Yamani had arrived in the U.S. Dec. 3 for a week-long stay as part of a tour of Western nations to explain Arab views. Yamani, accompanied by Algerian Minister of Industry and Energy Belaid Abdessalem, had toured West European countries Nov. 26–Dec. 1. Their discussions included meetings with French officials in Paris Nov. 26, with Belgian officials in Brussels Nov. 30 and with Dutch leaders and representatives of the European Economic Community (EEC) in Brussels Dec. 1.

Dutch Economic Affairs Minister Ruud Lubbers said Dec. 1 after his meeting with the two Arab oil representatives that their demands for his government's condemnation of Israel and a call for a complete Israeli withdrawal in exchange for a resumption of oil exports to the

Netherlands was "out of the question." Lubbers added: "We are not going to buy oil on a Saturday morning after making a declaration that could be misunderstood by others."

A statement issued by the Dutch government Dec. 4 for the first time referred to Israel's occupation of Arab lands as "illegal." A Foreign Office spokesman clarifying his government's Mideast policy, said that the Dutch-endorsed EEC statement of Nov. 6 "meant in principle that Israel should move out of the Arab territories she is holding, occupied since the 1967 six-day war. Fully adhering to that position the Dutch government considers that the Israeli presence in occupied territory is illegal."

Prior to endorsement of the EEC statement, the Dutch had interpreted the 1967 U.N. Security Countil resolution on Israeli withdrawal not to necessarily mean that Israel was to pull back to the pre-1967 borders.

In a TV interview in Washington Dec. 9, Yamani again said the Arabs would lift the oil embargo against the U.S. "when Israel accepts the withdrawal from the occupied Arab territory, and that acceptance is guaranteed" by the U.S. He said "there is nothing between the United States and Saudi Arabia as a bilateral dispute." He asserted that if "the political obstacle" to peace was removed, "What is left is an economic question and I think it is possible that Saudi Arabia will meet most of the world demand for oil."

Yamani said in return for withdrawal, Israel would get a "secure boundary as such, secured by the treaty of peace and possibly by the guarantee of superpowers, if this is what they want." He said Israel's immediate neighbors, Egypt, Jordan, Syria and Lebanon, "have to recognize the crisis and sign a peace treaty with Israel."

Arabs announce new cutback. Oil ministers of nine Arab nations agreed at a meeting in Kuwait Dec. 9 to reduce petroleum production by about 750,000 barrels a day starting Jan. 1, 1974. The new cutback, 5% of the current level of output, would largely affect Western Europe and Japan. It would bring the total cutback since September to about 28.75%.

A statement issued by the conferees said if Israel signed an agreement to withdraw its troops from occupied Arab lands and if the U.S. guaranteed that pullback, "the ban on oil exportation to the U.S. shall be lifted as soon as the implementation of the withdrawal time schedule begins."

A spokesman for the Kuwait Oil Ministry was quoted as saying that West Europe and Japan must "offer something more concrete and put more pressure on the United States and Israel" if they wanted to avoid more oil cutbacks.

The Kuwait meeting was attended by oil ministers of Abu Dhabi, Algeria, Bahrain, Egypt, Kuwait, Libya, Qatar, Saudi Arabia and Syria.

Italy seeks closer Arab ties. A meeting of Italy's top political leaders Dec. 12 called for closer relations with Arab oil-producing countries. The statement was drawn up after a 12-hour national strategy meeting that included Premier Mariano Rumor and the leaders of the four parties that comprised his government.

The conference discussed what action Italy should take in the coming months to cope with the energy crisis. The statement urged "a joint European initiative and strategy" to deal with the fuel shortage and the Middle East dispute.

Raffele Girotti, president of the state-owned fuel combine Ente Nazionale Idrocarburi (ENI), had called on the government to adopt "a new foreign policy" that would satisfy the Arab oil-producing states.

Iraq increasing oil output. Iraq announced Dec. 18 that it planned to increase its present oil output of 2.1 million barrels a day to 3.5 million barrels by 1975 despite the production cutoff of nine other Arab oil-producing states.

Oil and Minerals Minister Saadun Hammadi said "An oil production reduction means that we punish all countries of the world rather than just Israel and its backers." He said Iraq's national oil company was trying to help "friendly countries" that "have stood by us" in the Arab confrontation with Israel. Hammadi listed those friendly nations whose representatives had recently visited Iraq to discuss their fuel problems as Austria, Brazil, Bulgaria, India, Pakistan, Poland, Spain and Tanzania.

EEC summit for unity in crisis. The leaders of the nine member nations of the European Economic Community (EEC) agreed at their summit conference in Copenhagen Dec. 14–15 to develop a common energy policy to deal with the oil crisis.

The conference began Dec. 14 with the unexpected arrival in Copenhagen of the foreign ministers of Algeria, Tunisia, the Sudan and the Union of Arab Emirates, who later met with EEC foreign ministers. The Arabs reportedly stressed that the EEC nations would have to take a stronger pro-Arab position if they wanted an end to the oil squeeze. The Arabs were not officially invited to appear in Copenhagen.

Danish Foreign Minister K. B. Andersen, speaking for the rest of the EEC, warned the Arabs in a second meeting Dec. 15 that the oil squeeze could cause severe damage even to friendly European nations and that it was alienating public opinion, which could adversely affect Arab interests.

The final summit communique reaffirmed the EEC's Nov. 6 Middle East declaration calling for Israel to withdraw from Arab territories occupied since the 1967 war. It also called for the conclusion of Middle East peace agreements, including international guarantees and establishment of demilitarized zones. The EEC position would be conveyed to United Nations Secretary General Kurt Waldheim, an apparent concession to the Arab demand that the U.N. be responsible for the Middle East situation.

In an accompanying energy statement, the leaders said the oil crisis was "a threat to the world economy as a whole" and warned it would hurt developing as well as developed nations.

Japanese official tours oil states. Japanese Deputy Premier Takeo Miki returned to Tokyo Dec. 28 after a 19-day tour of the Middle East oil-producing states of Saudi Arabia, Egypt, Iran, Syria, Iraq, Kuwait and Abu Dhabi. Miki's mission was aimed at persuading those countries to reclassify Japan as a friendly nation to assure its "full oil needs."

After reporting to Premier Kakuei Tanaka, Miki said the premier "agreed with my view that our promises must, by all means, be carried out." The only commitment Miki was known to have made on his trip was disclosed after a meeting in Cairo with Egyptian President Anwar Sadat Dec. 18. Miki had offered Egypt a 25-year loan of $140 million to assist in widening and deepening the Suez Canal.

The Japanese government Dec. 13 had again called on Israel to withdraw to the Oct. 22 cease-fire lines as a first step toward a total pullback from occupied Arab territories.

Arabs double price, ease embargo. Oil producers of six Persian Gulf states announced after a two-day meeting in Teheran Dec. 23 that they would double the price of a barrel of oil effective Jan. 1, 1974. The decision was followed by an announcement by Arab petroleum producers in Kuwait Dec. 25 that starting Jan. 1 they would ease their embargo, but would continue the total ban against the U.S. and the Netherlands.

The gulf states of Iraq, Iran, Saudi Arabia, Kuwait, Abdu Dhabi and Qatar raised their posted price for crude oil to $11.65 a barrel from the current price of $5.11. The oil ministers' communique said the government income under the new price system would be $7 a barrel, compared with the present price of $3.09.

The six states were meeting under the aegis of the Organization of Petroleum Exporting Countries with five other OPEC members—Algeria, Indonesia, Libya, Nigeria and Venezuela—attending as observers.

Shah Mohammed Riza Pahlevi of Iran said after the meeting, "The industrial world will have to realize that the era of their terrific progress and even more terrific income and wealth based on cheap fuel is finished. They will have to find new sources of energy and tighten their belts."

Following a two-day meeting in Kuwait, the nine members of the 10-member Organization of Arab Petroleum Exporting Countries (OAPEC) announced Dec. 25 that starting Jan. 1 they would cancel a scheduled further 5% cut in production and would increase their output by 10% instead. Production, however, would remain 15% below what it had been in September when the oil countries began their cutbacks. Western Europe and Japan, hardest hit by the cutoff, would be the principal beneficiaries of the Arab decision.

The move was announced by Saudi Arabian Oil Minister Sheik Ahmed Zaki al-Yamani. He said the OAPEC had acted to ease their oil ban because Arab pressure had brought about favorable shifts in some countries' positions in the Arab-Israeli conflict. Yamani cited the change in the neutral policies adopted by Japan and Belgium, both of whom had called on Israel to withdraw from occupied Arab territory.

The countries that took action in Kuwait were Saudi Arabia, Kuwait, Abu Dhabi, Algeria, Libya, Bahrain, Qatar, Syria and Egypt. The 10th OAPEC member, Iraq, had expressed opposition to cutting oil production. Iraqi Oil and Minerals Minister Saadun Hammadi said Dec. 25 that the oil embargo was not affecting the U.S.

Other Developments

Dayan seeks U.S. arms. Israeli Defense Minister Moshe Dayan conferred in Washington Dec. 7 and 9, 1973 on more U.S. arms for his country.

Dayan held two separate meetings with Secretary of State Henry A. Kissinger Dec. 7 and also conferred that day with Deputy Defense Secretary William P. Clements and about 30 members of the Senate Foreign Relations Committee. Kissinger also met with Egyptian Ambassador Ashraf Ghorbal.

Dayan met Dec. 9 with Defense Secretary James R. Schlesinger on arms for Israel.

In a television interview Dec. 9, Dayan said that in his talks with Kissinger, the secretary had not pressured him to make concessions to attain a Middle East peace settlement. Dayan expressed opposition to total Israeli withdrawal from occupied Arab lands but said Israel would "give up some of the territory in order to reach an agreement." He again discounted international, including U.S., guarantees to secure his country's defense. This was no substitute, Dayan said, for Israeli arms and defensible borders.

Dayan had said in New York Dec. 8 that Israel was willing to give up some occupied Arab territory in exchange for a lasting peace. At the forthcoming Geneva conference, Israel would negotiate for "final, permanent boundaries," Dayan said. "We want to give them territory and we want them to give us peace."

Palestinians visit Moscow. Palestinian resistance leaders conferred with Soviet officials in Moscow Nov. 12–24. The delegation was headed by Palestine Liberation Organization (PLO) leader Yasir Arafat.

The Soviet news agency Tass reported Nov. 26 that Arafat and the other guerrilla leaders had been informed that Moscow would continue to provide the Palestinians with "assistance and support." Tass said the pledge was made by the Soviet Committee of Afro-Asian Solidarity, which had invited the group to Moscow.

Canadian Foreign Affairs Minister Mitchell Sharp had said in Moscow Nov. 20 that Foreign Minister Andrei A. Gromyko, in two days of talks, had stressed the need for the Palestinians to be represented at any Middle East peace conference.

The Lebanese newspaper An Nahar had reported Nov. 12 that Arafat and his group had been invited to Moscow by Soviet government officials to propose the formation of a Palestinian government in exile. The Soviet ambassador to Lebanon, Sarvar A. Azimov, was said to have met with Palestinian representatives in Beirut and discussed whether they would take part in a peace conference and whether they would accept the creation of a Palestinian state in the Israeli-occupied West Bank of the Jordan and Gaza Strip.

Israelis raid Lebanon. The Lebanese Defense Ministry reported that an Israeli armored force carried out a brief raid into southern Lebanon Nov. 16.

It was believed the strike was connected with Palestinian commando activity that the Israelis claim had been going on in the area. The ministry statement said that during a two-hour operation the Israeli force temporarily severed a road between the border villages of Yarin and Alma Chaab, four miles east of the Mediterranean coast. The ministry said the Israeli attackers were "inter-

Arabs hijack, free Dutch plane. A KLM Royal Dutch Airlines 747 passenger jet en route from Amsterdam to Tokyo was seized over Iraq Nov. 25 by three armed Palestinian hijackers. The plane and the last of its 11 hostages were released by the gunmen after landing in Dubai Nov. 28.

The plane, carrying 18 crew members and 247 passengers, mostly Japanese, was taken over by the hijackers Nov. 25 shortly after taking off from Beirut. The gunmen identified themselves as members of a little-known group called the Arab Nationalist Youth for the Liberation of Palestine. KLM said the men demanded that the airlines halt the transporting of arms to Israel and that the Dutch government drastically alter its "pro-Israel stance" and cease providing mediation or assistance in the emigration of Soviet Jews to Israel. They threatened to blow up the plane if their demands were not met.

The commandos forced the plane to turn back and land in Damascus, Syria, where it was denied refueling and then flew to Nicosia, Cyprus Nov. 26. It took off again after Cypriot officials rejected the hijackers' demand for release of seven Arabs jailed for the April attack on the home of Israel's ambassador to Cyprus and on an Israeli airliner. (The seven were granted amnesty by Cypriot President Makarias and flown to Cairo Dec. 6.)

The aircraft stopped briefly at Tripoli, Libya and then landed Nov. 27 at Valletta, Malta, where the gunmen freed all 247 passengers and eight stewardesses. Their release followed a Dutch government announcement Nov. 26 pledging not to "allow the opening of offices or camps for Soviet Jews going to Israel" and banning "transportation of weapons or volunteers for Israel."

(Jan J. de Roos, Dutch charge d'affaires in Tripoli, said Nov. 27 that his government never had transit facilities for Soviet Jews. He also denied that KLM had ever flown arms to Israel or that the Netherlands had ever given Israel military aid.)

The plane left Malta with 11 hostages—

10 crewmen and a KLM vice president, A.W. Withholt. It arrived in Dubai Nov. 28, then left for Aden, South Yemen and returned to Dubai later Nov. 28 after Yemeni authorities discouraged a landing. The three gunmen surrendered the plane and its 11 hostages in return for safe-conduct guarantees.

Israel expels 8 Palestinians. Israel Dec. 10 expelled eight Palestinians from the West Bank and East Jerusalem and sent them to Jordan in connection with an upsurge of terrorist bombings the previous week.

The men were charged with incitement and trying to undermine security, law, order and normal life and with advocating cooperation with Palestinian terrorist groups. Among those ousted were Mayor Abed Salah Ita of El Birah in the West Bank and Abed Abu Messager, a member of East Jerusalem's Supreme Moslem Council, which administrated the city's Moslem community affairs. The council had supported the resolutions adopted by the Arab summit meeting Nov. 26–28.

In related actions, Israeli forces Dec. 9 had demolished the homes of five Arabs in the West Bank town of Abu Daif in connection with a grenade attack in November.

Terror attacks in Israel—A hand grenade exploded in the Old City of Jerusalem Dec. 4, injuring 20 persons. Among those wounded were five Israeli women soldiers. A Palestinian commando group in Beirut, calling itself the Revolutionary Forces, claimed credit for the attack.

Israeli police reported that 15 persons were wounded Dec. 5 when a bomb exploded aboard a bus near Natanya, 15 miles north of Tel Aviv.

Col. Eliezer Segev, the Israeli military governor of Nablus (West Bank), and a soldier were wounded Dec. 8 when their car was hit by a grenade.

Eight West Bank Arabs were wounded when a guerrilla threw a hand grenade into a crowd at Hebron Dec. 12.

Commando massacre at Rome airport. Five armed Palestinian commandos attacked a U.S. jet airliner at Rome's international airport Dec. 17, killing 29 persons aboard the plane. Two other persons, including an Italian policeman, were shot to death as the gunmen were hijacking a West German Lufthansa airliner nearby. The hijacked plane was flown to Kuwait Dec. 18 after short stopovers at Athens and Damascus. The guerrillas released 12 hostages and surrendered.

The Palestinians began shooting as they removed submachineguns from luggage in the lounge of the airport at Fiumicino, 15 miles from Rome. The men made their way to a Pan American Boeing 707 that was preparing to take off for Beirut and Teheran. They hurled incendiary bombs inside the aircraft, killing the 29 people aboard and heavily damaging the plane. Among the dead were four Moroccan government officials en route to Teheran for a state visit and 14 U.S. employes of the Arabian-American Oil Co.

The guerrillas herded five Italian hostages into the Lufthansa plane and killed a sixth, the Italian customs policeman, as he tried to escape. The second man shot outside the plane died on the way to the hospital. The plane, carrying the guerrillas, the Italians and the crew, took off and the pilot was ordered to head for Beirut. Lebanese authorities, however, refused landing permission, and the jet was flown to Athens, where it landed Dec. 18.

In negotiations by radio with Greek authorities in the Athens airport control tower, the guerrillas reportedly demanded the release of two Arab terrorists held since August for an attack on the Athens airport. The guerrillas killed one of their Italian hostages and dumped his body from the plane before leaving Athens.

The plane's pilot, Capt. Joe Kroese, had urged the Greek authorities to meet the commandos' demands, reporting that four other hostages had been shot dead. Kroese was unaware at the time that the shootings were a hoax, that the guerrillas were merely firing their guns in the air to give the false impression that they were killing the other prisoners to put further pressure on the Greek officials.

The plane then flew to Damascus, where Syrian authorities permitted the loading of food and fuel during a two-hour layover.

On landing in Kuwait later Dec. 18, the five guerrillas released their hostages in return for "free passage" to an unknown destination.

A statement attributed to the group involved in the Rome attack said Dec. 21 that the assault was aimed at the U.S. because of its military airlift to Israel during the October war. The statement published in a Beirut newspaper did not specifically identify the guerrilla group but was merely signed "The Palestinian people."

U.S. officials Dec. 26 identified the Rome airport attackers as members of the Popular Front for the Liberation of Palestine (PFLP). They said Libya had provided and moved the arms used by the terrorists.

Guerrilla attack assailed—The guerrilla attack and hijacking was criticized in the Arab world and by the U.S. and the Soviet Union.

The Palestine Liberation Organization (PLO) said in Beirut Dec. 17 that the assault was against the interests "of our people." A PLO official said Dec. 18 his group would "do everything in our power to stop such acts."

The Soviet Union expressed concern Dec. 18 that the commando operation might undermine the Geneva peace conference. The Soviet press termed the guerrilla assault a "bloody provocation" carried out by "murderers" and "saboteurs."

Meir rule weakened in Israeli vote. The ruling Labor party of Premier Golda Meir lost several seats in Israeli parliamentary elections held Dec. 31 but was assured of retaining power as the country's dominant party. The Labor alignment lost five seats in the 120-seat Knesset and emerged with 51 seats.

The right-wing Likud coalition gained seven seats for a total of 39, the National Religious party, Labor's former coalition partner, lost one of its 11 seats, and another former Labor partner, the Independent Liberals, retained their four seats. The other parties in the new Knesset: Tora Religious Front (composed of four ultra Orthodox parties) 5; New Communists 4, Civil Rights list 3; Arabs supporting the government 3; and Moked (left-wing intellectuals) 1.

Peace Efforts ✓

Arab-Israeli Talks
Produce Pullback at Suez

Representatives of Israel and two Arab states—Egypt and Jordan—met in Geneva Dec. 21, 1973 to seek possible settlements of Arab-Israeli disputes arising from and preceding the October 1973 war. By mid-January 1974 their military bargainers had achieved an agreement for the disengagement of Egyptian and Israeli forces on the Suez-Sinai front. The U.S., which had played a major role in bringing about the Geneva meeting, was hard at work in an effort to initiate similar talks between Israel and Syria.

Geneva peace conference opens. The first peace conference between Israel and Arabs began in Geneva Dec. 21, 1973. The initial round of talks ended Dec. 22 and was followed by discussions between Egyptian and Israeli generals Dec. 26 and 28 on disengagement of their forces along the Suez Canal. These meetings and other military and political aspects of the dispute by the full conference were put off until January to mark time for the Israeli general elections, scheduled Dec. 31.

The Dec. 21 meeting was devoted to general policy speeches delivered by the foreign ministers of the participating nations—Egypt, Israel, Jordan, the So-viet Union and the U.S. United Nations Secretary General Kurt Waldheim, who attended as an observer, officially opened the meeting at the Palais des Nations, scene of other high-level conferences. Syria boycotted the conference.

Soviet Foreign Minister Andrei A. Gromyko and U.S. Secretary of State Henry A. Kissinger were co-chairmen of the conference. (Ellsworth Bunker headed the American delegation.) In his address, Kissinger said "Peace must bring a new relationship among the nations of the Middle East, a relationship that will not only put an end to the state of war which has persisted for the last quarter of a century but will also permit the peoples of the Middle East to live together in harmony and safety."

Kissinger pledged a determined U.S. effort to achieve a solution on the basis of a four-point approach: The truce must be "scrupulously adhered to"; separation of Egyptian and Israeli forces was "the most immediate problem"; the peace accord must include Israeli withdrawals, recognized borders, security arrangements, guarantees, settlement of the Palestinian problem; and recognition that Jerusalem "contains places considered holy by three great religions."

Gromyko also sounded a plea for peace and held out a possibility of re-establishing diplomatic relations with Israel, severed in 1967. But he expressed continued Soviet support for the Arab demand that Israel

152

withdraw from occupied territories. "The intolerable situation in the Middle East, created in view of Israeli policy, cannot go on any longer," he said. Gromyko assailed Israel's "policy of annexation, the trampling of norms of international law and decisions of the U.N."

The continued Middle East impasse was reflected in statements made by Foreign Ministers Ismail Fahmy of Egypt, Zaid al-Rifai of Jordan and Abba Eban of Israel. Both Arab ministers stressed the need for an Israeli pullout from Arab territories as the basis for a settlement. Fahmy, reiterating Cairo's stand, said it expressed the collective Arab position taken at their summit conference in Algeria in November.

He listed the following points as the "basic essentials for peace"; total Israeli withdrawal; "liberation of the Arab city of Jerusalem"; the Palestinians' "right to self-determination and to live in peace and dignity"; "the right of every state in the area to enjoy territorial inviolability and political independence; and guarantees by the major powers or the U.N. or both "as an added safeguard to international peace and security in the area."

A blueprint for peace outlined by Rifai was essentially similar to the one submitted by Fahmy. Referring to Syria's boycott of the conference, Rifai said its absence "should not in any way prejudice her right to full withdrawal of Israeli forces from all its occupied territory."

Eban described the conference as "a new opportunity" "to bring a halt to the spreading contagion of violence in the Middle East." He said Israel was seeking a treaty that would "provide for the permanent elimination of all forms of hostility, blockade and boycott." Any negotiated pact, he said, should "provide for the renunciation of force" and "contain specific and unequivocal recognition of each other's political independence, integrity and sovereignty." Eban called for an agreement that would establish permanent boundaries with "security arrangements and demilitarized areas." Israel, he said, was "ready for a territorial compromise."

As for the Palestinian refugee problem, Israel would "propose compensation for abandoned lands," Eban said. Replying to Arab demands on Jerusalem, Eban said

Israel "does not wish to exercise exclusive jurisdiction or unilateral responsibility in the holy places of Christendom and Islam, which should be under the administration of those who hold them sacred."

Eban's remarks were later rebutted by Fahmy, who charged they were "distorted" and meant for "home consumption." He accused Israel of continued violations of the cease-fire and of having killed Egyptian civilians during the war.

After a 20-minute closed session Dec. 22, the Geneva conferees issued a communique announcing that Israel and Egypt would enter into troop disengagement talks and that more committees would be established later to deal with other issues. The joint statement said "the conference at the foreign ministers level will reconvene in Geneva as needed in light of developments."

During the meeting, Foreign Minister Rifai said Jordan also wanted to negotiate with Israel on the separation of their forces along the Jordan River but would be flexible on the timing of such talks. Eban replied that Israel would not rule out such discussions with Jordan later.

Israeli-Soviet contacts—Israeli and Soviet Foreign Ministers Abba Eban and Andrei A. Gromyko held a private meeting at the Soviet diplomatic mission in Geneva Dec. 21. The discussions were the first high-level talks between Israeli and Russian officials since Moscow broke off diplomatic relations between the two countries during the 1967 war.

The meeting was held at Eban's initiative and was said by an Israeli spokesman to be connected with the Geneva conference.

Kissinger reports to Nixon on talks—Secretary of State Henry A. Kissinger returned to Washington Dec. 21 and reported to President Nixon Dec. 24-25 on the opening of the Geneva conference.

Kissinger told a year-end news conference Dec. 27 that improved U.S. relations with the Soviet Union depended on Moscow's behavior in the Middle East. He conceded that Soviet action at the Geneva conference "has been constructive and has been recognized to be constructive by all the parties there."

The secretary said there were "two schools of thought about Soviet behavior in the Middle East—the first that Moscow only wanted to stir up trouble and provoke anti-Americanism in the Arab world, and the other, that after sober reflection, the Russians now wanted to help stabilize the situation." The U.S., Kissinger emphasized, would "deal with the Soviet Union as long as its actions are consistent with the second interpretation. That is to say, if the Soviet Union makes a reasonable contribution to peace in the Middle East, we will be prepared to cooperate—not at the expense of our traditional friends, not by imposing a settlement made together with the Soviet Union."

Syria scores conference results—Syria Dec. 23 assailed the first phase of the Geneva conference, saying that the decision to form a military working committee to discuss disengagement of Israeli and Egyptian forces meant that the parley was dealing with marginal, not basic problems.

Syrian Deputy Foreign Minister Zakharia Ismail said Dec. 29 that his country might be willing to attend the peace conference if the talks showed signs of progress toward substantive matters. Before Syria ended its boycott of the sessions, Israel, the U.S. and the Soviet Union would have to agree "to try to resolve the essential problem instead of neglecting it and concentrating on the marginal aspect of this problem," Ismail said. He said Damascus' main conditions for attending was that the conferees "should declare that they are going to talk about withdrawal of Israeli forces from occupied Arab territories. The Israelis should stop talking about prisoners of war and disengagement. They should talk about the purpose of the conference."

Qaddafi opposes peace moves. Libyan leader Col. Muammar el-Qaddafi expressed opposition Dec. 28 to Egyptian-Israeli peace talks and advocated a revolution to prevent Cairo from concluding an agreement with the Israelis.

In an interview with the Lebanese weekly magazine Beirut Al Massa, Qaddafi declared: "Any Arab state may commit the crime of a unilateral peace.

The only possible measure to counter it is a revolution backed by the Arab revolutionary regimes." Qaddafi said the Palestinian guerrilla movement should help in preventing any Arab state from making peace with Israel.

The magazine said Qaddafi had sought unsuccessfully to get Egypt to boycott the Geneva peace conference.

Troop disengagement talks. The troop disengagement talks held by Israel and Egypt Dec. 26 and 28 were a continuation of a previous series of meetings on the subject that had broken off Nov. 29 at Kilometer 101 on the Cairo-Suez road.

Heading the Egyptian delegation at the talks was Brig. Gen. Taha el-Magdoub, assistant chief of operations. Israel was represented by Maj. Gen. Mordechai Gur, a former military attache in Washington.

Lt. Gen. Ensio Siilasvuo, commander of the United Nations Emergency Force who presided over the discussions, announced after the second meeting Dec. 28 that both parties had reached a "consensus of some principles of disengagement" and that another meeting would be held Jan. 2, 1974.

But the two sides remained deadlocked after discussions Jan. 2, 4, 7 and 9. It was then agreed to suspend the conference for six days to allow the Israeli and Egyptian governments to make political decisions and to give the U.S. and the Soviet Union an opportunity to help bring both sides closer together. U.S. Secretary of State Henry A. Kissinger left for Egypt and Israel Jan. 10 to press for a disengagement agreement, while Soviet leaders planned to discuss the matter in Moscow with Egyptian Foreign Minister Ismail Fahmy.

Kissinger had discussed the Suez troop separation problem with Israeli Defense Minister Moshe Dayan in Washington Jan. 4–5.

Israelis lift Suez blockade. Israeli forces imposed a blockade Jan. 2–3 of food and other non-military supplies for the Egyptian III Corps trapped on the east bank of the Suez Canal and for the city of Suez on the west bank. The lifting of the blockade was announced Jan. 4 by the United Nations Emergency Force

(UNEF) following U.N. intercession with the Israeli army and government.

The Israelis had barred the shipment of supplies to the III Corps to retaliate for Egyptian firing on an Israeli bulldozer two miles north of the truck-unloading point at Suez. An Israeli source said Jan. 3 that as long as the Egyptians violated the Nov. 11, 1973 cease-fire agreement, Israel was under no obligation to permit food, water and medicine to pass through its lines to Suez city or the III Corps.

Canal fighting tapers off—Intense fighting had been reported around Suez city and on the east bank of the canal Jan. 1–5, but the clashes tapered off considerably through Jan. 9. UNEF commander Lt. Gen. Ensio Siilasvuo discussed the deteriorating situation Jan. 1 in separate meetings in Cairo with Egyptian military chiefs—Gen. Ahmed Ismail, war minister, and Lt. Gen. Mohammed Abdel Ghany al-Gamasy, chief of operations—and in Jerusalem with Israeli Defense Minister Moshe Dayan. Siilasvuo's discussions followed a UNEF report of 72 shooting incidents along the canal Dec. 30, compared with a daily average of about 40 incidents.

Egyptian troops on the east bank of the canal were reported to have made two ground advances Jan. 1. In one incident UNEF said they moved 200 yards at a point about four and a half miles southeast of Qantara and were seen burying land mines.

Fighting was particularly heavy between Israeli and Egyptian forces around Suez city Jan. 5, with UNEF reporting both sides exchanging intense artillery, machine-gun and small-arms fire. UNEF said Israel had filed complaints with the peace-keeping force, charging 67 Egyptian cease-fire violations from Dec. 31 through Jan. 3, including eight Egyptian troop movements beyond the truce lines. Egypt had accused Israel of seven violations Jan. 3.

Egyptian soldiers advanced 200 yards south of Adabiya on the west bank of the Gulf of Suez Jan. 4, but withdrew Jan. 5 at UNEF's request.

According to an Israeli account reported Jan. 4, 14 Israelis had been killed and 85 wounded in cease-fire violations on the Egyptian and Syrian fronts in the past six weeks.

Egypt blocks UNEF patrols. Egyptian troops had blocked the movement of patrols of the United Nations Emergency Force (UNEF) on the Suez front and Egyptian advances in the Suez city area "again has heightened" tension, the U.N. reported Jan. 10.

U.N. spokesman Rudolf Stajduhar said UNEF vehicles were stopped by the Egyptians Jan. 8 from entering Port Said at the northern end of the Suez Canal and were barred from using a road on the eastern side of the waterway.

Stajduhar said an Austrian UNEF unit had rejected an Egyptian request to abandon a new observation position 11 miles west of Fayid on the west bank.

Egyptian troops that had occupied positions on the northwest outskirts of Suez city Jan. 7 refused a UNEF request to withdraw.

Israel accused Egypt of violating the cease-fire 12 times Jan. 8. The truce breaches included Egyptian troop advances near Uyun Musa on the eastern shore of the Gulf of Suez, west of Adabiya on the western shore of the gulf and east of the canal in the Sinai.

Israeli and Egyptian troops exchanged heavy gunfire Jan. 10 around Adabiya and in the Suez city area to the north. Two Israeli soldiers were killed in the clashes, according to the Israeli command.

Israeli forces Jan. 11 again blocked the flow of nonmilitary supplies to the trapped Egyptian III Corps on the east bank and to Suez city to retaliate for shelling of Israeli positions near Ismailia, about 50 miles north of Suez. The Israelis lifted the blockade Jan. 12, but fighting that broke out Jan. 15 prevented U.N. vehicles from bringing supplies to the Egyptians.

Suez troop separation. Egypt and Israel signed an accord Jan. 18, 1974 to separate their military forces along the Suez Canal. The agreement had been announced simultaneously Jan. 17 in Jerusalem, Cairo and Washington. The pact had been negotiated through the mediation of U.S. Secretary of State Henry A. Kissinger, who had held separate meetings with Egyptian and Israeli officials, shuttling between Aswan and Jerusalem Jan. 11–17.

The accord was in two parts: one dealt with the actual pullback of troops and establishment of disengagement zones; the other provided for the limitation of troops and arms in the zones. Details of the latter agreement were kept secret. Copies of it were signed by Premier Golda Meir in Jerusalem and by President Anwar Sadat in Aswan. Kissinger attended both ceremonies.

The troop withdrawal treaty was signed at Kilometer 101 on the Suez-Cairo road by the Egyptian and Israeli chiefs of staff—Maj. Gen. Mohammed Abdel el-Gamásy and Lt. Gen. David Elazar. The commander of the United Nations Emergency Force (UNEF), Lt. Gen. Ensio Siilasvuo, presided.

The text of the agreement was accompanied by a map delineating the zones of disengagement. Israel was to abandon its bridgehead on the west bank of the Suez Canal and withdraw its forces on the east bank 14–20 miles from the waterway. In the southern sector the Israelis would be deployed immediately west of the Mitla and Gidi Passes, which controlled the routes into the heart of the Sinai Peninsula. The Egyptians were to remain on the east bank in a 5–7½ mile-wide zone. The Israeli zone was to be of equal size. Both forces were to be separated by a buffer zone 3½–5 miles deep patrolled by UNEF troops.

According to unofficial reports, Egypt would reduce its forces on the east bank from 70,000 troops and 700 tanks to 7,000 troops and 30 tanks.

Israeli and Egyptian military representatives were to work out details of the disengagement process within five days. The pullback itself was to be completed within 40 days.

The accord pledged that Israel and Egypt would "scrupulously observe the cease-fire" and stressed that the agreement was only the first step toward a permanent peace.

Nixon announces agreement—In his announcement Jan. 17 of the Israeli-Egyptian troop disengagement accord, President Nixon congratulated President Anwar Sadat and Premier Golda Meir and their aides "for the very constructive spirit they have shown in reaching an agreement." He said the American people could "be proud of the role that our government has played, and particularly the role that has been played by Secretary Kissinger and his colleagues" in bringing both sides closer together.

Text of Disengagement Agreement Signed Jan. 18

[A]

Egypt and Israel will scrupulously observe the cease-fire on the land, sea and air called for by the U.N. Security Council and will refrain from the time of the signing of this document from all military or paramilitary actions against each other.

[B]

The military forces of Egypt and Israel will be separated in accordance with the following principles:

1. All Egyptian forces on the east side of the canal will be deployed west of the line designated as line A on the attached map. All Israeli forces including those west of the Suez Canal on the Bitter Lakes will be deployed east of the line designated as line B on the attached map.

2. The area between the Egyptian and Israeli lines will be a zone of disengagement in which the United Nations Emergency Force will be stationed. The UNEF will continue to consist of units from countries that are not permanent members of the Security Council.

3. The area between the Egyptian line and the Suez Canal will be limited in armament and forces.

4. The area between the Israeli line, line B on the attached map, and the line designated as line C on the attached map, which runs along the western base of the mountains where the Gidi and Mitla passes are located, will be limited in armament and forces.

5. The limitations referred to in paragraphs 3 and 4 will be inspected by UNEF. Existing procedures of the UNEF, including the attaching of Egyptian and Israeli liaison officers to UNEF, will be continued.

[C]

The detailed implementation of the disengagement of forces will be worked out by military representatives of Egypt and Israel, who will agree on the stages of this process. These representatives will meet no later than 48 hours after the signature of this agreement at Kilometer 101 under the aegis of the United Nations for this purpose. They will complete this task within five days. Disengagement will begin within 48 hours after the completion of the work of the military representatives, and in no event later than seven days after the signature of this agreement. The process of disengagement will be completed not later than 40 days after it begins.

[D]

This agreement is not regarded by Egypt and Israel as a final peace agreement. It constitutes a first step toward a final, just and durable peace according to the provisions of Security Council Resolution 338 and within the framework of the Geneva Conference.

For Egypt:

MOHAMMED ABDEL GHANY AL-GAMASY
Major General

For Israel:

DAVID ELAZAR
Lieut. Gen., Chief of Staff of Israel Defense Forces

While describing the pact as "the first significant step toward a permanent peace in the Middle East," the President stressed "the difficulties that lie ahead" in resolving other aspects of the dispute.

Nixon noted the mediative role the U.S. had conducted in bringing Egypt and Israel "together, to help them narrow differences, working toward a thorough and just settlement for all parties concerned where every nation in that region will be able to live in peace. . . ." The President pledged continued U.S. involvement to that end, saying "I personally shall see that all negotiations, any efforts, which could lead to a permanent peace, not only between Egypt and Israel but between other countries involved, have the full and complete support" of the U.S. government.

Kissinger negotiates accord—Kissinger had shuttled between Egypt and Israel Jan. 11–17 to negotiate the disengagement accord.

He held discussions with President Sadat in Aswan, rather than in Cairo. The Egyptian leader had been in the warmer climate of Aswan since December 1973, recovering from bronchitis. The secretary's meetings with the Israelis included all senior Cabinet officials except Premier Golda Meir, who was ill. Deputy Premier Yigal Allon was chairman of the discussions. Defense Minister Moshe Dayan and Foreign Minister Abba Eban also had participated in the seven days of negotiations with Kissinger.

Kissinger held his first round of talks with Sadat in Aswan Jan. 11–12. He flew to Jerusalem later Jan. 12 and met with Allon, Eban and Dayan. The secretary had paid a courtesy call on Premier Meir earlier. At the conclusion of those talks Jan. 13, it was announced that the Israeli government that day had approved a specific proposal on troop disengagement drawn up by U.S. and Israeli officials. The Cabinet approved the plan and Kissinger flew back to Aswan to present it to Sadat.

After presenting the proposal to Sadat and holding eight hours of talks with him Jan. 14, Kissinger announced that progress had been made in narrowing Israeli and Egyptian differences. The secretary then returned to Jerusalem the night of Jan. 14 with Sadat's reply, in the form of a detailed map and a counterproposal to the Israeli map.

Kissinger's discussions with Israeli leaders through Jan. 15 resulted in a new Israeli map. It was handed to the secretary as he boarded his plane to return to Aswan the morning of Jan. 16.

Kissinger conferred with Sadat Jan. 16, at which time U.S. officials indicated that a virtual agreement was at hand. Other U.S. and Egyptian officials later worked out the details.

The Egyptian-Israeli agreement was finally announced Jan. 17 after Kissinger had flown between those two countries three times that day.

Kissinger reports on mission—Kissinger returned to Washington Jan. 21, and he and President Nixon later that day briefed 16 Congressional leaders at a closed meeting on the secretary's latest trip to the Middle East.

A senior State Department official later disclosed the "eight or nine" assurances and understandings that Kissinger had developed with the Israelis and Egyptians in his discussions with them Jan. 11–17. These unwritten principles were in addition to the troop disengagement agreement and the arms limitation accord, still unpublished.

Among the statements:

■ The U.S. had informed Israel that it assumed that after the troop pullback along the Suez Canal Egypt would reopen the waterway to international shipping, including Israel-bound vessels.

■ Cairo told the U.S. that it could inform Israel that after signing of the disengagement accord Egypt would no longer blockade the Bab el Mandeb strait at the entrance to the Red Sea. The blockade actually had been lifted in November 1973 under a secret agreement with the U.S. and Israel.

■ The U.S. assured Israel that it would continue to receive American support for its existence, including military assistance, but there would be no formal commitment to this effect.

■ The U.S. told Israel it believed that the United Nations Emergency Force (UNEF) to be deployed in a buffer zone between the Israeli and Egyptian zones in the Suez Canal area could only be disbanded by the U.N. Security Council. The previous UNEF force had been unilaterally dispersed by Egypt in 1967 without a Council vote.

Kissinger disclosed at a news conference held Jan. 22 that he had been given assurances by Arab leaders that when the Israeli-Egyptian disengagement accord was reached, the Arab oil embargo against the U.S. would be lifted. He said failure to do so "in a reasonable time would be highly inappropriate and would raise serious questions of confidence in our minds with respect to the Arab nations with whom we have dealt on this issue."

Kissinger said the U.S. had no formal obligation to act in case the disengagement agreement was violated by either side. However, he foresaw American involvement if Egypt or Israel asked the U.S. for "diplomatic support."

Although the reopening of the Suez Canal would benefit the Soviet Union by permitting its fleet to move more readily from the Mediterranean to the Indian Ocean, the U.S. "can be compensated both by the greater ease with which we can transfer some of our ships to the Indian Ocean and other measures that can be taken of a different nature," Kissinger said.

Suez troop separation begins. Details of the agreement to separate the Israeli and Egyptian forces along the Suez Canal were completed Jan. 24 at a meeting held at Kilometer 101 on the Cairo-Suez road. Participants were the two armies' chiefs of staff—Lt. Gen. David Elazar and Maj. Gen. Mohammed Abdel el-Gamasy.

Military officers of both sides had been meeting since Jan. 20 to work out the technical arrangements that were based on the more general agreement reached by Israel and Egypt Jan. 18. The meetings were presided over by Lt. Gen. Ensio Siilasvuo, commander of the United Nations Emergency Force (UNEF).

The troop withdrawal formally got under way Jan. 25 and was to be completed within 40 days. Israel had begun moving troops and armor on the canal's west bank eastward to new positions in the Sinai Jan. 23, two days before the deadline. Engineers also had started removing minefields in the area. Each sector

of the bridgehead that was evacuated was to be occupied by UNEF troops for six hours and then turned over to the Egyptians. This pullback was to be completed in 28 days. In the following 12 days, Israeli and Egyptian forces were to withdraw to their new disengagement zones in the Sinai.

Israelis end siege of Suez city. Israeli forces continued to evacuate the western bank of the Suez Canal and by Jan. 28 they had lifted the siege of Suez city by withdrawing from the surrounding area. The Israeli pullout from part of the city they had seized in the October 1973 war freed the supply lines of the Egyptian III Corps on the eastern bank of the waterway opposite Suez.

United Nations Emergency Force (UNEF) troops moved into the areas evacuated by the Israelis and turned the territory over to the Egyptians six hours later. The key positions reoccupied by the Egyptians included the port of Adabiya, south of Suez, and the Ataqa mountains that commanded access to the port.

A small UNEF unit was deployed between the Egyptians and the Israelis in the remainder of the bridgehead.

U.S. monitors Suez troop pullback. American officials disclosed Feb. 7 that Egypt and Israel had approved a plan to have the U.S. monitor compliance of their troop disengagement agreement along the Suez Canal. The plan had been worked out by Secretary of State Henry A. Kissinger in his negotiations with Israeli and Egyptian officials in December 1973. It was part of the still unpublished annex of the disengagement accord signed Jan. 18.

The U.S. did not specify how the surveillance would be carried out, but it was believed that satellites and reconnaissance aircraft would be used.

Sadat tours Arab states. Egyptian President Anwar Sadat toured eight Arab states Jan. 18–23 to rally support for Egypt's troop disengagement agreement with Israel.

At his last stop in Rabat, Morocco Jan. 23, Sadat called his meetings with the

Arab leaders a "complete success." Sadat, who had met Jan. 19 with Syrian President Hafez al-Assad in Damascus, disclosed that Syria was willing to meet with Israel to discuss separation of their military forces along the Golan Heights front. The Geneva peace conference would not resume until that matter was settled, Sadat said.

Sadat said that in his meetings with U.S. Secretary of State Henry A. Kissinger in Aswan the previous week, he had expressed willingness to accept an Israeli withdrawal to the first Oct. 22, 1973 cease-fire line, which would have left the Israelis on both sides of the Suez Canal. Israel, however, preferred to pull back its forces to the east bank "because of the precarious position of its armed forces," Sadat said.

Sadat said the reopening of the Suez Canal was "purely a matter of Egyptian sovereignty" and was "in no way" linked to the disengagement accord. He said that pact dealt only with military matters and there had been no secret agreement with Israel. The U.S. was no longer following a policy of giving Israel "total and unconditional support," Sadat noted. The U.S., he said, "now says they favor a balance of power in the area."

After meeting with Algerian President Houari Boumedienne in Algiers Jan. 22, Sadat said at a news conference that the Arab oil-producing states should take note of "an evolution" in U.S. policy in the Middle East since Kissinger first visited the area in November 1973. Without mentioning the oil embargo against the U.S., Sadat said "now that the Americans have made a gesture, the Arabs should make one too."

Sadat had met previously on his tour with the leaders of Saudi Arabia, Kuwait, Abu Dhabi, Bahrain and Qatar Jan. 19–21.

Palestinians at odds over Suez pact— The Palestinian guerrilla movement was reported Jan. 21 to have split over the Egyptian-Israeli troop separation agreement.

Criticism of the accord came from the Palestine Liberation Organization (PLO), which represented the various commando groups. The position taken by its key members was regarded as a challenge to

Yasir Arafat, head of the organization's Executive Committee and leader of Al Fatah. President Sadat said Arafat endorsed the agreement.

The Executive Committee denounced the agreement at a meeting Jan. 20 and sent a cable to Sadat expressing its opposition. Arafat disavowed the criticism in a telegram to Sadat Jan. 21. Arafat said the committee meeting at which the statement was drawn up was illegal because he was not in attendance.

A member of the committee said Jan. 21 that the group regarded the Israeli-Egyptian agreement a "surrender to the American plan." He pledged continued war against Israel "until all occupied Palestinian soil is liberated."

A committee member denied a report Jan. 20 in the Egyptian newspaper Al Ahram that the committee had approved establishment of a PLO coordination group with Egypt following Arafat's meeting with Sadat in Aswan Jan. 18. Arafat was present at Sadat's signing of the troop separation agreement.

Government-controlled newspapers in Iraq and Libya Jan. 21 condemned the agreement, asserting that it "ushers American penetration and domination into the area." The Iraqi government newspaper Al Jomhouriya urged that progressive Arab forces prevent other countries from making similar agreements with Israel.

Israeli Parliament backs troop pact. The Israeli Knesset (Parliament) approved the troop disengagement agreement with Egypt Jan. 22 by a 76–35 vote following sharp debate in which right-wing Likud Party members denounced the accord as a surrender.

The debate opened with a statement by Premier Golda Meir in which she declared that the object of the agreement was to attain "a permanent peace settlement." The alternative, she warned, "is nothing but the renewal of the war."

Menachem Begin, leader of Likud, assailed the agreement as a unilateral pullback and a violation of the government's mandate, which he said was committed to make peace, not to carry out a withdrawal. Singling out Moshe Dayan for criticism, Begin addressed the defense minister: "Why don't you tell the Knesset what you mean by disengagement of forces? You mean retreat."

Another Likud member attacking the government's position was Maj. Gen. Ariel Sharon, who had announced his resignation from the army Jan. 18 to protest the disengagement accord.

Israelis end 2nd pullout phase. Israeli troops Feb. 4 completed the second phase of the withdrawal from their bridgehead on the western bank of the Suez Canal as their last rear-guard unit moved about five-six miles north of the Cairo-Suez road. They were replaced by about 600 troops of the United Nations Emergency Force (UNEF).

UNEF troops turned over the newly evacuated territory to the Egyptians Feb. 5, giving them control of the entire area south of the Little Bitter Lake.

UNEF troops had started to move into the area on the eastern bank of the canal Feb. 4 that would eventually be part of a buffer zone between Israeli and Egyptian forces. At the same time, the armies of both nations were reducing their forces in the two zones on either side of the UNEF buffer strip. UNEF officers, accompanied by Egyptian and Israeli officers, inspected the thinning-out operations Feb. 5–6.

Israelis end Suez bridgehead pullout. Israeli troops Feb. 21 completed their withdrawal from the west bank of the Suez Canal seized in the October 1973 war. It was the fourth and final phase of the pullback from the bridgehead that had started Jan. 25.

The Israelis gave up the northernmost segment of the salient to troops of the United Nations Emergency Force (UNEF), who turned the area over to Egyptian soldiers six hours later. The Israelis withdrew to their zone on the east bank through a corridor 7–10 miles wide that ran through the Egyptian zone and the UNEF buffer zone.

UNEF soldiers completed deployment in the northern part of their buffer zone Feb. 21.

Israel Feb. 21 released 22 Egyptian soldiers captured on the Suez front during the war. The captives were turned over at a UNEF checkpoint near Qantara as a goodwill gesture in return for Egyptian cooperation in recovering the bodies of Israeli soldiers.

Two Finnish UNEF soldiers had been killed and six wounded when their vehicle struck a land mine on the west bank of the canal Feb. 14. This brought to five the number of UNEF soldiers killed on the Suez front since October 1973.

Suez troop separation completed. Israeli and Egyptian troops completed the disengagement of their forces along the Suez Canal March 4. Israeli forces withdrew to their prescribed zone in the Sinai Desert after turning over the east bank of the waterway to troops of the United Nations Emergency Force (UNEF). Egyptian troops moved in six hours later and assumed control of both banks of the canal for the first time since the 1967 war.

UNEF troops then completed deployment in their buffer zone between the Israeli and Egyptian sectors.

The U.S. Navy had sent demolition experts to the Suez Canal to advise Egypt on clearing mines and other explosives from the waterway, an American official disclosed Feb. 26. The mission was being undertaken at Egypt's request.

U.S. & Egypt resume relations. The U.S. and Egypt announced Feb. 28 the immediate resumption of full-scale diplomatic relations severed in 1967. The announcement was made in Cairo and Washington after President Anwar Sadat had met that day with U.S. Secretary of State Henry A. Kissinger, who had just arrived from Israel where he had presented Premier Golda Meir with a list of Israeli war prisoners held in Syria following a visit to Damascus Feb. 26–27.

Kissinger was in the Middle East on another round of personal diplomacy to help negotiate a troop disengagement agreement between Syria and Israel. He arrived in Cairo to formalize the renewal of U.S.-Egyptian ties and to apprise Sadat of the start of his negotiations in Jerusalem and Damascus.

A text of the accord to establish U.S.-Egyptian relations expressed the two governments' hope that "this step will develop and strengthen relations between their countries and contribute substantially to better mutual understanding and cooperation." The statement said Ashraf Ghorbal had been renamed ambassador to Washington and that Hermann Eilts was to be reappointed to his post in Cairo.

Egypt starts Suez Canal clearance. Egypt had begun work on clearing the Suez Canal blocked by sunken ships and mines and shells since the 1967 war in the first phase of reopening the waterway, the Egyptian government newspaper Al Ahram reported Feb. 7. The government hoped to return the canal to operation within six months. It would be capable of handling ships of up to 60,000 tons. After two weeks, Egyptian workers had cleared several miles of the waterway of mines and shells, Reconstruction Minister Ahmed Osman reported Feb. 20. (Osman had been a major contractor for Egypt's Aswan dam.)

A project drafted by Osman to reconstruct the canal and its banks had been published Feb. 4. The plans included enlarging the canal to accommodate tankers of as much as 300,000 tons, rebuilding and expanding Suez city to 10 times its present area and constructing an eight-lane highway tunneled under the canal.

Britain lifts arms embargo. Britain Jan. 21 lifted the arms embargo to the Middle East which it had imposed during the October 1973 war.

In announcing the decision in the House of Commons, Foreign Secretary Sir Alec Douglas-Home said removal of the ban was made possible by the Israeli-Egyptian troop disengagement agreement. He said, however, that Britain would send no new military supplies into the region that could "escalate the danger of war in the area" and pledged that his country would continue to closely examine any future arms requests. Douglas-Home proposed a "rationing system" among the major powers for arms deliveries to the Middle East.

Syria prodded on pullback accord. The Soviet Union urged Syria Jan. 30 to agree to a military disengagement with Israel, similar to the accord Egypt had reached with Israel.

The Soviet statement, appearing in the Communist Party newspaper Pravda,

said, "The issue of disengagement of troops as a first step toward the settlement of the issue" of Arab territories occupied by Israel "directly involves Syria." Damascus' refusal to enter into such an agreement played into the hands of Israel, which was "persistently pursuing a line toward weakening the unity of Arab countries," Pravda said.

Egyptian Foreign Minister Ismail Fahmy had briefed Soviet leaders on the accord with Israel during a visit to Moscow Jan. 21–24.

The Soviet Union endorsed the Israeli-Egyptian agreement in a joint communique Jan. 24. It cautioned, however, that the pact had a "positive significance" only if it was followed by "a radical settlement in the Middle East" that was based on the United Nations Security Council resolutions of 1967 and 1973 calling for Israeli withdrawal from Arab territories.

Egyptian officials said Jan. 27 that the Soviet leaders had promised Fahmy they would exert their influence on Syria to reach agreement with Israel. Egypt was said to be seeking a more active Soviet role in the Geneva conference.

Premier Golda Meir, expressing interest Jan. 30 in negotiations between Israel and Syria on military disengagement, said her country had no intention of retaining Syrian territory captured in the October 1973 war. But she reiterated Israeli opposition to enter into such discussions until Syria provided a list of its Israeli prisoners and permitted International Red Cross officials to visit them. Mrs. Meir also ruled out Israeli negotiations with "Arab terrorist organizations" at the Geneva conference. She said they were "not interested in territorial questions but only in expelling Jews from the land of Israel."

Syria Urged to Negotiate

Kissinger presses Syria on talks. U.S. Secretary of State Henry A. Kissinger visited Damascus Jan. 20 to urge Syria to enter into negotiations with Israel.

After a four-hour meeting with President Hafez al-Assad, Kissinger stopped briefly in Tel Aviv to convey to Israeli officials Syria's latest stand. He said Assad had submitted to him "very constructive suggestions" on disengagement of Israeli and Syrian forces on the Golan Heights and on a final peace settlement. Assad had given him assurances that the Israeli prisoners held by Syria "are being treated in a humane fashion," Kissinger disclosed. The secretary was not given a list of the prisoners demanded by Israel as its condition for negotiating with Syria. But another U.S. official said later that Assad had agreed to turn over the list when Syrian-Israeli discussions started. Damascus had previously insisted that the names of the POWs would not be handed over until after conclusion of the talks.

The Israeli officials apprised of Assad's views by Kissinger were Deputy Prime Minister Yigal Allon, Defense Minister Moshe Dayan and Foreign Minister Abba Eban.

Before flying to Damascus, Kissinger had stopped briefly at Aqaba, Jordan where he conferred Jan. 19–20 with King Hussein and Premier Zaid al-Rifai. Rifai announced after the talks that Israel and Jordan would "shortly" start negotiations. Jordan would insist that "the first item of discussion" be the disengagement of Israeli and Jordanian forces along the Jordan Valley, the premier said.

Jordanian troops that had fought on the Syrian front had been withdrawn to Jordan, the Amman government had announced Jan. 3. According to Amman sources, Jordan's forces in Syria had totaled 8,000–10,000 men and had suffered about 50 killed and wounded during the war.

Syrian-Israeli clashes. Syria reported clashes with Israeli forces on the northern front Jan. 2 and 7, 1974.

Israel acknowledged that three of its soldiers were killed Jan. 2 when a mortar shell hit their positions.

Damascus claimed Syrian artillery Jan. 7 inflicted heavy casualties on an Israeli unit that attempted to advance. Israeli sources denied there had been a serious clash.

A Damascus communique said Syrian artillery attacked Israeli forces Jan. 10–11 during attempts to strengthen their positions. The shelling destroyed several Israeli vehicles and killed or wounded 10 Israeli soldiers, the statement said.

Another Israeli attempt to consolidate front-line positions led to a clash Jan. 12, resulting "in putting the enemy's artillery out of action and inflicting some casualties," according to Damascus.

Israeli acknowledged that one of its soldiers was killed in an artillery exchange Jan. 13. The Syrians claimed 20 Israelis were killed or wounded in a clash Jan. 15, but Israel did not confirm the high losses.

Sporadic fighting resumed on the Golan Heights Jan. 26 and continued through Feb. 5, with the Syrians claiming to have inflicted heavy casualties on the Israelis.

Syria reported that 40 Israelis were killed or wounded in two separate clashes Jan. 27. A Damascus communique said 11 Israeli artillery batteries had been knocked out by Syrian artillery and that other Israeli equipment had been destroyed.

The Israeli command acknowledged shelling incidents Jan. 27 but said they were not serious. The command said one Israeli died of wounds received Jan. 26.

A Damascus communique said at least 10 Israelis were killed Feb. 1 when they tried to ambush a Syrian force. An Israeli command spokesman denied there was any ground contact between the two sides.

Syria said its artillery caused high casualties among the Israelis during a three-hour exchange Feb. 2. An Israeli bulldozer and several tanks were destroyed, according to the report. Israel acknowledged the artillery duel but said there had been no Israeli casualties.

The two sides fought tank and artillery duels Feb. 3, with the fighting centered largely in the bulge jutting toward Damascus. A United Nations observer interceded and both sides agreed to a truce, but the fighting resumed two hours later. The Israelis described the shooting as intermittent and sparse and denied the Syrian report that the fighting was full-scale and intense.

Four Israeli soldiers were wounded Feb. 10 when Syrian shells fell on their positions. The firing and counterbombardment lasted two hours.

Syrian guns continued the shelling Feb. 11, killing a policeman in El Quneitra on the Golan Heights and a woman in the Israeli settlement of Ramat Magshimim, 20 miles south of El Quneitra. Five Israeli soldiers were wounded in El Quneitra.

A Damascus spokesman said the firing was in response to an Israeli shelling attack against several densely inhabited Syrian villages.

Syria and Israel claimed their forces killed four soldiers in a ground clash Feb. 15. Two Israeli tanks, one missile position and one heavy artillery site were destroyed in two artillery duels during the day, according to Damascus.

16, with Syria reporting the destruction of an Israeli engineering unit. Israel denied the Damascus claim of casualties inflicted on its troops.

Syria claimed the destruction of an Israeli machine-gun position and its crew in a 15-minute clash Feb. 20.

According to Israeli estimates, 13 Israelis, including 11 soldiers, had been killed and 39 wounded on the Syrian front since the Oct. 24, 1973 cease-fire, it was reported Feb. 19. Of the 208 reported incidents, more than one-third had occurred in the past three weeks.

Syrian Foreign Minister Abdel Halim Khaddam had said Feb. 3 that Syria was deliberately fighting a "war of attrition" on the Golan Heights in order to "paralyze" Israel's economy by forcing it to keep its reserves mobilized.

Syrian guns fired across the truce line March 9. Israeli positions near the occupied Syrian village of Jaba were the principal targets. Syria claimed the shelling destroyed an Israeli bulldozer and another vehicle. Israel reported no casualties. Israel moved more reinforcements to the front.

Israel reported that one of its unmanned reconnaissance planes crashed on Jordanian territory March 10. The report followed an earlier Damascus claim that Syrian defense forces shot down an Israeli aircraft when it violated Syrian airspace and that it fell in Jordan.

The Syrians and Israelis traded heavy artillery fire March 12-13. Israel denied a Syrian claim that several Israelis had been killed in the March 13 exchanges.

Damascus conceded that four Syrian soldiers were slain in a three-hour artillery exchange March 17.

An Israeli army announcement March 18 said two Israeli soldiers were killed in artillery and tank duels that day.

Another Israeli soldier was killed and two United Nations truce observers were wounded March 19 in the heaviest artillery exchange on the Golan Heights

U.S. seeks Syrian-Israeli accord. President Nixon announced Feb. 19 that Secretary of State Henry A. Kissinger would go to the Middle East in a personal effort to bring about negotiations between Israel and Syria on disengagement of their forces on the Golan Heights.

Nixon made the announcement in the presence of Ismail Fahmy and Omar Saqqaf, the Egyptian and Saudi Arabian foreign ministers, who had conferred with Kissinger Feb. 16-18. They submitted to Kissinger a plan for Syrian-Israeli disengagement drawn up at a summit conference in Algiers Feb. 13-14 of the leaders of Egypt, Syria, Saudi Arabia and Algeria. Kissinger held another meeting with Ismail Feb. 20 and with Sabah Kabani, Syria's chief diplomat in Washington. The secretary also held separate discussions Feb. 17 and 19 with Simcha Dinitz, Israeli ambassador to Washington.

Neither Kissinger nor the Arab diplomats would disclose what they had discussed, but it was known their meetings dealt with the Arab oil embargo against the U.S. and the Syrian-Israeli negotiations. Kissinger was believed to have expressed objections to some Arab demands to link the end of the oil ban with withdrawal of Israeli forces from occupied Arab territories.

A final communique issued at the Algiers summit Feb. 14 did not mention the oil embargo or the proposed Israeli-Syrian talks. The joint statement only reaffirmed the call for withdrawal of Israel from all Arab territories and a guarantee of Palestinian rights. The conferees decided to send Fahmy and Saqqaf on their mission to Washington.

Attending the summit were President Anwar Sadat of Egypt, King Faisal of Saudi Arabia, President Houari Boumedienne of Algeria and President Hafez al-Assad of Syria.

Syrian Foreign Minister Abdel Halim Khaddam had announced Feb. 3 Damascus' terms for disengagement as follows: "Syria will accept military disengagement on the Golan Heights front only if it is made a part of a plan for a total Israeli withdrawal from Arab territories conquered in the 1973 and 1967 wars. A disengagement by itself without an Israeli commitment for total withdrawal and an assurance of Palestinian rights is not acceptable to Syria under any circumstances ."

State Department officials had said Feb. 9 that the U.S. had begun to sound out Syria and Israel on a formula to negotiate an agreement to disengage their troops on the Golan Heights and to have Syria issue a list of Israeli war prisoners they held.

State Department officials had informed Israel that the Soviet Union would try to use its influence to get Syria to submit the POW list and to permit International Red Cross officials to visit the captives, Foreign Minister Abba Eban disclosed Feb. 10. It was believed Soviet Foreign Minister Andrei A. Gromyko had given Kissinger such assurances in their talks in Washington Feb. 4.

Israeli government sources had reported Feb. 5 Cabinet rejection of a U.S. compromise proposal to get talks started with Syria. Under the plan, Syria would meet one of Israel's conditions for agreeing to negotiations by providing a list of prisoners. Syria, however, would not permit Red Cross officials to visit the prisoners, as demanded by Israel, until progress had been made in the talks. Premier Golda Meir was said to have polled her ministers on the U.S. formula Feb. 4 and they rejected it.

Meir had told settlers in the Golan Heights Feb. 8 that Israel considered the Syrian territory taken in 1967 "an inseparable part of Israel." She was quoted as saying that Israel would not withdraw beyond the cease-fire lines that were established in that conflict.

Plans for building a city on the heights were announced by the Israeli government Feb. 10. Construction was scheduled to start in March, with the town housing 5,000–7,000 persons in the first phase, and 20,000 within a decade.

Syria gives Israel POW list. A list of the Israeli prisoners of war held in Syria was presented to Israeli Premier Golda Meir Feb. 27 by U.S. Secretary of State Kissinger.

Before his trip to Israel, Kissinger had flown to Damascus Feb. 26 and conferred with Syrian President Hafez al-Assad to pave the way for possible negotiations with the Israelis on disengaging the forces of the two belligerents on the Golan front. Kissinger was said by officials to have been in possession of the roster of 65 Israeli POWs held by Syria before his arrival in Damascus but was unable to turn it over to Israel until he was authorized by Assad in their seven hours of talks.

The secretary flew to Jerusalem Feb. 27 and gave the list to Premier Golda Meir. He also gave her Assad's assurances that International Red Cross officials would be permitted to visit the captives starting March 1.

Israeli officials said the release of the prisoner list and the promise of Red Cross visits fulfilled Israel's conditions for holding talks with Syria. A U.S. official said an understanding had been reached that the 65 Israeli prisoners and the 386 Syrians held by Israel would be exchanged as soon as a disengagement accord was arranged.

In a television address to the nation, Premier Meir expressed gratitude to Kissinger "for his unceasing efforts" in getting Syria to release the prisoner list and permit Red Cross visits.

Kissinger, back in Israel March 1, received from Premier Meir an Israeli proposal for separation of troops. He then transmitted the plan to President Hafez al-Assad in Damascus later March 1. Assad found the plan unacceptable and gave Kissinger an undisclosed counterproposal for relay to the Israelis "in order to continue the talks on disengagement of troops," a Damascus official said.

The Israeli plan was said to have called for a demilitarized zone between Israeli and Syrian front lines within the territory captured by Israel during the war. United Nations troops would be stationed in the zone, while both sides would thin out their forces and weapons.

Red Cross visits Israeli POWS—Israel's 65 prisoners of war in Syria were visited for the first time March 1 by three representatives of the International Committee of the Red Cross. The visit had been arranged by Kissinger in his recent meetings with Egyptian, Israeli and Syrian officials.

A report stating that the prisoners were found to be in good physical and mental health was given to Israeli Foreign Minister Abba Eban March 4 by Red Cross official Michel Convere. Convere said March 5 that some of the POWs were recovering from wounds received at the time of their capture, but declined to give the number of wounded.

Gromyko visits Syria, Egypt. Soviet Foreign Minister Andrei A. Gromyko visited Syria and Egypt Feb. 27–March 6.

Kissinger's round of talks in the Egyptian and Syrian capitals had been critically alluded to by the Soviet Communist Party newspaper Pravda Feb. 24. An article warned the Arabs, including Syria, that the main goal of U.S. diplomacy was "not a settlement of the Middle East problem, but the lifting as soon as possible" of the Arab oil embargo against the U.S. "The peoples of Arabic countries are maintaining their vigilance toward any maneuvers directed at infringing upon their legal rights," Pravda said.

Gromyko echoed Pravda's sentiments in a speech in Damascus Feb. 28, one day after arriving in the Syrian capital. He said, "The opponents of a just and lasting peace both in Israel and beyond [an apparent reference to the U.S.] want to retain the Arab lands captured by them. In this they hope by means of various maneuvers and tricks they will manage to split the Arabs and their friends and allies."

After conferring with President Hafez al-Assad and other Syrian officials, Gromyko flew to Cairo March 1, a few hours after Kissinger ended his 24-hour visit to the Egyptian capital. Gromyko met with President Anwar Sadat during his stay until March 5, at which time a joint communique was issued. It stressed that both governments would work closely toward a settlement of the Arab-Israeli conflict.

Gromyko returned to Damascus and held more discussions with President Assad March 5–6. A joint communique March 7 declared that a Syrian-Israeli disengagement agreement should be "an inseparable part" of a final peace settlement—"a first step for full Israeli withdrawal from all occupied territories according to a fixed timetable."

Syria demands total Israeli pullout— President Hafez al-Assad declared March 8 that Syria would continue its state of belligerency against Israel until "all the Arab territory is liberated." Assad told a Damascus rally, "If Israeli leaders think we are tired of fighting or making sacrifices, then they have made another serious mistake." Challenging Israel's claim to the Golan Heights, Assad said Palestine, including the state of Israel, was "a basic part of southern Syria."

For the first time, Assad publicly endorsed Resolution 242 adopted by the United Nations Security Council after the 1967 war. However, the president said his government accepted the resolution as a basis for a political settlement only "if it fulfills there two conditions": total Israeli withdrawal from occupied Arab territories and Israeli recognition of the full "rights" of the Palestinians.

Israel lists 2,552 casualties. Israel distributed a booklet March 11 listing 2,-552 Israeli servicemen killed or missing in action between the start of the war in October 1973 and Feb. 12. Included were 581 officers and 691 sergeants. Only 190 of the casualties were full-time soldiers, sailors or airmen; the remaining 2,332 were reservists.

Israeli military sources March 10 had placed Egyptian war casualties at about 9,000 killed and 11,000 wounded.

Other Developments

Vatican changes stand on Jerusalem. The Vatican no longer favored internationalization of Jerusalem and dropped its objections to Israeli control of its holy shrines, a papal officer said Feb. 5, 1974 in an interview with the Israeli newspaper Haaretz.

The spokesman, Federico Alessandrini, said, "Internationalization of Jerusalem, which the church originally supported is not a realistic solution today. The church wishes free access to holy places for freedom of religion."

Vatican sources had reported Jan. 8 that Pope Paul VI was intensifying his efforts to have a voice in settling the Jerusalem problem. The Vatican had earlier made public a memorandum the pope had written after a pilgrimage to the Holy Land and Jerusalem in 1964. It said he hoped his trip would renew the desire of Catholics for "guardianship over the Holy Places."

Israeli Cabinet backs Elazar. The Israeli Cabinet expressed full confidence Jan. 27 in Lt. Gen. David Elazar, chief of staff, for his role in the October 1973 war.

The Cabinet did not delve into the charges raised against Elazar by Maj. Gen. Ariel Sharon, who had questioned Elazar's decisions during the conflict.

The Cabinet received a report on Sharon from Attorney General Meir Shamgar, who headed a judicial commission that was investigating the country's alleged failures and shortcomings in the war.

Sadat dismisses Heykal. Mohammed Hassanien Heykal was dismissed Feb. 1 as chief editor and chairman of the board of the influential Egyptian newspaper Al Ahram under a decree issued by President Anwar Sadat. Heykal was appointed special press adviser to Sadat, a post he had thus far refused.

No official reason was given for Heykal's removal, but a source close to the government said Feb. 5 that Heykal had attempted to turn Al Ahram into "a power center that was tantamount to a state within a state." This was "a practice that President Sadat put an end to once and for all in May 1971," a reference to the alleged conspiracy activities of former Vice President Aly Sabry.

Heykal had been a confidant of Egyptian government leaders since the time of President Gamal Abdel Nasser. He had recently been critical of Sadat's policies, including his disengagement agreement with Israel and his decision to move away from Libyan leader Muammar el-Qaddafi in favor of King Faisal of Saudi Arabia.

Qaddafi threatens Arab revolt. Libyan leader Muammar el-Qaddafi threatened Feb. 10 to arm and train guerrillas to overthrow the leaders of Tunisia, Egypt and Algeria "if [Arab] unity cannot be brought about by normal means." He said the people of those three countries would pressure their leaders to achieve this unity.

The editor of the official Libyan news agency ARNA denied that Qaddafi had called for a revolt against Tunisia, Algeria and Egypt, the Times of London reported Feb. 14. In a letter to the newspaper, Suleiman Azbai said Qaddafi's remarks had been misrepresented, that he "did not remotely suggest at any time in his speech that Libya contemplated giving support to the movements bent on toppling Arab governments."

In a surprise statement, Qaddafi apologized to President Anwar Sadat Feb. 19 for criticizing the Egyptian leader's policy in accepting a cease-fire with Israel in the October 1973 war and for his subsequent negotiations and accord with Israel. Speaking in the presence of Sadat at a meeting of the National Assembly in Cairo to honor Egyptian soldiers killed in the war, Qaddafi praised Egypt for being "the fortress of the Arab struggle."

Sadat promised in a speech that "Egypt will continue to carry arms until all Arab territories are liberated. Our pledge is not to bargain over the rights of the people of Palestine."

Palestinians discuss future state. The Central Council of the Palestine Liberation Organization (PLO) met in Damascus, Syria Feb. 16 to discuss possible establishment of a Palestinian state in territories now held by Israel and whether to attend the Geneva peace conference when it resumed.

A working paper drawn up at the conference called for the right of Palestinians to "establish a national authority on any lands that can be wrested from Zionist occupation." This was the first time the commando groups agreed to consider accepting control of any territory now held by Israel. Previously they had insisted that all territories occupied by Israel, including Israel itself, be taken over by the Palestinians for establishment of a secular state of Moslems, Christians and Jews.

The areas specifically referred to in the document were the West Bank, the Gaza Strip and the El Hamma region south of the Golan Heights on the Jordanian border. El Hamma was included in a Palestinian state that was to have been established in 1948. It was captured by the Syrians in the 1948–49 Arab-Israeli war and was taken by Israel in the 1967 war.

The working paper was drawn up by Al Fatah and was also endorsed by As Saiqa and the Marxist Popular Democratic Front for the Liberation of Palestine. Two other commando groups, the Popular Front for the Liberation of Palestine (PFLP) and the Arab Liberation Front, rejected the proposal.

The PFLP submitted its own working paper, which rejected the Middle East peace settlement, the Geneva conference and establishment of a Palestinian state in the West Bank and Gaza Strip.

Meir forms new Cabinet. Israel's political crisis was resolved with an announcement by Premier Golda Meir March 6 of formation of a new majority coalition Cabinet. Defense Minister Moshe Dayan, who had threatened to quit, agreed to continue to serve in the new government.

The decision to end the nine weeks of political stalemate was spurred by an urgent need for domestic unity in the face of a reported threatening Syrian buildup on the Golan Heights front.

The protracted deadlock in drawing up a new Cabinet had prompted Meir to announce March 3 that she would not head the next government. She reversed herself the following day.

The new Cabinet commanded a majority of 68 votes in the 120-seat Knesset. It would embrace Meir's Labor Party (51 seats), the National Religious Party (NRP) (10), the Arab Lists (3), and the Independent Liberals (4). The Executive Committee of the NRP had reversed itself and voted to rejoin the coalition an hour before Meir advised President Ephraim Katzir of the formation of the new Cabinet. The NRP action assured Meir of a majority in the Knesset.

In addition to Dayan, the other key ministers remaining in the Cabinet were Transport Minister Shimon Peres, who had threatened to remain out of the new government, Foreign Minister Abba Eban, Deputy Premier Yigal Allon and Finance Minister Pinhas Sapir. The new members included Itzhak Rabin, former chief of staff and ambassador to Washington, who was named labor minister.

Dayan's sudden decision to join the new government had been made after an emergency Cabinet meeting March 5 to consider the reported Syrian buildup. Dayan had been insisting that he would not serve with Meir again unless she included the right-wing opposition Likud in her Cabinet, a demand the premier had rejected. After the Cabinet meeting, Dayan and Peres informed Meir they were prepared to continue to serve.

Dayan confirmed in a television broadcast March 6 that he had reversed his resignation decision because of tension on the Syrian front. He said there were indications that the Iraqis and Jordanians might send troops to that front, as they did during the October 1973 war. In view of this, the immediate formation of a new government was vital, Dayan said.

Dayan had toured the Syrian front earlier March 6. He later reported that the Syrians had deployed more than 1,000 tanks along the truce line, 200–300 more than before the war.

Oil

U.S. Seeks End to Embargo

As the Arab embargo on oil to the U.S. continued on into 1974, U.S. leaders stepped up their warnings that the Arabs might suffer retaliation. The U.S. also led in efforts to muster oil-consumer unity in dealing with the oil producers.

U.S. warns Arabs on embargo. U.S. Defense Secretary James R. Schlesinger said in a TV interview Jan. 7, 1974 that if the Arabs continued their oil embargo against the U.S., the American public might be provoked into demanding force be taken to end the ban. But Schlesinger said he believed the oil producers recognized the problem and would not push too far.

Another warning on the oil boycott was voiced Jan. 8 by Vice President Gerald R. Ford, who said the economic disorder caused by the cutoff might result in a reduction of U.S. food shipments to the Middle East and North Africa. Ford did not threaten a deliberate American move to end food shipments to those regions but emphasized the "circular flow" of the world economy "that requires the cooperation of all to keep things moving."

Kuwait and Saudi Arabia, regarding Schlesinger's remarks as a threat of military intervention, were reported Jan. 9 to have made plans to blow up their oil wells in the event of an American attempt to occupy them. Kuwaiti newspapers quoted Foreign Minister Sheik Ahmed Sabah al-Jaber as saying that mines had been planted near the fields and could be detonated at a moment's notice.

Arab press reports from Riyadh said Saudi Arabia also had wired its oil fields with explosives that would be set off in the event of a U.S. attack.

U.S. seeks foreign ministers' meeting. Secretary of State Henry A. Kissinger Jan. 10 called on oil-producing and oil-consuming nations to seek a long-term multinational agreement to deal with the energy shortage.

Kissinger's appeal followed an announcement by the White House Jan. 9 that President Richard M. Nixon had asked foreign ministers of eight oil-consuming nations meet in Washington Feb. 11 to discuss world energy problems. Invitations were sent to the heads of government of Britain, Canada, France, Italy, Japan, the Netherlands, Norway and West Germany. Nixon also had sent messages to the 13 states belonging to the Organization of Petroleum Exporting Countries (OPEC), inviting them to join in the discussions with the consumer nations at a later date.

According to the text of the letter to the eight nations made public by the White House Jan. 10, Nixon warned that "the energy situation threatens to unleash political and economic forces that could cause severe and irreparable damage to the prosperity and stability of the world."

The President said the purpose of the foreign ministers' meeting would be to analyze the situation and then "establish a task force" to "formulate a consumer action program." The program, he said, would "deal with the explosive growth of global energy demand" and would "accelerate the coordinated development of new energy sources." According to Nixon, the oil-consuming nations would seek to "meet the legitimate interests of oil-producing countries while assuring the consumer nations adequate supplies at fair and reasonable prices."

Kissinger's remarks on the fuel crisis were made at a joint news conference with William E. Simon, head of the Federal Energy Office. The secretary said the goal of, multilateral agreements lay behind President Nixon's proposal for the Feb. 11 energy conference. Kissinger advised the oil-consuming nations not to seek individual agreements with oil-producers to protect their supplies because such "unrestricted bilateral competition will be ruinous for all countries concerned."

Kissinger also cited the problems of the developing nations, most of whom, he noted, could not pay for the increased price of Arab oil.

Saudis warn oil consumers. Saudi Arabian Petroleum Minister Sheik Zaki al-Yamani warned major oil-consuming nations Jan. 12 that any counteraction they might take against the Arab oil embargo would result in international economic "disaster" and a possible head-on "confrontation."

Speaking at a news conference in Rome on a tour of European capitals, Yamani rejected a suggestion by a Kuwait newspaper that Arab oil producers blacklist all nations that attended the U.S. energy conference.

Yamani said Saudi Arabia was not supplying "a drop of oil" to the U.S. and was boycotting "any refinery that supplies petroleum products" to the U.S.

Yamani reversed himself in Bonn Jan. 17 when he admitted the boycott against the U.S. and the Netherlands was ineffective.

Libya warned on oil leakage to U.S. The Organization of Arab Petroleum Exporting Countries (OAPEC) warned Libya of "serious consequences" of refusing to comply with the organization's oil boycott against the U.S., a Beirut newspaper reported Jan. 5.

The newspaper Al Hayat said that at its meeting in Kuwait, Dec. 25, 1973, the OAPEC had called Libya's attention to the "large quantities" of its oil that was finding its way into American hands. The Libyan delegation had been told that "between 60% and 90% of the oil exported to the United States originated from Libya," the report said.

U.S. bank to fund Egypt pipeline. The U.S. government-owned Export-Import Bank Jan. 10 approved a loan and financial guarantee of $100 million to finance the building of an Egyptian pipeline between the Red Sea and the Mediterranean. The funds would be used for American equipment and services for the Suez-Mediterranean (SUMED) Petroleum Corp. project to be built by Bechtel, Inc. of the U.S. SUMED was owned half by the Egyptian government and half by the governments of Saudi Arabia, Kuwait, Abu Dhabi and Qatar.

U.S. Rep. Thomas Rees (D, Calif.) criticized Eximbank's decision to provide the loan to SUMED. He said it would be "arming Egypt at a time when our policy has been to establish a status quo in this area as the basis for equality of bargaining in talks between Egypt and Israel." Rees charged that Egypt was "the main instigator of the current" Arab oil embargo against the U.S.

Japanese-Iraqi deal. Under an agreement signed in Tokyo Jan. 17, Japan was to lend Iraq $1 billion to construct oil refining and other industrial facilities in exchange for crude oil and petroleum products. Japan also was to provide Baghdad with technical and training assistance and tanker ships.

Algeria raises oil price. Algeria announced Jan. 17 that the posted prices of its oil would be increased 75% effective Jan. 1. The boost raised the price of a barrel from $9.25 to $16.21. The Algerian action appeared to contradict a decision Jan. 9 by the Organization of Petroleum Exporting Countries (OPEC), of which Algeria was a member, that there would be no price increases until April 1.

Saudis pledge oil price cut. Saudi Arabian Petroleum Minister Sheik Ahmed Zaki al-Yamani said Jan. 27 that King Faisal was preparing to "take very important steps" aimed at reducing the price of crude oil to avoid harming the world economy.

Yamani made the statement in Tokyo where he had arrived Jan. 26 on a five-day mission to explain his government's oil policy to Japanese officials. He told a news conference that although Saudi Arabia regarded current prices as "fair and reasonable," it was concerned that the "present prices of oil will create some serious problems in the balance of payments of so many nations, whether they are developing nations or industrialized nations."

Algerian Industry and Energy Minister Belaid Abdelsalam, who accompanied Yamani, expressed disagreement and said he was opposed to any cut in petroleum prices. He said the current high rates were necessary in view of Algeria's balance of payments deficit and its heavy indebtedness to foreign countries.

Yamani said Jan. 28 that any cut in oil prices must be taken jointly by the oil producers. "If we can convince the others, we will reduce our prices," Yamani said. He reiterated his warning against participation by other countries in the forthcoming U.S.-sponsored world energy conference to be held in Washington Feb. 11. Yamani said Japan and other oil-consuming nations "cannot afford any sort of confrontation."

Italy urges Israeli withdrawal. Italian Foreign Minister Aldo Moro called on Israel Jan. 23 to withdraw from "all occupied territories," including the Golan Heights. "The acknowledgment and the certainty of being able to live within safe and recognized frontiers certainly have a price," Moro told the Senate Foreign Affairs Committee.

Moro denied that his statement had been urged by the Arab nations to show sympathy for their cause. Saudi Arabian Petroleum Minister Sheik Ahmed Zaki al-Yamani had said during a visit to Rome Jan. 12 that Italy had been asked to call for Israeli withdrawal in order to be recognized as a "friendly" nation by the Arabs and thus qualify for guaranteed oil shipments.

Italy renews withdrawal call—Italy reiterated its appeal to Israel Feb. 28 to withdraw from occupied Arab lands and recognize "the national rights of the Palestinian people" as the "bitter" price of peace.

In a report to the Foreign Affairs Committee of the Chamber of Deputies, Foreign Minister Aldo Moro said Israel's acceptance of these conditions would release it "from her unhappy condition of being a powerful fortress besieged by an enemy becoming steadily more numerous, better armed and trained, . . . and would give her a chance for an important dialogue with a world no longer hostile to her."

Arab recognition of Israel "would free the Arab world from the curse of war without end," Moro said.

The foreign minister defended Italy's bilateral oil deals with Middle East nations, but said his country would not hesitate to abandon such transactions if there were an international energy agency, at least within the European framework.

Italy frees 3 Arab plotters on bail—Three Arabs accused of planning to shoot down an El Al Israeli airliner with missiles near Rome Sept. 5, 1973 were sentenced in a Rome court Feb. 27. They received prison terms of five years and two months and were fined $2,500 each. Then they were freed on bail.

Two other Arabs involved in the plot had been released soon after the incident in their own recognizance and were assumed to have left Italy.

French mission to Arab states. French Foreign Minister Michel Jobert visited Saudi Arabia, Kuwait and Syria Jan. 24–29 in a move aimed at establishing French economic, political and military influence in the region.

In his meetings with Saudi Arabian

King Faisal Jan. 24–26, Jobert discussed a proposed 20-year agreement in which France would receive 800 million tons of oil in return for sophisticated arms and industrial equipment.

Jobert was said to have sought a similar oil-arms agreement in his discussions in Kuwait Jan. 27–28. Kuwait government sources reported Jan. 28 that France was ready to supply fighter planes, tanks and anti-aircraft missiles without political conditions. Jobert, the sources said, offered French participation in petrochemical and oil refinery projects in Kuwait in return for a yearly guarantee of oil delivery.

The French foreign minister conferred in Damascus Jan. 29 with Syrian President Hafez al-Assad and Foreign Minister Abdel Halim Khaddam. Jobert criticized the exclusion of European states from the Geneva conference on the Middle East.

On his return to Paris Jan. 30, Jobert said the U.S. had made some "spectacular initiatives" in the Middle East but with "perhaps less spectacular results."

Jobert had defended his government's policy of bilateral arms-oil agreements with Arab countries Jan. 21. He charged that this policy was being criticized in some quarters "because France might take someone else's place or ask that a little room be made for her."

French-Saudi Arabian deal—France had confirmed Jan. 9 that it had signed an oil agreement with Saudi Arabia. The government announcement said France would receive 27 million tons of crude oil from Saudi Arabia over the next three years.

The Paris statement did not say what the Saudis would receive in return, but Saudi Petroleum Minister Sheik Ahmed Zaki al-Yamani had said Jan. 7 that his country would get French warplanes and other military equipment in exchange. Other sources said the French also would provide industrial machinery and technical advice.

France proposes world energy meeting— French Foreign Minister Michel Jobert, in a letter to United Nations Secretary General Kurt Waldheim dated Jan. 18,

proposed the urgent convening of a world energy conference under U.N. auspices. Jobert wrote that the conference should aim at determining the general principles of future cooperation between the energy producers and consumers and to devise practical steps likely to achieve such cooperation.

Britain gets more Saudi oil. Saudi Arabia had given the Arabian American Oil Co. permission to increase the quota of oil to Britain, it was reported in London Jan. 15. The size of the greater allocation was not immediately disclosed, but a New York Times report from Beirut Feb. 3 said Britain was receiving an immediate supply increase of 200,000 barrels a day.

Libya, Iraq oppose lifting embargo. Libya and Iraq were reported opposed to efforts by Egyptian President Anwar Sadat to have the Arab oil-producing states lift their embargo against the U.S.

Libyan Premier Abdel Salam Jalloud was quoted by the government radio Jan. 23 as saying that, contrary to Sadat's views, the U.S. had not changed its policies in the Middle East enough to warrant an end to the ban. If the Arab states abandoned the embargo, Jalloud added, "they would be condemning the oil weapon as a failure."

The Baghdad press reported Jan. 24 that Iraqi President Ahmed Hassan al-Bakr had refused to receive a special envoy sent by Sadat Jan. 22 to explain Egypt's troop disengagement agreement with Israel. The Iraqi government also announced that Bakr had rejected an invitation by President Nixon to attend a world energy conference in Washington with other oil exporters.

Arabs see no end to boycott—Saudi Arabian Petroleum Minister Sheik Ahmed Zaki al-Yamani said Feb. 5 that he had "no knowledge of any Arab country promising to lift the embargo against the United States." Yamani's statement was in reply to a question about President Nixon's Jan. 30 announcement that an early meeting of Arab oil producers would end the boycott. As for Saudi Arabia's intentions of lifting the ban against the U.S., Yamani said this would have to be decided jointly "at the meeting of Arab oil ministers." This was a reference to a conference to be held in Tripoli, Libya Feb. 14.

Yamani spoke in Lebanon where he was on a tour to explain Arab oil policies.

Beirut newspapers reported Feb. 4 that Saudi Arabia and Kuwait had assured Syrian President Hafez al-Assad that they would continue the oil stoppage against the U.S. until Israel and Syria agreed to disengagement of their forces on Syrian terms. Assad was given the pledge in meetings with Saudi Arabian King Faisal in Riyadh Feb. 2 and in talks with officials in Kuwait Feb. 3.

Kuwaiti Foreign Minister Sheikh Sabah al-Ahmad al-Jaber Jan. 21 had dismissed as "premature" speculation that the Arabs might ease their oil embargo against the U.S. because of the Israeli-Egyptian pullback agreement. "Lifting the oil measures is still linked to Israeli withdrawal from occupied Arab territories and the restoration of the rights of the Palestinian people," he said.

A U.S. government official in Washington said Jan. 29 that Sadat's appeal to other Arab leaders to lift the oil embargo was in response to a pledge to Secretary of State Henry A. Kissinger that he would urge such a move in appreciation for the secretary's efforts in helping achieve the Israeli-Egyptian troop disengagement agreement. Sadat had informed Arab leaders during his eight-nation tour Jan. 18–23 that Kissinger's mediation was a reflection of change in American policy in the Middle East that warranted a shift in Arab oil policy, the U.S. official said.

U.S. warns Arabs on oil embargo. Secretary of State Henry A. Kissinger declared Feb. 6 that the U.S. had been led to expect an end to the Arab oil embargo in view of recent American peace efforts in the Middle East. The continuance of this ban "under these conditions must be construed as a form of blackmail and would be considered highly inappropriate by the United States and cannot but affect the attitude with which we will have to pursue our diplomacy," he said.

This was the first time Kissinger had used the word blackmail to describe the embargo.

President Nixon had said in his State of the Union message Jan. 30 that he had been assured by friendly Arab leaders that a meeting would be held to discuss the lifting of the embargo.

The secretary also sought to assure oil producers and some European countries that were apprehensive about the forthcoming international energy conference to be held in Washington Feb. 11–12. Kissinger discounted as untrue reports that the U.S. would try to use the parley "to organize a consumers' cooperative" or "to produce a confrontation with the producers."

Kissinger reiterated his criticism of bilateral oil deals, saying "they tend to support a price which is ruinous to nations making them and generally to the world economy."

Oil-consumer conference. The conference of foreign ministers of 13 major oil-consuming nations, called by President Nixon, was held in Washington Feb. 11–13, 1974, and it endorsed a U.S. proposal for international cooperation in overcoming the world energy crisis.

Attending the U.S.-sponsored meeting were the foreign ministers of Belgium, Britain, Canada, Denmark, France, West Germany, Ireland, Italy, Japan, Luxembourg, the Netherlands, Norway and the U.S. The finance ministers of all those countries, except France, also were present.

French Foreign Minister Michel Jobert criticized the conference, asserting that energy matters were used by the U.S. as "a pretext." The parley's real purpose, he said, was a "political" desire by the U.S. to dominate the relationships of Western Europe and Japan.

Arabs assail energy conference—The conference in Washington was criticized Feb. 10 by the major Arab oil-producing states of Libya, Kuwait and Saudi Arabia.

Tripoli radio called the meeting "an aggressive act against the oil-producing states, particularly the Arab states." It said the parley was "an American trap to sanction an American tutelage in Europe and internationalize oil resources by means of force."

Kuwaiti Petroleum Minister Abdel Rahman Atiki said his government approved of the conference in principle but opposed "the idea of allowing opposing blocs to discuss such an important topic."

Prince Saud of Saudi Arabia said "if the aim of the Washington conference is to mount pressure on the producing states, then we do not think it will be fruitful."

Algerian President Houari Boumedienne had said Feb. 4 that the conference was "directed toward creation of an imperialist protectorate over energy resources." He said it would bring no results "because the oil-producing states are opposed to it."

The Soviet Communist Party newspaper Pravda described the conference Feb. 11 as a U.S. attempt "to create a coalition of industrial states against the oil-exporting developing countries."

Arabs cancel oil conference—The Arab oil-producing conference scheduled to open in Tripoli, Libya Feb. 14 was suddenly canceled indefinitely.

The official Libyan press agency reported Feb. 13 that the decision was taken "at the request of Saudi Arabia and Egypt." No official clarification for the action was given, but diplomatic sources in Cairo said Egypt and Saudi Arabia needed more time to persuade other Arab leaders that the oil embargo against the U.S. must be lifted soon.

Soviets back continued oil ban—The Soviet Union called for the continued oil embargo against the U.S. and criticized those Arab states that favored lifting the ban.

One Moscow broadcast monitored in London March 12 said if "some Arab leaders are ready to surrender in the face of American pressure and lift the oil ban before those demands [for Israeli withdrawal] are fulfilled, they are taking a chance by challenging the whole Arab world and the progressive forces of the world, which insist on the continued use of the oil weapon."

Another Soviet broadcast March 5 had said "United States imperialism has hidden behind the mask of a friend of the Arabs in order to break up Arab unity."

U.S. officials in Washington March 12 conceded that the Soviet Union was taking the side of the radical Arab states on the oil embargo but said this was only a reiteration of a standing policy and did not represent a major shift.

Arabs offered cooperation plan. The European Economic Community (EEC) offered March 4 to explore long-term economic, technical and cultural cooperation with 20 Arab nations. The joint offer was approved at a meeting of EEC foreign ministers in Brussels.

The pro-Arab move omitted mention of cooperation on political and oil questions. According to reports, France had wanted to include those issues.

Three initial steps were envisaged as part of the plan: diplomatic contacts in Bonn between the Arabs and West German Foreign Minister Walter Scheel, current president of the EEC Council of Ministers; establishment of joint working groups to discuss possible areas of cooperation; and eventually an EEC-Arab ministerial meeting.

Shah says U.S. continues to get oil. Shah Mohammed Riza Pahlevi of Iran said Feb. 24 that the U.S. was importing at least as much oil as it did before the Arabs imposed their embargo during the October 1973 war in the Middle East and indicated that the American oil industry may have deliberately manipulated gasoline shortages in the U.S. to increase their profits. The charge was disputed by U.S. officials.

The shah's statement was made to interviewer Mike Wallace and broadcast on WCBS-TV. Suggesting that the U.S. may be getting oil surreptitiously, the Iranian leader told of tankers changing their destinations "two or three times" in mid-ocean and of oil being sold for one destination and being delivered somewhere else.

U.S. probes charges vs. oil companies. Hearings held Jan. 21–23 by the Senate Permanent Investigations Subcommittee provided a forum for airing of charges that the fuel shortage had been contrived, that oil industry profits were excessive, particularly during the period of the Arab embargo, and that at least one major oil company had cut off supplies to U.S. military forces during the Middle East crisis at the order of Saudi Arabia. Oil

executives from seven major companies—
Exxon, Texaco, Mobil, Gulf, Shell, Standard Oil (California) and Amoco, a sub-
sidiary of Standard Oil (Indiana)—
testified in rebuttal over the three-day period.

Sen. Henry M. Jackson (D, Wash.),
chairman of the subcommittee, said
that Mobil and Gulf had been the only
companies to reply fully to a question-
naire about their business operations.

Despite the lack of cooperation from
the industry in providing complete information on the extent of the fuel
shortage, the subcommittee concluded
that at the end of 1973, inventories in all
petroleum products held by the seven
companies were 5.5% higher than at the
end of 1972.

Oil cutoff to military charged—Jackson
said Jan. 23 that he had documentary evidence that Exxon had cut off fuel supplies
to U.S. military forces abroad at the bid-
ding of the Saudi Arabian government.

Jackson said he based his charges on
the Dec. 1, 1973 issue of Business Week
and corroboration from "independent
[government] documentation." According to the magazine, Saudi Arabia's
King Faisal ordered U.S. companies participating in the Arabian American Oil
Co. (Aramco) to cease supplying U.S.
troops with fuel derived from Saudi crude
oil. Faisal threatened to "retaliate against
any breach by extending the oil embargo
to the company involved and the country
in which the violation took place,"
Business Week stated.

According to Jackson, the order was
issued in October 1973 during the U.S.
military alert, but Business Week said the
incident occurred during a meeting of the
consortium in Jeddah Nov. 4, 1973.

Spokesmen for Aramco members—Exxon, Mobil, Standard Oil (California) and
Texaco—denied personal knowledge of
the alleged shutoff but said they would
check further on the charge. Jackson la-
beled the action a "flagrant act of corpo-
rate disloyalty to the U.S. government."

In a statement issued Jan. 24, Exxon
Corp. Chairman J. K. Jamieson did not
deny that fuel shipments to the U.S.
military were shut off, but he refuted
Jackson's charge that the incident constituted a "disloyal act."

"As is generally known," Jamieson
said, "the Saudi Arabian government in
late October [1973] imposed an embargo
on the export of crude oil and products to
the U.S. and certain other countries. Included in this embargo were deliveries to
the U.S. military of products derived
from Saudi Arabian crude. These developments and actions taken by Exxon were
promptly reported to the Department of
Defense and the Defense Fuel Supply
Center."

Z. D. Bonner, chairman of Gulf's U.S.
affiliate, issued a similar statement the
same day:

"The oil industries in the Middle East
were simply told by the Arab governments that 'You will not be allowed to
supply the U.S. military overseas from
our oil and if you do you'll be cut off completely,' " Bonner said. "The U.S. government of course was completely informed. . . . And the decision was made to
increase military supplies out of the
United States."

Aramco officials conceded Jan. 25 that
fuel had been withheld from the U.S.
military since Oct. 21, 1973, when King
Faisal issued the embargo instructions.
"The embargo action was taken by a
sovereign state and Aramco's compliance came as the result of a direct order
which had nothing to do with patriotism,"
officials said, adding that the threat of
harsh, but unspecified reprisals, was explicit in the king's order.

Embargo Partially Lifted

7 of 9 states remove ban. Seven of nine
Arab petroleum-producing countries
agreed at a meeting in Vienna March 18
to lift the oil embargo they had imposed
against the U.S. in October 1973.

One of the seven nations, Algeria, said
it was removing the ban provisionally until
June 1. The Arab producers were to meet
again on that date in Cairo to review their
decision. The embargo was to remain in
effect against the Netherlands and Denmark. The delegates placed Italy and
West Germany on the list of "friendly nations," assuring them of larger supplies.

The Arab action, taken at a meeting of
the Organization of Petroleum Exporting
Countries (OPEC), was approved by Al-

geria, Saudi Arabia, Kuwait, Qatar, Bahrain, Egypt and Abu Dhabi. Libya and Syria refused to join the majority. Iraq boycotted the talks.

The OPEC meeting, which had begun March 16, confirmed the Arab decision which had been approved in principle at a conference in Tripoli, Libya March 13. The Vienna delegates had agreed at the March 17 meeting that oil prices would not be rolled back, despite protests and appeals from consumer nations.

Saudi Arabia was the only country which pressed for a lower price for oil. Other countries, led by Indonesia, Algeria, Nigeria and Iran, sought an increase above the $11.65 posted price.

With the announcement of the agreement to end the oil embargo, Saudi Arabia pledged March 18 an immediate production increase of a million barrels a day for the U.S. market.

A formal statement on the Arab decision did not mention the restoration of production cutbacks. The communique explained that a shift in American policy away from Israel had prompted the producers to terminate the embargo. The new U.S. "dimension, if maintained, will lead America to assume a position which is more compatible with the principle of what is right and just toward the Arab-occupied territories and the legitimate rights of the Palestinian people."

Algerian Petroleum Minister Belaid Abdelsalam said March 18 his country believed the U.S. had shown enough "goodwill" in using its influence to get Israel to carry out military disengagement with Egypt and to agree to contacts with Syria to negotiate a similar pullback to warrant lifting the embargo. Libya and Syria, however, were not convinced of this and decided not to go along with the majority opinion, Abdelsalam said.

Syrian resistance to abandoning the "oil weapon" because of its stand that the U.S. had not done enough to insure Israeli withdrawal had delayed until March 18 the formal announcement of the end of the embargo, despite the majority decision taken at the Tripoli meeting March 13.

Saudi Arabia Petroleum Minister Sheik Ahmed Zaki al-Yamani said March 18 the decision against resuming the flow of Arab oil to the Netherlands and Denmark was taken because these two countries "have not made clear their position on asking for a full [Israeli] withdrawal from occupied territories."

On leaving Vienna March 20, Kuwaiti Oil Minister Abdel Rahman Atiki said his country regarded the Arab production cutback ordered in December 1973 to still be in effect.

Libyan Oil Minister Ezzedin Mabrouk said March 20 that his country would not only continue the embargo against the U.S., but also would retain its current production level of 1,850,000 barrels a day, compared with 2,300,000 barrels in September 1973.

Soviets back continued oil ban—The Soviet Union called for the continued oil embargo against the U.S. and criticized those Arab states that favored lifting the ban.

One Moscow broadcast monitored in London March 12 said if "some Arab leaders are ready to surrender in the face of American pressure and lift the oil ban before those demands [for Israeli withdrawal] are fulfilled, they are taking a chance by challenging the whole Arab world and the progressive forces of the world, which insist on the continued use of the oil weapon."

Another Soviet broadcast March 5 had said "United States imperialism has hidden behind the mask of a friend of the Arabs in order to break up Arab unity."

Index